In Search Of Love

Ata Servati

> To obtain more information about the writer, go to
>
> *www.eeiff.com*

Copyright@ 2007 Library of the congress of USA.
Registrations # TXu001360565/06/13/2007
Registrations # TXu002021-337/06/02/2021

ISBN print: 978-1-7358163-4-0
ISBN eBook: 978-1-7358163-5-7
WGAW NO: 5143701989/

All right reserved. No part of this book maybe reproduced or transmitted in any form or by any means, electronic or mechanical, including photocopying, recording, or by any information storage and retrieval system, without permission in writing from the copyright owner.

This book was released in 2022.
This book was printed and bound in the United State of America

ALSO BY ATA SERVATI

I AM A LOTUS (Spiritual Poems From the Heart.)
IN SEARCH OF HEAVEN (The Howard Baskerville story)
MARRIED TO THE WELL (INCLUDES 3 volumes)
ASYEH (Volume 1)
THE SILENT BEGGER (Volume 2)
THE SHRINE (Vallum 3)

========

Plays (In Farsi)
OVER THE BRIDGE, BOTTOM OF THE RIVER
The Window

Dedication

I am humbled to dedicate this book to a gentle soul who taught me how to care for others, respect the poor, and not worship the rich. She taught me that respect, kindness, forgiveness, and love are the only tools that reach toward heaven. She is a soul that I miss, my late mother, Hajji Rogheyeh Servati. Also, to a most caring person who encouraged me to write and gave me the most precious gift of my life, my beautiful daughter Senna, to a soul whom I respect tremendously, Kristy Servati.

Ata Servati.

Table of Contents

Foreword vii

Chapter 1 He Learned How To Hate And How To Love.... 1

Chapter 2 Encountering Indifference And Opposition... 20

Chapter 3 Lost In Tehran... 30

Chapter 4 Rites Of Passage... 39

Chapter 5 It's Over For You. It's All Over For You Now, So What's Next .. 46

Chapter 6 Then Came A Defining Moment In His Young Life... 64

Chapter 7 Mysterious Infatuation With The Violin Girl... Love Connection... 76

Chapter 8 The Unspoken Rule... 89

Chapter 9 Love Has No Boundaries, But Is Forbidden By Traditions, What Would You Do? 104

Chapter 10 No Advice Or Lecture Would Have The Same Impact As Life Lessons... 114

Chapter 11 There Is A Magic That Can Be Derived From Nature... 128

Chapter 12 Vultures On The Loose... 135

Chapter 13 The Search Is On For Bahman Reesh... 149

Chapter 14 The Way He Wanted To Be, But Couldn't Change The Course Of Nature And Century Of Traditions... 153

Chapter 15 You Need It, You Little Writer You... 167

Chapter 16 When Unfair And Unjust Traditions Become Intertwined... 175

Chapter 17 Certain Events In Life Will Shape And Alter Your Existence... 187

Chapter 18 Do You Believe In Dreams? 199

Chapter 19 Up Close And Personal With The Dervish... 209

Chapter 20 You Can Run, But Where Can You Hide? 220

Chapter 21 His Second Home Land, Is It In Exile Or Born Of A New Life For Him? 227

Chapter 22 Still Searching For A Childhood Crush A Decade Later... 235

Chapter 23 Weeds That Always Reappear Right After Picking... 251

Chapter 24 Are You rom Saudi Arabia? 258

Chapter 25 Revolution, The New Direction Of Iran/Persia... 266

Chapter 26 A Lot Of Sadness And Doubt.................................... 274

Chapter 27 Please Go To The Living Room. I Will Be There... 290

Chapter 28 Smiling While Torment And Sadness Festered Inside; Moving House To House And Every Other Day..................................... 299

Chapter 29 The Revelation Of His Life... 308

Chapter 30 The Bird Had Found A New Home Now... 318

Chapter 31 After Spending So Many Years In Another Country; What Used To Be Normal Isn't... 332

Chapter 32 I Miss My Son; I Want To See Him... 344

Chapter 33 To Claim What Once Belonged To Him 355

Foreword

It took him about 10 years to finish the book, but the first 9 years and 11 months, he only had 10 pages typed. And then one day, he finds himself sitting in Starbucks, waiting for his film manager/agent to arrive to figure out what to do with his life. It is not an easy task to understand and accept being over 55 years old, having just lost everything, and realizing that you are homeless. Where do you go? Whom do you talk to when you only have $85.00 and some pennies to your name?

He had just arrived from Vancouver; he had to borrow some money from a neighbor to take a plane back to the United States. Supposedly he had escaped from the States due to disappointments in the legal system. It was his kindness toward others that got him in trouble. He is always there for others. But this time, he was set up by a greedy old man whom he thought was helping. For the first time in his life, he was getting a taste of the court system and dealing with an attorney. He found out that he had lost everything. He had lost all of his friends, and his short marriage of two years was also over. It was hard for him to digest and understand what had really happened. He found himself becoming a lonely man.

He was looking for a file to contact a friend for a possible job, and he accidentally found a file. It was a story about his mother, which he had started over 9 years ago. He never thought about it and began to read it, and in the process, began to correct it. A voice got his attention; he looked up and saw a Starbucks employee, "Sorry, but we will be closing shortly." He looked up and noticed that it was almost 10 PM He had no idea how time had passed so quickly. He had been writing for about 4 hours and discovered that he had typed over 20 pages. He realized that he had forgotten about his manager. He also knew that his phone had not rung.

He walked out of Starbucks, looked around, and did not know what to do or where to go. He stopped, looked around, and realized that he was really homeless.

He looks up and sees a bag lady sitting on the corner, smiling at him. The next time he checked the time, it was late, 1:00 A.M., and he was still talking to her. Her name was Alexa. She told him she came from Canada with $250.00 and a bus ticket that was given to her by her church because of the warm weather in California.

Lying on his car, lonely, looking around, he was thinking about his new life. The story continued over 23 days, typing every day at Starbucks, eating a 49c bean burrito per day, and drinking ginger tea. He had 407 pages typed, typing with one finger, and sometimes not even able to spell his own name. And somehow, he called it "IN SEARCH OF LOVE." A month later, his second book, also over 400 pages, was typed, entitled: "TAR." Interestingly enough, he found peace and found that his new life was a pleasant one. He did not need to be worried about bills. He had stopped talking to all but his daughter and one of his nephews he loved a lot. Then some American friends, Tony and Julie, found out about him and sheltered him at their house.

He used to come and take me out to lunch sometime, usually on Friday. He calmly looked into my eyes and deeply touched, he continued, "Bill," Ata said, "the nights I was sleeping outside and watching the stars while sitting among other homeless people around a small fire and chatting with them, these were the most peaceful moments of my entire life. I understood a lot about what life really means. I learned from them and especially from Alexa, an older Canadian lady. She helped me understand and fit into her gang of new friends. Alexa sometimes fed me, and then suddenly, one day, she was gone. Yes, it was God's destiny for me to lose everything in order to realize who I was and the purpose God had for my life. This had to happen in order for me to leave the sadness of the past behind and live in the future." And, the result was five novels in one year and a short film entitled "CELLFISH," and a movie script for CELLFISH. And his poetry book, "I AM A LOTUS." And after I read the new script to give him my thoughts, I liked it so much I asked him if I could write the forward, and he said, "Yes."

Bill Huff

Man is born innocent but learns to love and hate through his journey from birth to death.

Chapter 1

He Learned How To Hate And How To Love...

There were a multitude of beautiful creeks and streams surrounded by enormous mountains. These colorful giants were covered with wildflowers in spring and summer, then white snow in the winter. There was a wild, crystal clear river surrounded by green trees. Water flowed over the rocks with a swift liveliness. This was the place where he was born. His birthplace, called Khansar, the place which was known for its vibrant spring, its hanging wild mountain tulips, multi-colored wildflowers, an all-around freshness that was indescribable. It was there that he was given the name Nader. His earliest memories are of the river, a black and white puppy called Khaly, and the chickens, cows, donkeys, and horses. He also remembers the red-headed rooster that he was afraid of. He remembers his mother, who he always felt safe with. He remembers she was always busy doing things around the house, talking to the workers, her foreman, and dealing with his father. He remembers wandering around his father, who was stoned on opium all the time. And most time, he did not notice that he was ever there. His father began using opium at age twelve because of intense pain in his feet. Now he was addicted and smoked the drug recreationally. His father was a rich farmer, and there were never any worries about living in comfort. His mother, who came from another rich family, had her own wealth. She, in fact, was the leader of her family; and she was the one running the farm. Nader had early memories of his father fighting with his mother; on one horrific occasion, he actually beat her up, right in front of Nader's eyes. This became an ongoing event. The most painful memory was when his father broke a wooden car he built with his playmates at the farm race with and used a broken board amid the mess to hit his mother, badly hurting her.

When Nader turned seven years old, and it was time for him to go to school, he lived in Tehran in the fall, winter, spring, and during the summer, he would be with his mother on the farm. There was another boy named Haddi. He was the youngest son of a rich farmer to the south. All the boys use to have their own gangs of friends, and the most exciting part of the summer was their race competition. Haddi was leading the team, which was in competition with the team Nader was leading. They saw each other as real enemies. Their team would design a car which they would then take to the main road outside of the village for a race. The project of building their racing car was a complete secret until the day of the race. He remembers one year he had to work all winter to design the car, and he worked really hard to build it with the help of his village friends. The night before the race, he brought the car home and placed it in their huge guestroom. This room could fit over six hundred people, and his family used the room for big parties and weddings. Or, if there was a death in the family, it was converted into a wake room. It required more than six very large oversized rugs to fill the room. The floor was made of hard soil and was joined by a balcony that broke off into other rooms. Nader's father would sit in this room for hours on end, enjoying the warmth and colors of the fire. There was a portion of the floor that was left uncovered, he would sometimes wash his face and hands there, the water would sink into the hard soil floor and disappear as if the ground had quenched its thirst. His father was a nice and kind person, but when he was late for his next dose of opium, evil boiled out of his heart. He would not recognize anyone. His fire and teapot had to be ready to go at all times for his family to have peace in the house. The night Nader brought home the car, he was so proud. It was made of the finest wood they could find. He placed this cherished car in the covered part of the room to keep dirt out; he had planned to sleep in the same room in order to guard the precious car. He did not want to take his eyes off the car until the race was done. His team had been beaten two years in a row, and he was determined to win this time.

It was a dark night; many farmers had gathered on the large balcony to open a massive amount of walnuts and pecans. Over fifty people sat using small rocks to take the soft shell off nuts, and then when they dried out by the winter, the people would gather again and crack the hard shells of the nuts; the nourishing seeds were removed whole. Sometimes the large sitting room was used if more people came. One farmer, Mohammed Bagher, was playing the kamancheh, a traditional Iranian musical instrument, similar to a violin and sing. A few were serving food as the melody of the music combined with the cracking of the shells created their own personal orchestra. Nader was walking around taking in the night; every so often, he would march straight to the wooden car and check on it up close. When he wasn't present, one of his teammates would keep a watchful eye; after all, this was the highlight of their young lives. As the workers continued to gossip between cracking shells, Nader's mother walked in with a huge platter of fruit for all. Moments later, Nader's father rushed up the stairs and entered the balcony with his blood pumping. He did not notice anyone, but Beby immediately noticed him and began watching him like a hawk. Beby was the family's helper; she was middle-aged and was like a loving aunt to Nader. Beby was nervous, his father's fire and tea were not ready yet, and she rushed to prepare it. Everyone knew what his father needed, and this night he arrived in his familiar room a bit earlier than usual. Nader followed Beby, worried for her.

His father's voice hit Nader within seconds, screaming and yelling curses at Beby, his hand lifted with a slight arch ready to swing. Nader called for his mother, who was engaged in conversation with two of her team leaders from the farm; they were in the process of making some important decisions. He stopped in his tracks and realized that if his mother did respond, his father might start hitting her. It had happened before. So, he came back and sat few yards away, across from his father, wrapping his legs with his two hands, placed his chin on his knees, and stared at the car, trying to ignore his father. To his dismay, his father would not stop cursing at Beby. Nader was completely fed up with his periodic abuse towards her and his mother and until that day had never stood up to his father. He rose to his feet, walk to his father, and stood in front of him right across from the metal container holding fire and few teapots, staring right at him in madness, and after he threatened Beby to punish her badly, Nader listed and began yelling, insulting his father. In shock, his father's whole body pivoted and aimed for his small son.

Nader could not even remember what he said as he watched his father jump over a tea set and slap him with a heavy sting. Nader fell and rolled several yards as Baby called for his mother. She rushed in, taking in the scene within seconds. She threw her shoe at her husband so hard it smacked his head and came to a halt in the special metal container called Manghal, which was full of domes of fire, used for his opium and teapots. Tea, domes of fire, and ash scattered around, and on his father, watching his opium pipe fall off the metal container, his father, who now in pain, jumped up like a mad wolf. Then, something unspeakable happened. He spotted Nader's treasured wooden car; he quickly grabbed it, breaking it, then cracked off a piece of wood and attacked his mother with it while Nader still held onto her legs as frightened as he could be.

Nader saw the wood landing, crashing down on his mother's body as she was holding him in protection mode. Soon the music stopped, and workers rushed in to help. A few men grabbed his father and forced him off the balcony, which connected all six rooms. But it was too late, he had severely hurt his mother, and Nader could see tears running down her face. She was still holding on to him, acting as if the danger was still present.

This was not the first time he had watched his mother being beaten. He remembered as early as three years old, or maybe younger. From the first time as he witnessed his mother tearing up, in pain from his father's unjust punishment, he hated his father. That hate stayed with him for many years to come. The fighting was a normal event, and that night, as usual, a cousin and neighbor came rushing in as well when they heard his father's screams. They truly loved his mother and would always come immediately to help protect her from the violent outbursts.

His father, who was being held on the patio by several men, wanted to come in and smoke his opium. Nader knew his father was not himself; the opium had such a strong hold on him, it created a nasty and ruthless man. After smoking, you could see his demeanor change; he became the nice and kind man he used to be when he was clean. Once, he saw his father begging Beby for forgiveness with tears and helplessness stretched across his face. Nader swore he would never touch the stuff. By coincidence, his second oldest brother Bijan, who used to live in Tehran and hardly ever came to the farm, arrived in the middle of the horror. He walked in and sat by the large fireplace, facing the door. Nader could see and feel his brother's embarrassment. He was stunned. He did not utter a word, just like a lion that is in meditation preparing to wake up. Nader could see the rage in his eyes boiling over into the lines on his face. In his heart, Nader was begging him to rise and punish their father for what he had done to their mother. His mother was now being treated in another room, trying to recover, but he still could hear his mother's cries. And also, his father's voice from the patio, trying to get in to get his next fix of opium. But the men were holding on to him. He was mumbling to himself and, out of madness, began to hurl the rocks used to crack the nuts through the open doorway. One flew straight in and hit Nader's brother directly in the middle of his chest. It was enough to provoke the lion, putting him on full alert and attack. Bijan suddenly jumped up and stormed through the door, lunging at their father. Over eight men could barely contain him. He began furiously punching his father, landing some intense blows to his head. More men rushed in to help, finally holding his brother so that his father could run away down the stairway to the first floor and out of the house.

Nader never forgot that night of horror. He felt guilty for such a long time to come, thinking he was the cause. His brother Bijan was taken to his cousin's house so he could be controlled. Now it was just Nader and his Mother. Sadly, he watched his mother pacing in the large room holding onto her legs and began to cry, calling out to God. Nader was questioning who God was? How can God help? He had never seen God come into their house. At that moment, the name God began to register into Nader's conscious memory as someone who is good and is going to help his mother; therefore, he must be a great man. As Nader began to rub his mother's leg where she was rubbing to ease her pain, rolling her pants up, he noticed his mother's legs were entirely black from the beating by his father. His eyes began to tear up as he begged his mother to lie down, and as she became more concerned and worried about him than her pain, she lied down. He hugged her and began to rub her legs. She was playing with his hair, something he really loved even when he was older. As little as he was, still, he pretended to go to sleep and waited until his mother fell asleep.

The sound of a barking dog outside captured his attention, and for a moment, he stared at the four tall glass doors facing the small balcony; one was open. He quietly rose, as to not awaken his mother, and walked to the open door, stepping onto the balcony, and was careful to close the door gently, but not entirely, lest he wakes his mother. There was a gigantic moon lighting the land. Staring at this fantastic moon, he wondered if this was God, and maybe he could ask for help. In the silence of the night, he took in the tall wall which surrounded their house and the other houses shimmering in the moonlight.

Maybe the sun is God. The barking dog was heard again, and he broke the silence as Nader began talking to the oversized moon.

> -Please, God, help me. I do not know who you are, but can you hear me? Please help my mother to feel better, please God, can you hear me?

His voice was so quiet he hardly could hear himself. By then, silent tears were running down his cheeks. He did not even notice he was tearing up. He closed his eyes and experienced the relief of the tears. Then, he heard the words,

> -God can hear you and did hear you.

He opened his eyes and found a slender, older man in his sixties, with a short white beard, sitting next to him. He continued:

-God always hears you, and he always sees everything. Do not worry; some things do happen for a reason. Your mother is fine; just like nothing happened, no pain. Nader began to speak with the old man, and it didn't occur to him how the man came to be on the balcony. Nader had never seen him before, and he had never been to his house. Nor was he one of the farmers or family friends, yet this did not seem odd.

Their house was built in such a way that it would be almost impossible for anyone to get in. This was because of the fight that his grandfather had with another farm's inhabitants. In fact, his mother, at age thirteen, was given to his father basically to bring peace between his father's side of the family and his mother's. She used to tell him, her older uncle had practically carried her from their farm to his father's family farm. She said that at the time, she did not know what "husband" meant, nor did she know what being married meant. After all, she was only thirteen years old. She was told that she must obey her father-in-law Hajji Gholam Hussein. And whatever he said, she had to follow, and that was all she knew about marriage. She basically became a servant to her father-in-law. His grandfather's wife had passed away, and everyone had a story about it. Some said she died because she could not handle the pressure and kind of life the family had. However, his mother was the favorite among all three daughters-in-law, and this did benefit her on occasion. That was why the house had to be built in such a way, so their enemies could not attack them during the nighttime. There was a tall wall about two stories high around the building and just one entry door, which was so short that you could not enter while riding a horse or even a donkey. The first floor was only used for the animals. There was a large yard for the animals to mingle, along with storage for the hay and other food for the animals. There were three different stables for the horses, cows, sheep, and goats. The second floor was very large, and this was where the family stayed. To enter the house was almost impossible without being caught, especially for this peaceful, calm old man sitting next to him, giving him comfort. He told Nader about life, about his father and his mother. But Nader was so young, and as the years passed, he could not remember all the man spoke about. It seemed he did understand him at the time, but he could not remember it after he was gone. This man helped him not hate his father and advised him to let a higher power handle such unfairness and unjust acts. It was such a great conversation; he knew everything about Nader and knew more about what he felt than he did. The tears stopped flowing down his face, but he still did not know who God was. He looked up at the moon once again and turned to the older man and asked him,

-Are you, God?

A smile appeared on the older man's peaceful illuminated face, and with his soft voice, whispered. "No, you are." He did not know what he meant by this, but Nader quietly started to laugh. Suddenly the tall door opened and his mother appeared next to him where the older man was sitting. But there was no older man next to him. The balcony was just enough for two people. She was standing there looking at Nader with concern. Worried, confused, and concern, Nader search for the older man to see he was standing at the lower balcony smiling at Nader. The lower balcony was a bit larger, with enough room for about fifteen people. Nader was worried that she would see the older man and ask who he was or be frightened and make him leave. To his amazement, she said nothing about the older man as if she didn't even notice his presence. It was as though she could not see him. She sat next to him,

-Nader, what are you doing here? whom are you talking to?" Nader nervously looks at the older man than his mother and, as his voice started, whispered, Go…God… I was asking him to help you…

Tear appears in his mother's eyes once again, and she reached for him and began hugging him. As she played with his hair, she whispered into his ears,

> -I guess God heard you! An older man came to my dream and touched my leg, and the pain went away… no more black spots on my entire legs. You should not be worried, see…

His mother showed him her legs where they had been entirely black because of the beating. Nader was shocked and happy when he saw no black spots, and they were white as snow. Surprisingly, as Nader turned and looked towards the older man through his mother's arms, He was still surprised about why his mother did not say anything about the older man's presence. He looked at his mother and then at the older man. But he was no longer there. He kept looking around for him, but he was nowhere to be found. He had simply vanished as quickly as he had appeared. No one else was there besides his mother and him. He was scared for a moment, but he soon felt a fantastic sense of peace when his mother began telling him that she felt no more pain. Somehow the sleep took the pain away. Then, she said something astounding. She began to describe a dream she just had in which an older man was telling her to wake up. She continued,

> -The old man said that I would not have any more pain. Then, I woke up, and the pain was all gone.

Nader cut in.

> -Do you think this old man was God?

Mother answered,

> -Yes, it was… I guess he heard you cry….

His mother then hugged him tightly, and the warmth of being in her arms was wonderfully soothing. He peered out from beneath his mother's embrace and was astonished to see the old man standing on the balcony again, just a few yards from them. He smiled at Nader, and then suddenly, he just vanished. Like he was playing a kind game with Nader. His eyes were wide open with disbelief, but he did not say anything to his mother. Somehow, he knew he should not mention the old man's presence. He felt he should keep this one to himself. Later that same night, he was lying in bed next to his mother; his eyes were fixed on the tall window, thinking about the older man. He closed his eyes in calmness and then sadly remembered the car and his sense of peace left. He looked around very carefully, not to wake his mother up, but he could not see anything. He had forgotten about the race and the car they built. He remembered the boys on his racing team who helped him build the car; they were going to be crushed about the loss. He remembered them during the fight, watching them collect the pieces of the broken car. He knew the next day he would see sadness deep within the eyes of his friends. He also knew they would not say a word even if they were heartbroken about the car they had built. But at the time, he was more concerned about his mother and could not even think about the race or the wooden car. He did not even notice that the broken wooden car was gone. The thought of the older man had engaged his mind once again. He forgot about the wooden car and the race he had the next morning. Finally, he fell into a deep sleep. And there was the old man again. He appeared and sat next to Nader. But this time, they're under a white berry tree in an alley, and it was snowing; he began telling Nader about life, his father, and his mother. But he was so young, and as the years passed, could not remember all he spoke about. It seemed he did understand the old man at the time, but he could not remember it after he was gone. This man helped him not hate his father and advised him to let a higher power handle such unfairness and unjust acts. It was such a great conversation; he knew everything about Nader and knew more about what he felt than he did. The sounds of his friend woke him from his dream; he was awakened by one of his friends.

-We are going to be late for our race! Why are you still sleeping? Let's go…

Nader was a bit confused at first; it was way past the time he usually used to wake up. Right away, he realized the wooden car they had built was not in the room.

-I am sorry, we don't have a car to race with… my father broke our car….

His friend laughed and said,

-Wrong, we do have a car… hurry up, we are late….

Then he took off and exited the room. Confused, Nader got up and walked down to the yard and delightfully found his friends there. Then a friend spoke up and said,

-After the fight was over, we took the wooden car out of the room and began to put most of it back together during the night. Then there was this older man, one of your guests, came to help…Nader, he was like a magician, in less than a few hours he fixed everything, it looks like it was before.

A smile appeared on Nader's face and soul. Perhaps, he knew who the older man was but said nothing. A bit later, they took off toward the racing area. When Nader and his team got there, Haddi and his team were waiting for them. His heart was calm. He believed that everything would now be okay; they could still participate in the race. The race started quickly, and off they went. They got about 100 yards, and then their little car broke in the middle of the race. Once again, they lost. But for some reason, he was not unhappy as he'd been the previous years. He noticed one of his friends began to dance and celebrate their loss as others joined in. Maybe this was because of the older man Nader saw the night before. Maybe life had taught them something more valuable than winning. Their celebrations made Haddi and his team mad. They almost broke into a fight if it wasn't for a couple of men who were passing by, who separated them and sent them on their way, in opposite directions.

The old bearded man began visiting Nader regularly after that first night, and whenever he was sad or unhappy, he would appear. It was as though he had been summoned by the energy Nader released. There was an alley behind a place called Housinieh, which was used for religious ceremonies for ten days during the month of Moharam. Housinieh was built just like a large open theater. There was a large stage in the middle, and the place was so large that over 100 horses could be used for a fighting scene. Encircling it was two stories of small rooms with one side open towards the stage. Each family had its own booth. One was three times larger than the rest; this belonged to Nader's family. Before the ceremony started, the families used to design their booths for 10 days with colorful fabrics, decorative goods, and Persian rugs. The ceremony would start around 1 PM and go on for several hours; each day, they had different performances, mostly religious plays, almost all work stopped in the villages. Those ten days were the best time of all for the children.

It was outside of the Housinieh under a large berry tree called "toot" that the old man used to come and talk to Nader. What Nader had never mentioned to anyone was that this old man would come to visit him in his dreams. Nader would often fall asleep to see him sitting by a well under the tree; it would always seem to snow when he appeared to chat with him. He could never remember all of their conversations, only that this old man was a friend and would take his hard feelings out of his system and leave him in happiness and balance. It was an unknown force he never questioned.

The old man's visits continued every so often until Nader was about sixteen years old. As he became a young man, the visits stopped. He used to ponder as to why he never questioned these visits, he knew if he told most people, they would just laugh, and he never wanted to scare the man away with too many questions. He grew quite fond of the old man because he was helping him untangle his inner turmoil. Up until then, Nader had a war deep within his soul, and this gentleman had helped him. The newfound peace he was discovering was an immense growth for him; he felt reborn because of his bearded older friend. Sadly, the last time he saw him was when he was almost eighteen years old. But now, he was able to have visions, accompanied by very lucid dreams, which he accredits to his bearded older friend.

***

After the horrible night of his father's violent fit, wife-beating, and car-breaking, his oldest brother Abbass decided to become a protective father figure for his family. He had previously lived a somewhat secluded life on the farm. Everything changed when his older brother joined the military. He remembered one late afternoon he was playing in the yard and saw several rigid men riding their horses toward his house. These men appeared to be lawmen; they were very daunting, especially for a five-year-old boy. Every kid used to hide from them or run away when they saw them coming. Nader was playing with a few of his friends in front of his house by a small creek as the scary lawmen approached with the representative of the village. His name was Kadkhoda, he was the mayor of the village. They slowly rode up to the front of Nader's house, and Kadkhoda walked to the door. The lawmen were sporting thick over-exaggerated mustaches and their army uniforms. When they saw the kids playing, they would stop and ominously stare at them, then play with their mustaches to tease and frighten them. Nader was not as afraid of them as the other kids were. Their chief used to be a guest at his family house on occasion, and during his visits, Nader was always running around. He was the baby of the family. He was seven years younger than his brother before him. You could say he was a bit spoiled, especially by his mother and sisters.

Kadkhoda walked out and asked the lawmen to enter with him. Nader watched them enter his house, not liking the situation, and displayed the grimmest look he could conjure up. His mother rushed out and, to him, whisked him away from the menacing men. She leaned in and whispered,

"Run to your brother and tell him not to show up at the house. Tell him the lawmen are here to take him away. Run, he is on the way home." As Nader started running to find his brother, he felt himself filling up with even more hatred for the uniformed men. He was tired and sweating, but he did not stop. He ran through beautiful swaying trees along the clean, crisp creek that ran across the farm. Though surrounded by beauty, he did not notice it on this day. He spotted his brother Abbass walking toward him. As he reached him, he shouted the message to him, talking as fast as he could. His brother looked at him calmly and said,

-Good. Now let's go home.

To his surprise, they just continued walking towards the house. Maybe his brother didn't understand what he was telling him, so he repeated his message. Raising his voice, he exclaimed,

-Hajji Khanoom said you must not go home.

For a reason unbeknown to him, his brother just lifted him up and carried him toward the house. He was confused; his brother was walking so calmly in the wrong direction. They reached the house, and everyone, including his mother, Hjji Khanoom, was surprised and a bit angry as to why he showed up.

It was later that Nader watched the lawmen take his brother, with tears in his eyes, holding onto his mother. He couldn't understand why. What had Abbass done wrong? He wanted to have the power to attack and kill the lawmen, stopping them in their tracks from taking his brother. Now, feeling distraught, he asked God for help, but no help came this time, and his brother was gone. Later his questions were answered. Abbass had done nothing wrong and, in fact, was doing something great. He was joining the military to serve and defend his country. Going into the military in Iran, even now, is mandatory; unless you know someone with influence who can help you avoid it. But if you have a physical problem or an elderly father or mother, and you are the only caregiver, you can be released from military duties.

It was many years later, he realized the main reason his brother wanted to go into the military. He wanted to get away from the farm and start a new life for himself and his family. The situation with his father greatly bothered his brother, and he needed to get away. After his military duties, he took a job with the government while simultaneously working on his education with hard work. He received his desired degrees and was extremely dedicated to his job. Within a short time, he had become a man of influence in the Iranian secret police, the Savak. Nader remembered several years later that his brother used to quietly come to his room with one request. Nader was living in Tehran in his mother's new house and attending the College of Dramatic Arts. Abbass would come in from time to time and request to use a typewriter that he had stashed away in Nader's closet, wrapped in plastic. He would ask Nader to leave his room for a while. But Nader used to peek through the window and observed the most unusual thing. Abbass would type while wearing gloves as though he was typing some type of secret document. When he was done typing, he would put the typewriter away, ask Nader to put on the gloves, and go mail the letter he had just typed. On the envelope were just a few numbers, no name or any address. Later he discovered that his brother was reporting directly to the Shah concerning wrongdoings by high government officials.

Nader's sister Parry was the first family member who left the village for Tehran with her husband. She was young but still much older than Nader. After she got married and moved to Tehran, this was the beginning of the slow trickle of the whole family relocating. His brother Abbass was next to move to the city. He never returned to the farm after his military service. And then it was Bijan, his other brother, who left without a trace. They finally received word that he was with Parry in Tehran. Then it was Kamaal and after, him when Nader turned the age of seven. Abbass and his sister Parry, who was only 4 years older than Abbass, would look out for Nader in Tehran. She and Boloor, Abbass's wife, were like his second mothers. Upon moving to Tehran, Parry registered Nader in first grade. Nader didn't know this at the time, but he was sent to Tehran mainly because he was creating unwanted problems back in the village school. He had organized a rally to get rid of one of his teachers when he was only six years old; he was a little troublemaker. The school had been organized by some members of his family. The teacher's daughter also attended this school in the same class that Nader was in. They were both six years old. She was the only girl at school. Nader and this particular little girl did not get along because she acted rudely toward Nader and others. He was not accustomed to this bad behavior. He thought she felt that she was above most of the other kids because her father was the teacher. Nader had been spoiled by his family. Nader had been treated like the king of his village. So, when this girl treated him as though he was beneath her, Nader didn't let it go. He couldn't recall exactly what he did one day, but Nader did something that this girl didn't like, and she told her father. Her father punished Nader by hitting him on his palm with a wooden stick, not extremely hard like he had punished other students. He just wanted to embarrass Nader. Students would be afraid of teachers for this very reason. Teachers were very strict, and they would punish them regularly. The worse punishment was to hold your feet up and have the bottom slapped hard with a wooden stick. Students would always walk the other way when they saw their teachers coming. When this teacher hit Nader, it didn't hurt physically as much as it hurt his pride. He was embarrassed at being punished in front of the other boys for what seemed to be nothing. The teacher wanted to show the students that no one could disrespect his daughter, and Nader was used as an example. Nader did not cry during this punishment, but he was humiliated. He planned revenge in his head. He gathered his gang of a few brave boys and organized a trip to the city of Khansar. He told the boys that they needed to go to the city to complain about this teacher because he was a bad teacher who had to go. As the school bell rang to announce the closing of the school for the day, his friends all joined him, and they started their journey towards Tehran. It was 4 o'clock in the afternoon. He was preaching along the way, sprawling his arms across the clear sky, emphasizing each word about how they were doing a brave and necessary thing. But it never crossed their minds that within a few hours, night would fall, and they had to stop. It did not occur to them that the office they were headed to would be closed. They were traveling on the only dirt road. They felt they were all grown up, completing a great journey. They were still bellowing with their chests stuck out as they came to a one-room monument. This monument was engulfed in a mood-altering realization. It was told that a lady had entered this room one day and never came out. So now, her spirit was lingering around the monument and could appear anytime and take you away with her. None of them wanted to encounter a ghost at this time. Nader was the leader, and he couldn't let them turn back. He had to think of a way for them to get around this monument without being frightened to death and carried away for eternity. They were all scared, and no one wanted to take another step. He was as scared as the rest, but he couldn't show the other boys his fear, so he tried to act calm. He told them he would walk past the scary building, and when nothing happened to him, they could all follow. He started to walk towards the building. His heart was pumping, about to explode from his chest. He was cold yet sweating, very afraid, and began whispering to God. He asked for help out of this situation and promised he would be good for the rest of his life if he just saved him from the dead lady's spirit. As he walked by the door of the monument, he was so frightened that he could only stare straight ahead. His knees were shaking, and he could not even talk to God anymore. Somehow, he pushed himself forward. He was out of breath from the fear and thought he was going to die. He made it a few yards past the door and managed to get his breath back, feeling very brave again. He forced a smile onto his face and called out,

-See, nothing happened to me. Come on, you chickens.

But the gang was scared, and no one could move. It was really getting dark, and if they didn't get past this monument now, they never would. Nader began loudly pleading with the other boys to follow him. They should just get a move on, and they could be past the building and safely on their way. He was coaxing them to hurry up. They really thought the lady's spirit would jump out and attack them. Nader was about to give up, realizing that they weren't coming. The sun was setting, and he heard a voice exclaim,

-Agha Nader, what are you doing here?

He jumped three feet, thinking it was the dead lady's spirit talking. But to his surprise, it was his older cousin. He was standing there with his bicycle, which was an impressive thing in those days. He thought that maybe his cousin was God, or he at least had saved the day for God. He told him that they were headed to the city. He was no longer afraid now, and he was able to speak with confidence again. They were all relieved and began to relax. Nader told his cousin, with a boost of confidence, that they were going to go and talk to the office educations in the city to get their teacher removed. He continued,

-His daughter is in our class, and he hit me because she said I did something wrong.

Nader stopped talking, he remembered that their teacher was his cousin's friend, and his cousin helped him get the teaching job.

-OK, then I will help you,

His cousin surprisingly informed him. He began to think that maybe he really was God now or was sent by God. He was going to help them by this scary monument, which none of the kids would look at. A fake smile of victory sprawled across his face as they all believed they could move forward with his cousin's help. Nader was about to proudly tell all his friends that his cousin was going to be the hero. But no sooner than they had gotten past the monument, his cousin reached for his belt buckle and began to rush around and beat the boys, yelling,

-I am going to take all of you and leave you in this building so that the spirit lady will take you away! You damn boys! Your teacher is a good man.

They realized that this cousin of Nader's was not interested in helping them at all, so off they ran in all directions. He began chasing some of them, trying to scare them, and boy did he succeed! Most of them were running towards a farm. Nader didn't know how they gained the strength to do this, but they all climbed a very tall wall for them and jumped over it to get away from his cousin. They kept running through a multitude of trees, and soon they were in two groups running side by side. They just kept running and jumping over walls. The belt and the spirit lady gave them stamina. Now it was dark, and they were lost. They were still worried about the dead woman's spirit finding them. The smallest boy who had bravely followed Nader was now in tears, and he believed this was entirely Nader's fault. He had never been caught up in a situation as scary as this one. To make matters worse, they thought they might be on the property of their enemies. If they saw them, they might harm them or kill them.

By now, Nader's mother had sent farmers to search for the boys. When they heard them coming, they thought they were angels. They turned and ran towards the saviors, thanking God for sending angels to them. Nader never forgot this night which was the catalyst for his move to Tehran.

*****

Chapter 2

Encountering Indifference And Opposition...

Shortly after the spirit lady episode, Nader arrived in Tehran to live with his brother Abbass, his wife Boloor, and his sister Parry, despite his mother not wanting him to leave. His older brother was hardly ever home because he traveled a lot. This was a blessing for all of them. Nader soon realized that his kind brother had been turned into a strict and rigid military sergeant. He was not the man Nader remembered from the farm. When his brother was gone, they would have peace. No one would be complaining and bossing them around. In his brother's eyes, no one could do anything right. It felt like they were in jail when he was home. Nader didn't like Tehran to begin with, partly because it was so different from what he was used to. It wasn't exciting like he had thought it would be and was especially dull for someone coming from a farm. They were rich among the farmers, but their money didn't assure that they were welcomed into Tehran society. He was considered a village boy, and he was not accepted by the city boys. If you were a city person, you were considered to be sophisticated and upscale. Nader felt like an outsider in this strange place. He realized that he was no longer the boss' son, leader of the pack. He was considered "uncultured"; he was a "nobody" and played by himself most of the time. He had a few friends, which were the kids who were shy or already outcasts. He hated his school and became disgruntled about being there. He wanted to fight because he was disoriented, disrespected, and lonely. He dreamed of the farm and became shy and depressed. He asked Parry if he could go back to the village, but everyone felt that it would be better for him to remain in the city. He was told he would get used to it. This started to affect his small first-grade mind and would soon change his life. He realized that maybe all people should be treated the same regardless of race, color, or stature. He developed compassion for the underdog and respect for the working class. His disdain grew for those who ruled as if they were Gods.

Some days were really difficult. He would be standing in the schoolyard watching the other boys play soccer - and he wasn't invited. He would watch these boys having fun, and he was still an outsider. On the farm, he was the leader of the team. He would be the one calling the shots. He decided who played and who didn't. He could even change the rules if he wanted to. In this strange new city, he was invisible and alone. He was nobody. He managed to survive his awful first year at his new school. But it was such a culture shock and a hurtful memory. He felt as though all the happiness in his life had been taken away. All he encountered was indifference and opposition from most of his classmates.

When summer finally arrived, he was able to go back to the farm. He needed relief from his unfriendly new school. After his arrival on the farm, he realized that it was somehow different. Something was missing, and he couldn't put his finger on it. City life had affected him in ways he would never have imagined. He had been so unhappy in the city. Yet now, he felt a great distance between him and farm life. His friends in the village were elated to see him. They wanted to build another wooden car, so they could win the race this year. He didn't care very much about the race anymore. He felt confused and surprisingly wanted to return to the city.

*****

After Nader moved to Tehran to start his schooling, his mother began to spend most of the winter and fall seasons with them in Tehran. His brother's personality had taken on a new attitude due to his military training. He was in control and in charge. He had become well-respected by the government, and he had established a position as the most likable and highly influential member of the Savak. He had somehow kept his modesty and patience. His belief was to serve people, not himself, and that respect gained him respect. This position helped the family financially and in getting in the door at any government office. If you were connected to someone with high influence, you had it made. Although the home in Tehran was beginning to feel like a military base, Nader resisted this atmosphere. He did not want to be like his father or brother. His brother's point of view was that education was all that mattered. If you were anything other than a doctor, lawyer, or engineer, you were nothing. Nader knew from that point on that he would have to work very hard to create his own identity.

Just sitting in the same room with his brother was painful enough. He was so overbearing about how much time had to be spent on homework. Nader would just stare at his books and move his lips in silence as if he cared about what he was reading. The truth was that he wasn't reading at all. He hated schoolwork, and at those moments, he hated his brother for being so obsessive. In essence, his drive to push Nader into education did the opposite; he began hating school and despised studying. His brother's strict watch during his study time was excruciating. He had to sit and study every day for several hours after school in the living room. It began to feel like a prison. Escaping to the bathroom every hour was the only way he could get a break from this monotonous routine. Sometimes Nader would just sit on the toilet for no reason just so he didn't have to stare at his boring books.

Nader's family finally settled in a huge house with almost an acre of land. Now Bloor, Nader, Bigian, and Abaass were living away from Parry. Their bathroom was outside. The interior of their home was quite luxurious, and the kitchen and the bathroom were on the same side of the building as the helper's room. The land was covered with trees, but there were several unsafe wells that were very deep. Nighttime was scary because there were thieves who would enter the property. The police who would chase them would always be afraid of falling down a hidden well as they ran through the thick patches of trees. In the beginning, there were hardly any families living around the house. Neighbors slowly trickled into the midst of all the unhappiness in Tehran. They were a saving grace. Nader had neighbors to the east. They were a Jewish family. Muslims and Jews have not been amicable. Being Muslim, you tended to have contempt for Jewish people, and they had equal disdain for Muslims. But this Jewish family was much more interesting to Nader than the rest. This family had a daughter who was learning to play the violin. She was very good at her young age. He would go to the end of his backyard and climb up the old large tree and secretly watch her. Sometimes he thought that she could see him. Sometimes he thought this Violin Girl knew he was there and pretended not to see him. She would look his way and smile as she continued playing. He would try to hide from her view as much as possible and bury himself among the branches of the tree. Before long, he had built a simple treehouse with branches and wood. This became his regular hang-out. He had stocked the treehouse with everything he needed to assure his comfort while secretly watching his neighbor practice her delightful music. This secret little spot was cleverly hidden amongst the branches of a huge tree, and he didn't think anyone could see him. He never told anyone about his treehouse, not even his sister or Boloor. It was a secret he kept from everyone. He was lucky his treehouse was so far from his house, and no one could even see him when he used to get lost between the trees. He would stare for many hours at her. Dreaming about her long hair as thick and sleek as a horse's mane. Her big eyes were shaped like almonds with thick black lashes. He began to feel as though she was teasing him, enticing him. She wouldn't let on that she was aware of his presence. He both hated and loved this little game. He would try to figure out a way to talk to this beautiful girl who he had started calling "my love."

In his little seven-year-old mind, he was already planning to marry this girl. He didn't even know her name. He wondered how wrong it was for people to hate each other because of differences in their religion or culture. He would marry her in a second, even though he knew that he would not be allowed to have a friendship with this Jewish girl. He would get sick thinking about how Muslims and Jews thought so poorly of each other. This belief was wrong and should be changed.

He hated for summer to arrive because he knew he had to go to the farm with his mother. Before he had his Violin Girl, he could not wait for summer to arrive. He had no choice and left for the farm. When summer ended, his main thoughts were about getting back to the treehouse to see the beautiful young violinist. He saw smiles filled with happiness from Boloor and Parry. Their eyes told Nadar they genuinely missed him. It was good to see them as well. He realized how much they all cared for each other. The women had prepared a glass of juice for him that he downed quickly. He was anxious to get to his treehouse. After chatting a bit with Boloor and Parry, he escaped to his tree. As he climbed up, he had been listening for the sound of the violin, but none could be heard. He sat on his treehouse for a long, but her window never opened, and there was no sign of her. Disappointed, he left the tree and headed back to the house. All night he thought about the girl and her violin, hoping he would hear the poignant sound of her music. A week passed, and still, there was no sign of her. He went back to school, and when he would come home, he would look for his treasured neighbor, but her window remained closed, and she was nowhere to be found. He was becoming depressed and worried that maybe she was gone. Then, suddenly one day, he was in the back of the house, and he heard the glorious sound of a violin. He ran outside and climbed up into his treehouse. He was so delighted to see his friend smiling and playing. She was back, and he was in heaven.

He created a view-finder through the leaves so that he could see his neighbor better. He still had not met this girl, but he was sure she knew that he was watching her. He would look forward to watching her every day. He loved her music dearly. He would make up lyrics to the music as she played. He would sing with the lyrics he made. This continued for about a year, and it was like a game of cat and mouse. He would do most of his homework in the treehouse. Still, no one in his family knew about his secret spot in the tree. Their yard was so huge; a few film crews had even shot movies using their tree-filled property as a location to mimic the Caspian Sea. Sometimes he would use the street to get to his treehouse, so no one would get suspicious about why he always disappears into the tree and in the same direction. Then he would quickly climb a telephone pole next to the wall of their property and jump over a wall and disappear into the trees and to his treehouse. Soon another summer had come again, and this time when he came back, his Violin Girl was gone again. He looked for her for several days, but there were no curtains on the windows, and there appeared to be no movement inside the house. He walked by the house a few times to see if he could find her, but she was never home. Feeling desperate, several times, he went up to ring the doorbell. Nader waited for a long time, debating if he should or not. He walked away every time neighbors drove up or walked by. Several years passed, and the girl never came back. He had been very sad about her for a while, but he would never forget her face or violin.

*****

After his Violin Girl had vanished, he was often bored, and he missed her. It was then he realized how much he liked her or loved her, how much he cared, and what she meant to him. He began missing his friends at the farm as well; there were so few things for a child to do in the big city. Nader started to invent different activities to entertain himself. He still hated schoolwork, and he wanted to rebel against his brother's pressure on him to study all the time. He also became a rebel against his family's traditions and beliefs. He had learned patience from the wise bearded old man who had visited him. It became a game that he would play, rejecting all the rules that his brothers would try to enforce upon him. His mother would be the mediator between his brothers and him. But soon, he knew that he had to find other means to get away from home and fill his time with something more fun. He slowly made more friends at school, and one day, Nader was introduced to the game of soccer. He was beginning to enjoy his life again. But his brother would still interrupt his happiness by trying to stop him from playing. He would have to sneak out of the house to play soccer. It was difficult; he had to lie about playing until grade school ended. What his brother never understood was that soccer is a force that runs in the blood of any young Iranian. Sneaking out of school, playing all sorts of tricks, lying to your parents and teachers just to get a chance to play with your friends is a rite of passage. Parents saw education as your only vehicle of success. A sport did not matter in the long run. Each night, when his family was asleep, Nader's brain would be concocting a plan to sneak out early to get a chance to play for a few minutes before school started. Normally their game would start out in the street in front of the school before classes began, then they would move into the schoolyard. The plastic soccer ball was kind to them. It became an addiction, and without it, they would almost be lost. His day would usually start very early in the morning, around 6 A.M. Sometimes, his duties would be to rush to the bakery and get fresh hot bread. Three kinds of bread were very popular: Sangak, Taftoon, and Barbary, the most popular being Sangak. In Iran, they are accustomed to eating fresh food every day, every meal. He remembered when they began to bring frozen meat in from Australia, and people refused to eat it. In Iran, you purchase vegetables, meats, fruits, and dairy products fresh. Especially bread has to be fresh every morning, noon, and night. It could be delivered by the bakery. But if you wanted it hot out of the oven for every meal, you had to make a trip three times a day to the local bakery. This was usually done by a young boy, helper, or the women. Often half of the bread would be gone before you arrived home. Hot Sangak bread was just impossible to resist. After his trip to the bakery, it was breakfast time. If his mother didn't force him, he would not wait for breakfast. This would allow a couple of extra minutes to get to school to kick the ball, which was far more exciting than eating breakfast. He also got used to eating fast, and in fact, would just gulp his food down and run a half-mile to school. He was called "the fastest eating kid around." His routine would be to drink milk at the local store on the way to school; this helped him boost his energy. He believed he was growing into a big, strong, invincible man. He remembers studying harder to get better grades so that if Abbass caught him playing soccer, he would be in less trouble. Having good grades helped him a lot. Nader would pay any price to be able to play a few minutes more. His right arm had been broken three times, but he never revealed this to anyone. He let it heal itself because he was afraid that if his brother found out, he wouldn't be allowed to play. However, he paid the price later on when the same arm would break for the fourth time.

Usually, every neighborhood had its own soccer team. The boys would find a large piece of property that was empty and flat. Then, they would go to work vigorously cleaning the land. Next, the soccer gate would rise, and the games began. Soon everyone from the neighborhood would arrive and introduce themselves; it would be the start of new friendships. The team members often recruited more friends from other neighborhoods to join them. The team uniform would be chosen along with the captain of the team. The person who started the team was the Captain, and he was usually the best player. After the team was organized, they invited another team to play against them. The night before the match, no one could sleep in anticipation.

To play just a simple game of soccer, you had a giant challenge ahead. The most difficult part was buying the uniforms, which was quite expensive for most players. The most exciting part of the game was dreaming about playing with a real leather ball for the first time. As a beginner and young boy, you would always start with a plastic ball and play in your neighborhood alley. Then, when you got older, about sixteen or so, you would have developed into a decent player and join a team. You could join a local soccer team which always played with a leather ball and full uniforms. Nader used to hide his soccer outfit in the bushes or at a friend's house so his brother would not see it. He would carry some kind of a book to make his brother think that he was studying with his friend. His brother was often abusive and a tyrant. Abbass wasn't always wrong. Later on, when he was older, Nader understood the mentality of the Iranian society was that education was the only way to have a successful life. When his brother would come home, the house became quiet, and everyone would act like they were completely engaged in reading or doing homework. It was mostly pretense, but they did not wish to provoke the wrath of this overprotective family member.

Nadar had become good enough to play for a local team called Shahrzard. They would play in a field located by a small river on the east side of it. He had organized the team with a couple of his friends, Abraham and Mohammad Mandeghari. There was a wall surrounding their field on the north, south, and west corner; the east had a small river flowing. On the south side of this wall was an alley that connected to a small river. That was the entry to their soccer field. One of the team members, Hamidy, who was also their classmate, lived directly across from the field on the other side of the alley on the south side. He was not a good player, but he was always fun. They were always nice to him because of his pretty sister, Freshdeh. Her bedroom was on the second floor facing the field, and somehow all of them dreamed that one day she would go out with them, even though she was several years older than them. But what made Freshdeh more interesting to Nader was she played the violin, always reminding him of his Violin Girl. She might have been gone, but her image was ingrained in Nader's mind.

Later their team developed into one of the best around. The soccer tournament started once again, and their team was one of the top favorites to win. His position was 'right back, and he had become very strong and rough to the point that all the other players would run away from him. His regular routine of swimming nearly every day had carved his body into one strong, lean footballer. His legs and chest were becoming very muscular, especially his legs. As a teenager, he would wear his shirts unbuttoned a bit to show off his increasing chest hair. Nader thought he was a young stud, not knowing as an old man, he would laugh at himself recalling these times.

By now, his visits to the farm were growing fewer, and his mother began to visit by herself. He would worry about his mother's safety, fearing that if she were alone with his father at the farm, she might get into a fight with him, and no one would be there to protect her. This disturbing thought never left his mind. But luckily, the boys were older now. Bijan had ferociously threatened their father, putting his foot down. There would be no more abuse towards their mother. But Nader's father was still addicted to opium, and it was difficult for him to find treatment. He had used it now for over forty years. He would still be having trouble containing his devil-like nature when he would try to withdraw. Paradoxically, he was the nicest man when he was high. Nader managed to visit his mother twice a year during his school year while she was at their farm.

*****

Chapter 3

Lost In Tehran...

Nader was beginning to find his place in Tehran. He had created his own group of friends. His life was ruled by soccer; everything else was behind it on his priorities list. The older he got, the more his struggles with his brother increased. During this time, his older brothers and sisters convinced Hajji Khnoom to move to Tehran. She ended up being alone, and finally, she gave up the farm. She hired other farmers to run it and move to Tehran. By now most of the people in the village had moved to the big city for a better life. The villages became empty, and the cities crowded. But leaving the farm was not easy for her. It was very hard for her. She had been so active, running the daily activities as a landlord. Now she became inactive, sitting in a house in Tehran. Every time the family used to have lunch or dinner, they had several farmers join them. It was his mother's policy that the whole family had to sit on the floor and eat with them. They rarely used the dinner table, which was practically new, but there was not enough room for everyone at the table, and his mother didn't want any of the farmers to feel that they were beneath them and had to sit on the floor. He knew his mother missed all the commotion and life that used to fill her days on the farm. Leaving had also created another problem for his mother and the family. As the farming business continued to fail, farmers began to move to Tehran, and the first place they came to was his house to see his mother. Somehow, someway, they expected his mother to continue taking care of their needs in Tehran as she had done on the farm. So, his mother enlisted the help of her sons to find work for them, which worked out well. Surprisingly, they all became very successful and were able to start their own businesses. Two of those farmers who moved to Tehran were clergy. His mother asked them to come to the house once a week and pray, hoping other relatives and friends would follow suit. It was intriguing how the clergy used to come to the house, sit alone in one room reading their prayers, and then collect their payment which was in an envelope waiting for them. On one occasion, one of them was late. There were a couple of older ladies in attendance whose husbands worked in the garden where Nader's brother grew a multitude of flowers. These ladies would normally come and sit downstairs for the prayer session while the clergy were upstairs, reading their prayers. When the prayer would commence, the ladies would cry so loud that they could be heard on the second floor. The clergymen were brothers, and the eldest used to go first. The younger brother had a great voice which was especially inspirational, and his prayers and chant would move the women to feel deep emotion. He was the one who was late.

The clergy were manipulating the women by concocting sad stories about Muhammad. But these made-up stories had very little to do with the basic principles of Islam. The sadder the story, the more women would cry. The women were unschooled and easily controlled by the clergy into thinking that the more they cried, the more of God's mercy they would receive. Thus, they believed they were gaining a passageway into heaven. This was an ongoing method that they used to control large groups of poor, uneducated people in Iran. It always bothered Nader. The clergy developed this storytelling in order to get the people to pay them. As part of their tactic, the clergy would tell the same stories over and over, and this would convince the people that they were getting closer to God. In some eyes, they had hijacked religion and utilized it as a tool to create a lucrative business for themselves. On the day the clergymen were late coming to Nader's mother's house, Nader snuck in the living room on the second floor and pretended to be the clergy and was quite convincing. Since the clergy were not really praying in Islam's true expression, he felt he was not hurting anyone by mimicking their prayers and chants. As he was leaving from his mock session of prayer-leading, the real clergy walked into the stairwell to go to the second floor upstairs. The women were confused, seeing him through the open door, questioning then who is upstairs performing the prayer. The clergy was even more confused than the women. Nader noticed the crying stopped downstairs, knew perhaps the real clergy must have arrived, then he heard his mother ask the clergy if he did not find the envelope that his pay was inside of. He informed his mother that he was just arriving and were late because they had to attend a funeral service. As the clergy headed upstairs, Nader ran up to the roof and escaped onto his sister's house living next door. He knew his mother was on the way up to see who was responsible for the occurrence. He did not inform his mother that he had performed the prayer. He knew she would be upset, and he never wanted his mother upset, so this mysterious prayer was talked about for a long time, becoming family folklore, the real culprit never caught. His mother believed some type of miracle had occurred. Eventually, Nader told her the truth. Upon learning of this, his mother became a bit sad. He instantly felt awful, realizing she would rather have believed the event had been a miracle.

Soon, life for his entire family took a turn for the worse. The family was struggling, money had become tight, and every member was forced to go out and find work. Everyone except Nader, he was not even informed about the bad situation. By this time, his mother was completely settled in Tehran, and Nader was still the baby of the family, her baby boy no matter his age. Nader could never have imagined the repercussions he would experience later in life from being a momma's boy. He didn't fully understand what being pampered meant, sheltered from negative experiences and daily struggles, he would have to grow up fast and deal with the harsh realities of life. When everything is always provided for you, money has no value. However, with his mother taking permanent residence in Tehran, things got more complicated. His mother and oldest brother Amir constantly fought an unspoken battle for who was the leader of the family. His mother was the leader of their farm, running all aspects and intertwined in family and friends' lives on a daily basis. In her mind, she was still in charge, constantly informing all members of the family as to what they should be doing.

Living in the city for Hajji Khanoom was a different ball game. Losing the farm had never really registered. She was not familiar with the intricate systems of major cities, and in Tehran, she was lost just as Nader was before. No one was able to deal with this issue besides Nader. She listened to him, and he did not hold back his opinions. They would argue, and he would always win. What made the matter more delicate was that in Tehran, Amir had taken on leadership as the head of the family. He was the oldest male. Amir did not hide the fact that he naturally was supposed to take the lead, knowing the ways of the city and smart business moves that would help them flourish. He felt Hajji Khanoom should simply accept retirement and follow his lead, but this was almost impossible for a strong Persian mother who had been the ruling fist of their entire family for decades. The social impact began to take its toll on Hajji Khanoom. She sank into depression. She strangely became more worried about her two cats left behind on the farm than leaving the farm itself. She was constantly talking about them, concerned if they would be fed by Beby, who generally took care of them during fall and winter. Interestingly, it seemed that the cats knew the exact time of his mother's return each year. It was as if they sensed her presence the second she put her feet on the ground. They would be sitting behind the door waiting, and the minute they heard her voice from downstairs, they frantically ran to greet her, embracing her feet as if she was royalty. Beby would crack jokes about how they had no loyalty for her.

One day Nader came home and saw his mother coming out of the bushes that ran along the side of their home. Quietly she looked around as if she had hidden something. He pretended like he did not see her. Later he crept into this passageway and found a little open area she had created; she was secretly feeding the wild cats. This was definitely something she needed to hide from his older brother because he felt wild cats brought diseases and would not approve. He was a fanatic about cleanliness, and the last thing he wanted was wild cats congregating in their yard as a safe haven. Besides, Abaass would not stop short to critic whatever anyone did.

Nader kept her secret, and later he found out that Parry and Boloor also knew about the cats. They even helped her feed them to make her happy. Nader overheard his mother one day wishing that she could fetch the cats from the farm. Joking about driving for hours to check on wild animals was a nonchalant response to something that meant the world to her. He began to realize her fascination with the wild cats was probably because she was filled with guilt about abandoning her cats on the farm.

Shortly after this, Nader witnessed his mother crying, mumbling about her poor cats, and decided to visit the farm to check on them and see if he could bring them back. No one would let Nader go alone, so he came up with a plan. He saved some money and told everyone he was going mountain climbing for the day with his friends. He had twenty-four hours to visit the farm and return home. Early one morning, he left the house to start the secret trip. He took a taxi to the bus station and the bus to the farm. It was about a six-hour drive. This was his first time he was riding the bus to go to the farm by himself. He felt great, like a grown man. The bus was traveling through the countryside, and he was sitting in the first seat behind the driver, having a conversation with the bus driver and his assistant. Talking as if he knew it all. To speak with the driver who was in charge was a big deal at the time for a young man Nader's age. The bus used to stop once for the passengers to eat or drink, use the bathroom, and pray. The drivers were greatly respected by the restaurant owners because they brought them customers; they were fed for free and usually given their best Kabob. He was sitting close by the driver and his assistant when they brought his kabob out. Before he could touch it, a waiter approached and took it away. Then another one quickly replaced it with another kabob, then he turned to the driver and gestured that he had done what he was asked. The driver leaned over and, with a smirk, said,

-This is real kabob. Eat, it is so tender.

Nader realized the driver had taken a liking to him, making sure he was brought the best. And what made it even better, he did not have to pay for it. The bus took off again as he fiddled around in anticipation. Finally, the bus approached the small two-bedroom building located at the front of the farm on the top of a small hill. A family of three used to live there; they ran a small tea house using one of the rooms and outside to serve travelers and the second one for their family. He stepped down the rigid steps, and he felt a very strange feeling. He felt as if he didn't belong there, as if he was a stranger in his own land. Nothing was the same as before,

> -Welcome back, Nader Khan. God bless you. You have grown into a man.

The voice broke him away from his strange thoughts. It was the older man who used to run the tea house. Soon he was walking down the narrow alley towards the main houses. But still, nothing looked the same. There was a slight feeling of sadness all throughout the farm. It was apparent on the faces of the people as well. Not only were there no happy faces looking on contently, but there were also barely any people. He was walking through a ghost town. He walked past the solemn creek which fed water to the land. He slowed his step and walked back to examine the creek. The water level was low and murky. With every step he took more unanswered questions began to loom. He reached the large bridge that crossed the big river leading to his family farmhouse. The sound of the water traveling down the path was not the same loud and wild river he was afraid of when he was younger. The water had no passion or gusto as it traveled the worn path. His steps were getting shorter and shorter. The farmers were passing by and showing their respect. They began to chat with him, and he quickly had four farmers escorting him. Each expressed their problems and were curious as to whether his mother would ever return, desiring for all to be how it was. Finally, they reached the house, he saw Beby, his mother's helper. She had been living next to their house and was responsible for taking care of the cats when his mother wasn't around. She approached him, seeming a bit nervous. She handed him the key to their house but one of the men immediately took the key out of his hand. Out of respect, he went to the gate and opened the door and motioned for him to enter. It was a good feeling to have the workers treat him with the same respect that they had shown his mother and brothers. As he passed Beby, he realized she wanted to tell him something but couldn't get the words out.

-I mostly came to check on the cats. My mother is worried about them. How are they?

This was the last question Beby wanted to hear. She just stood there speechless, staring blankly. A farmer broke the silence,

-It seems they disappeared; we have not been able to find them.

For a few moments, Nader became concerned and worried if he could not find and take the cat with him. Nader decided to check the house first, and if they were not there, they would look elsewhere. He walked away from Beby with concern. He entered the house, followed by three other farmers and Beby. He did not like what he saw. There were bushes growing in the yard in the area that once had many horses, cows, sheep, and goats. The sight of this depressed him to the point that he felt as if he wanted to sit down. The men stood there watching him, feeling the sorrow but remained speechless. They appeared to be hiding something. He wanted to just turn around and leave, but he could not because he had to check on the house and cats. He told himself the sooner he checked the house and found the cats he could leave. He quickened his step, walked through the yard, and entered the lower pathway, heading up the stairs. It was dark; he used a match to light his way up. Just as he turned the first curve to reach the top, his eyes landed on one of the cats sitting behind the door to the large room. She was staring right at him with her eyes wide open. This cat was yellowish and white. For a moment, he stopped and smiled because he had found the cat, and he knew if she was there, the other one must be around. But he still could not see the entire area. He squinted his eyes, noticing the other black and white cat sitting on his feet in the same position as the other. His eyes wide open, staring right at him as well. He felt relieved to find the cats, yet suddenly it hit him, why are they not moving? Why were they not running to him? He let out a soft whisper, beckoning for them to move, there was no movement.

-There they are.

Beby's voice broke his silent confusion.

-They disappeared a couple of months ago. I never saw them until now. I should have come and checked here.

He could not speak or move. In shock, he reached out his hand to stop Beby from taking the cats away. Beby did not realize they had frozen to death, remaining loyal, waiting for his mother's shadow to fall upon them. Nader stepped over and sat between them, overtaken with sadness. The cold had kept them intact. It was as if they were alive, frozen in time. Despite his embarrassment, tears began streaming down his face. The men were watching Nader, but he could not stop crying. Hoping to subdue his sorrow, one of the men started making jokes. They approached him as one man delicately grabbed the dead cats.

-Let's go bury them under the cherry tree. You will never forget their sweetness when you look at those trees or eat their fruit.

Nader helped place the cats in the damp, hard soil, remembering the day he planted these trees as a small boy with the help of his mother. This was a special tree to him; it was located inside a beautiful garden in front of their family house. There were several creeks running through the garden, with a large river flowing on the east and a big creek on the west side. Hanging over all was a huge walnut tree that covered most of the garden like an umbrella. They silently left the garden and walked back down the small pathway. Towards the end, there were two very large rocks on either side. These rocks indicated where the path broke off and led to a small one-room mosque that his family had built. It was used for prayer and for travelers passing by in rainy or cold weather. This mosque brought a flood of memories once again. He just wanted to leave. After he left the farm that day, he did not return for a very long time. He never told his mother about what happened to her cats. He told her a lie. It was the first time he had ever lied to his mother, and it was not easy to look her in the eyes for a long time. He told her that they were healthy and happy.

*****

Chapter 4

Rites Of Passage...

Time was passing quickly, and Nader was growing and maturing into a young man. There was a house being built on a large piece of property across the street from Nader's, and he watched the daily progress of this event, amazed at how quickly things can come into existence. He was happy to see there was a new family moving by his house. There were hardly any families around but a few Jewish families to the east leading towards a small river. The property he used to live on was so big that there was a large cross dividing their property into four equal pieces that two cars could pass through. In the middle of the cross was a round square with a beautiful fountain in the middle, surrounded by flower beds with all kinds of flowers. When he could not go to the soccer field, or when there was no game, he used this space to practice. He kept his ball hidden from his brother, and he had to practice when he was not around. Sometimes he would practice right across from the building that was being constructed. Within few months, the building was done, and a family moved in. On the second floor facing the driveway where he would practice, three teenagers moved into the rooms which had a direct view. They would watch him play from their windows. Then one day he noticed the older boy watching him, he heard a voice call,

-Can I play with you?

He looked up to observe a tall, handsome guy standing in the window. Later he found out his name was Hussein, Navabsafavai.

-Yes, you can.

He answered back. Within a few minutes, they were playing a game. Nader was much better than him in soccer, but he was more skilled at basketball. From the first day, they created a bond. They used to play together every day. Then, suddenly he did not see or hear from Hussein for a week. He checked in his windows, but there was no sign of him anywhere. He wanted to go knock on the door, but he didn't. He had a feeling that he did not want him to go to his house. Hussein had been playing with Nader without his father's permission. Otherwise, he would have invited Nader to his house. Also, when his father was home, he would not come out of the house. He had a feeling there was a problem. Hussien called out,

-Do you want to play?

Nader asked no more - not mentioning Hussein's disappearance. Within minutes they were playing. Hussein was not his usual self. He was very angry and sullen. He started arguing with Nader for no reason, got upset, and left. Nader was shocked at his friend's behavior since he had never seen him like this before. He wanted to know what was going on. He kept thinking of Hussein throughout the next day at school. Hussein went to a different school, and he would only see him after school, but they both were in the same grade. For a few days, he was thinking about him, debating on whether or not to go make up. Nader heard a knock at his window toward the alley where Hussien's house was; he opened it to see Hussein standing there looking depressed. He sadly declared,

-I just wanted to say I am sorry to have yelled at you. It wasn't you. I should have controlled myself. I have to leave before my father gets home.

Then, he turned and walked away, leaving Nader concerned and full of unanswered questions. Nader was relieved that it wasn't him that drove his friend to such anger and suddenly realized that he might be in a similar situation as himself. He lived with the wrath of his brother looming over him, but Hussein must feel the same pressure and restrictions. His father was chief justice of the family court in Tehran, a strict man, yet he could not rule his own family. Hussein had never told him anything about his father, but after that day, he let his guard down and spoke of the abuse they took from their father. Tears welled up in Hussein's eyes like a dam bursting. His father had beaten his mother regularly, he blamed him for her death, and he hated him. Nader could feel the deep anguish, the burden of watching these events unfold and unable to do anything. He had watched the life being stripped from his mother. He realized how similar they were, how their paths crossed for a reason. Their bond was now stronger than ever, and it occurred to him that they would be friends for life. As the weeks passed, Hussein seemed calmer and almost normal again. They would hang out and play soccer regularly. One day they were going to get a bite to eat at a local sandwich shop. Nader wanted to know more about Hussein's home life but could not find the right moment to bring it up. He felt that Hussein did not want to speak of it, so mostly he let it go. But his concern festered in the back of his mind.

The next year Hussein attended Nader's school, and they were classmates, partners in crime enjoying their youth as much as they could. It was at this time that half the property of Nader's house was leased out to a local bank and was turned into a nice athletic club for bank Saderat's employees. It was unfortunate, but the upside was that Nader's family had full access to the facility; he especially enjoyed the huge international-sized pool. Thus, began his regular swimming activities. He was practically in the pool all the time if he wasn't at the soccer field. His school studies were still avoided as much as possible. Throughout the weeks, Hussein's anger started to implode, Nader knew the situation at his house was not improving. No one would have guessed, Hussein, his three brothers, father, and stepmother appeared to be a happy family. Nader was also unaware of some of the issues within his own family. What he did not know was that their financial difficulties were growing. While all of his family members were experiencing great trepidation, he was living in his fantasy world of soccer and swimming. Nothing else could distract him, and most of the family let him be, thinking it was better if he did not know. He was now a respected soccer player, and if there was a game to be won, he had to be there. He was still playing in secret behind his older brother's back. Still, he would hide his soccer shoes and uniform in some trees or with friends and picked them up on the way out. This took magnificent planning not to get caught by anyone. He was obsessed with the game of soccer and swimming but had not forgotten about his treehouse and the girl with the violin. Sometimes, he really needed to be alone and think, he would hide at his treehouse for a long time and get lost and live in her memory. Hussein's addition to his life helped him forget his thoughts of the Violin Girl. But every time he was around music or heard the music, it seemed as though her face crept into his mind. To Nader's surprise, Hussein began to criticize him regularly. He would accuse him of wasting his time in the soccer field and in the pool. He tried to advise him to study more as he became almost like his older brother. But the truth was Hussein was not doing much better in his schoolwork either. They both had about the same marks. But his time spent in the pool was paying off. He was becoming a great swimmer, and soon Nader would be able to compete for the national championship.

Unfortunately, this was the wrong message to send to Abbass. In the beginning, Abbass was pleased with his brother's progress in swimming. But the moment he realized he was being distracted from his studies because of swimming, all hell broke loose, and he could not hear the end of it. Nader had to become a doctor, engineer, or attorney, and there was no other choice. Swimming, soccer were just hobbies, never careers. His brother had made the decision that Nader was one of his "soldiers" under his command, and following orders was the only option, no questions asked. Nader knew in his heart that he was not going to follow his brother's will, but traditions require you to respect your elders. Especially since his oldest brother was like a father to him, he was not allowed to disrespect him by doing what he wanted to do. He could not tell him to his face that he was not going to be what he wanted him to be. He had to play a game of politics, but he did not possess the skill to finesse him. He knew Abbass was not a bad man, and he was doing what he thought was best for Nader, which made the situation even more difficult. They all felt as though he was running a military base, not a family. He was his brother who loved them all, but living like soldiers under his command made life miserable.

As time went on, he found out that Abbass had been trained by the CIA, which had helped to create the Savak. Their father's unpopular, unjust, and embarrassing behavior had much to do with his brother's way of treating them. He was strongly against drugs and alcohol. When they were about to lose everything, Abbass had realized that their wealth could disappear at a moment's notice, but education always stayed with you. As a young teenage boy, Nader did not have a clue of any of this, nor could he comprehend the lessons which were shoved down his throat. He just wanted to do what he wanted to do and have fun. He watched all of his brother's earnings being spent on his family. Some money would go to the college students among the relatives. This showed them all that he meant well, he loved them all in his own way. Abbass was not the only one that Nader had to keep happy. There was his other older brother, Bijan, who had his own agenda. He was showing his position by constantly giving Nader daily advice about his future. They each had a different philosophy and were as different from each other as day and night. And then his mother, who was also constantly advising him that he should get hired in a government office. He should get a base salary, so he knew what he had coming to him every month. Her constant example was of one of the men who had gotten a job at the registry office in the town next to their farm and was living like a king with his small pay. Later in life, he understood where her logic came from. You could have great wealth, like a pot of gold stashed away, but if it disappears, it can't help you, but your regular paycheck can. Even though his salary was modest, his income did not dry up, and he was living in peace, whereas his mother was constantly worried about her loss. And there was his father, whose support Nader needed badly, but he was never there. He was in the world of opium dens. Nader did not want him around because he was embarrassed by him. At the same time, Nader felt bad for him because he was left alone on the farm, becoming old and only in his forties. And it was his other brother Kamaale who sometimes would force his ideas on him. And finally, it was his own feelings and ideas that were much different from everyone else's.

Nader was relaxing by the pool, soaking up the warm eastern sun contemplating the different aspects of his life. He wished that the older wise man would come to visit him and calm him down again, but he had stopped appearing some time ago. It occurred to him that he had never really thought to ask or question himself in regards to who the older wise man was. Why did he not ask him his name or what he wanted from him? Or who he was? He still did not know why, up to this day, it remained a mystery to him. Nothing could affect his spirits when his wise older man friend would visit. He wished he was around so he could ask him about Hussein; he must have an answer for him. But it seemed he had forgotten him. His friendship with Hussein was turbulent. Overall, Hussein was much less peaceful than when they first met. They would fight, not speak for a few days, and then things went back to normal. Construction on a new house had started right next to Hussein's house, and within few months, a family had moved in. The second floor of this house had shown images of a beautiful slim girl. At the time, Nader was not much into girls, being obsessed with swimming and soccer. The first time he saw the girl on her window sill, it immediately reminded him of his Violin Girl, and he wondered where she was. Each time he recalled her, the sound of her instrument would echo in his ears. Seeing this new neighbor kept bringing back tugs at his heart. He would look toward the treehouse he had built long ago for a moment and then be lost in thought for an hour. The angelic appearance of this slender girl changed his relationship with Hussein. Hussein himself had become friendlier and less judgmental; after all, what is there to critique when there is a pretty girl to watch. They now had a reason to hang out in Nader's backyard on a regular basis.

The competition officially began to impress the newcomer. It was around this time that Hussein began to take karate classes. One day, he showed up with a couple of bricks and placed them upon each other. After a few minutes of meditation and collecting his energy, he broke the top brick by chopping it with his hand. The girl and her friends could hear his scream. Actually, several houses down the block heard as well. They always made sure that the girls were watching when something impressive was about to occur. They were surprised that he was okay, and both boys were sure they would question them the next day about the state of his hand. But what the girls did not know was that the boys were cheating by sawing the bricks to a point just before breaking. Just a small chop, and they would break into pieces. This was the greatest trick. Hussein even got Nader with it the first time he tried it. The girl and her friends were always impressed. They were cheating, pumping out their chests, and putting on a show for the girls. Nader started to gain an interest in karate from the brick-breaking day. Within a few days, he was obsessed with it. Both he and Hussein wanted to become masters at karate. They were competitors with each other. Both were trying to impress the girls. Soon things got out of hand, and their pleasant competitions changed course and became unmerciful fighting within them, but they hid it from one another. One morning at the bus stop, the girl was giving them a sign that they wanted to talk to them. Both Nader and Hussein were so shy when it came to girls, there was no way they could step forward to open up a conversation. Nader was especially shy coming from the farm, and he was afraid of rejection. As the days passed, Nader and Hussein's relationship became strained. They were both the best of friends yet resented each other in complicated ways. As young men, they were moving in different directions, and sometimes they tried to completely avoid each other. Other times they were all laughs and smiles trying to impress girls they didn't have the courage to even speak to.

*****

Chapter 5

It's Over For You. It's All Over For You Now, So What's Next

Summer was arriving, and Nader could not hold back his excitement. This was when the real fun started. Now began the soccer tournaments, gathering around the pool and taking in all the movement and activity that took over the city. In addition, Nader now had new friends from his swimming group. Every day from one in the afternoon until five or six, he was at the pool, practicing swimming. And in between, they had games of soccer, always bare-foot with a small goal. He remembers the game was much more fun when Parviz Ghylech Khani, one of the well-known stars of the national team, joined them to play. A couple of players were there from other known clubs, but none were as well known as Ghylech. He was famous for his free kicks and playing the same position that Nader was. Now Nader was engaged with sports on a level of professional competition on two fronts, soccer and swimming. Abbass was not so much in opposition to swimming because he did not see it as a sport for the average people. Or it could have been because Nader had saved Abbass and his friend's life at the same pool. At the time, Abbass was joking with one of his friends, taking him into the deeper part of the pool, not knowing he couldn't swim. The friend grabbed his brother, and both quickly sunk to the bottom as his friend frantically pulled Abbass down with him. It was after hours, and there were no lifeguards at the pool. His brother always used to use the pool when it was closed to others. It was about seven in the evening, and Nader was eating dinner at the house when someone began to yell from the pool area,

-Help Nader khan, help, Nader khan...

And then Boloor began yelling for him. Nader jumped out of the window and began running towards the pool through the garden area so he could get there faster since it was about eleven hundred yards away. The gardener was panicking,

-Your brother, your brother is drowning!

Nader reached a small hill to get to the poolside, and he couldn't see anyone. The gardener ran to the deep side and pointed to his brother and his friend. Within minutes, Nader had both of them out of the pool and did not even feel the cut he acquired on his chest. He guessed his brother's friend was so scared when he got to them that he reached to grab him and scratched his hairy chest. He had to force him to let go of him and Abbass so he could separate and pull them out. More importantly, they were safe, and long after that, they both always bickered over whose fault it was. His brother never played a joke on anyone else again, and his friend never came around the pool area after that. Somehow his brother was impressed by what Nader had done, and he now thought that swimming was a respectable sport, yet still felt he was wasting his life. After that, Nader became the youngest licensed lifeguard in the country.

Summer arrived, and the time for all to prepare for competitions on the two fronts, soccer and swimming, that had started. Nader always thought Abbass was not aware that he was playing soccer, but he was wrong. Nothing was unknown to Abbass. He knew it all, about everyone. After all, he was a trained secret agent with information pouring in from all walks of life. It was the middle of August, and soccer tournaments were starting within a week, as well as the swimming championship. The schedule for both came out, and there was only one soccer game that conflicted with the swimming championship. Nader was happy as can be. By now, he hardly ever saw Hussein and missed conversing with him about all that was occurring in their lives. It had been about a month since they last crossed paths, and he knew something was wrong. He thought maybe he had taken a trip to his home city, Brojerd, at least he hoped so. Nader was playing in a major soccer tournament with a professional club -- with the big boys. He was playing under an alias name so his real name would not appear in the paper. This was to protect him from having his brother see any writings about him; in addition, he would not pose for photos or try to promote himself in public. He was just so happy to be on the field with the most known players in the country; that was his real enjoyment. They won the first game, and he was a significant part of their win. He began to get compliments for his free kicks. The next game was six days later, and for some reason, he could not relax. He felt a negative vibration in the air, the energy surrounding him was just not right. He felt as if he shouldn't attend the game, but how could he not show up for such an important game? That night, he hardly slept and woke up earlier than usual. He walked out of his room in a haze to see his Abbass doing exercises outside. He did them every morning for about forty-five minutes or so. He saw Nader and looked into his eyes and said,

-It is right that you do not have school now, but you should plan your study hours for the next year. You must build a strong foundation so you can enter into a good major at the university.

Nader hated such speeches so early in the morning. He was sorry he got out of bed at that exact moment. Before he could muster up a reply, he heard,

-He is. He will. He will enter the university.

Their mother always interjected when Nader needed rescuing. The two of them began to argue while Nader pretended he had to use the bathroom, rushing away swiftly and closing the door. He had a bond with their bathroom like it was his second room and the only place his privacy would not be invaded. Sitting in the bathroom, Nader began to realize that his brother's prolonged presence was unusual as well, he was barely ever around, and if he was in Tehran, he was not at home for such a long period of time. His brother knocked on the bathroom door, commenting he had been in there for quite a while and wanted to know if he was okay. He poured some water into the toilet, pretending to finish up in the bathroom. He just wanted him to finish his exercises and go to his room so he could quickly leave the house. But he had been in the bathroom for a long time, and when he opened the door, his mother was standing there. She was worried he was sick. He had to take some homemade traditional medicines, several of them, not just one or two. She had something for every part of your body, she seemed to know what was wrong with you right away, and surprisingly they all worked perfectly. Even if you didn't think something was wrong, you automatically felt better.

> -Mother, I am okay. I just wanted to get away from my brother, please, I don't need any more medicine. Please leave me be.

He walked away and knew after mentioning his brother she would leave him alone, and she did not follow. He quickly changed his clothes and rushed out of the house before Abbass could assign him with tasks that would take the entire day. It was Friday, and Friday in Iran is a holiday, or a day of rest, just like Sunday. If you didn't see Abbass all week, you could guarantee you would see him on Friday. This particular weekend he came home on Thursday, which was unusual, yet he was lucky to escape in the morning. He was wandering the streets trying to think of a way to occupy himself until four when the game was scheduled to start. It was only 7 AM, and he was tired. He couldn't go to his sister's house because his brother might decide to visit her. He thought of his friends, of Hamidi, who was a member of his first soccer team, might be awake. Hamidi had a store close to their house. He really wasn't a businessman or a scholar, so his parents opened a music store for him to run. He called him, and he showed up at the store. Hamidi led him to the balcony where Nader laid down. Regardless, Hamidi had a blanket and pillow up there, yet unable to sleep. But it felt good to be hidden from the world in anticipation of his game. As he was getting ready to leave, Hamidi had kabob waiting for him. He didn't want to eat because he couldn't risk being heavy before the game. He insisted that Nader eat, so he ate a little to be polite, thanked him, and left. It was normal to see Hamidi before practice or a game. He would keep his soccer equipment at his shop, so he knew he would see his friend again soon. He went on his way to visit another friend, Bahman. Bahman was on the swim team with him, they were also competing against each other. Nader had broken the free stroke record for the country, and Bahman had also broken another record. But they were ordered by their trainer, Mr. Sorory, not to reveal this to anyone. He felt that people would be more surprised if they unexpectedly took the championship. So, they respectfully honored their trainer's request and kept this information to themselves. The swimming championship was getting close, and Nader and Bahman were training heavily. His advantage over Bahman was that the pool was located where he lived, and he got extra practice time. After hours he would often sit at the side of the pool, close his eyes, and envision the length of the pool, the count of each stroke, the intensity of each breath. He had created his own method of meditation to psych himself up. He felt it always made him swim better. That morning his conversation with Bahman was about swimming, as usual. But he was extremely excited about his soccer game that day. He was anticipating the moment that he would walk onto the field and see the heated stadium filled with cheering fans. This was a dream come true, sort of like flying through the sky with no wings.

    He left Bahman and headed to the stadium. He wanted to get there before anyone else arrived so he could have the entire place to himself for a bit. He entered the empty stadium and sat in the front row all by himself. For a moment, he felt as though he owned the place and that he was "the man." But then, a feeling of melancholy came over him, as if he would not see this wonderful place again. He didn't pay much attention to that feeling as he continued to savor the moment. His whole life leading up to this moment was projecting out onto the field. He reflected back on the days when he was a little boy, playing soccer in the alley, hoping to one day replace the plastic ball with a leather one. All the shop owners knew him as the little boy who ran around doing the family errands. Now, being on the soccer team, he was growing into a man and had gained the respect of many. He was at the top. He was one of the few who soon would be considered a member of the national team. A few workers arrived, they did not bother him, which was great. In no time at all, it was time to go to the dressing room and get ready for the game. As he placed his bag on the bench, he was distracted by a voice,

> -You must not be worried. Whatever is going to happen will happen, and no one can do anything about it. Not me or even you. So be happy you are here, and remember that being here is a dream of thousands of young men like you. You are living this dream, even if it is for just one game or for a few minutes on the field.

He turned around to see an older man who was mopping the floor with exact precision. He reached Nader and politely gestured for him to move his feet. The maintenance man continued his work, keeping to himself as Nader began to go through his bag. He was worried about the old man's words, the lingered in the air and echoed in his mind,

> -Even if it's for one game or a few minutes on the field.

Nader turned around to see the old man was gone; he walked around the corner to find him to see that the entry door was still closed and locked. Just then, a few other players started coming in, glancing at him with puzzled expressions. He looked a little frantic. He asked them if they saw the older maintenance man, they responded with a shake of their heads from side to side. The maintenance man's soft voice suddenly reminded Nader of the wise old man that used to visit him in his youth. He had not been around for a while. He reasoned that his absence was because he had been very happy lately. At this moment, he became worried, yet pushed this to the back of his throat and channeled his energy to the field. As more teammates started to arrive, the excitement mounted. Soon they would be having the time of their lives. The moment arrived for them to enter onto the lush green field that was trimmed perfectly. As they jogged in, the crowd roared, chanting the names of a few star players. Nader was thinking that one day it was going to be his name echoing through the air. This would be an honor of a lifetime. Nothing could top this feeling for a boy from a small village to be honored in this fashion. As they walked through the pathway onto the field, he heard someone yell his name. He looked up to see Hamidi and a few other friends. He was glad to have their support. He raised his hand in thanks towards them. His eyes cut past them to a man staring at him in the crowd, he moved quickly, and Nader did not catch a good glimpse of him. But his eyes were familiar, and he suspected he knew him. Distracted, scanning the crowd for the man, standing alone on the field. One of his coaches approached him, asking if he was ok. He felt uneasy yet shook it off as he ran to join his team.

The referees entered the field, and each team settled on either side of the field to start the game. Then, he spotted a player on the opposite team who had just entered. He looked more closely and was stunned to see his old teammate from first and second grade, Abraham. He could not be mistaken in recognizing him, as they were the local team's stars, Sharzad, and the ones who organized everything together. Abraham, Nader, and their other friend Mohamad Mandeghari were the ones who would locate the property which would be made into their soccer field. At the time, the kids would locate a large piece of flat property that was not being used and use it to play soccer until the property owner began to build. They would gather other teammates to clean up and prepare the field, install wooden goalposts, and lay down the white powder boundary lines. They had been inseparable when it came to soccer for two years. They had built a new school for girls right next to their school. Now they could pass messages over the wall to the girls, and the girls would pass notes back to them. At this time, all schools were separate. Many boys were not into dating yet, but Abraham was a master when it came to approaching girls. There was a bushy area where they would pass their notes through, and one morning Nader messed everything up for everyone. He passed a note right into the hands of one of the girl's overprotective brothers. He wanted to have this girl as his girlfriend and asked him to give the note to his sister. In his mind, he thought if he showed his good intentions to her brother, he could gain the trust of her family, and he could date her freely instead of in secret as most did. Nader always used to go against the odds or traditions and hoped for the best. This is what set him apart from most and made his life a bit more interesting. However, this time he made a huge mistake. Traditionally men were very protective of women, whether it be a husband to a wife or brother to a sister. This particular brother took his note straight to his father, and the next thing he knew, he was called into the principal's office for questioning. This caused their secret passageway to be discovered, which ended all communication with the girls. As a result of this, Abraham lost his girlfriend due to further mishaps. This all was the result of Nader's foolish mistake, which wrecked his friendship with Abraham. He remembered Abraham's father, who would sometimes pick Abraham up from school in a giant Arhis motorcycle. His father would always be wearing Arhis uniforms. He was a big, bulky, intimidating man with a thick mustache. Nader was broken away from his thought when he was shocked to see Abraham lining up to play against him this day. This was the first time he had seen his old friend in a very long time. He didn't know he had signed with a major team, let alone playing against him. Within seconds Abraham approached him and began taunting him, with a smile on his face, trying to make friends again,

-I am going to kick your ass. I will walk through you and open that goal.

Nader quickly responded,

-Let's see if you can even stand on your feet, buddy boy.

They made snide remarks to each other while trying to smile and remember to be sportsman-like. After all, this was the first time they were playing against one another. At the time in Iran, you played sports for honor and fame, this wasn't about money, it was an important example to set for young kids, and respect could get you far. In Nader's mind, he was chanting to himself, shaking off this surprise and trying to stay positive and focused, playing well every single second was the goal. The head referee blew the whistle, the game instantly started. Nader's mind was fixated on stopping Abraham no matter what; from the first whistle blow, it was as if it was just the two of them on the field. They forgot they were playing on a team with other players. The past had caught up with them both, and proving who was better was all that mattered as unresolved feelings were brought to the surface. Slowly, their antics became more severe. Anytime they were facing each other, it seemed as though Abraham would aim his kicks at Nader's knuckles and body instead of the ball. Kicks were flying, and Nader quickly caught on. Since Nader had a strong build, Abraham had to hit him relatively hard in order to hurt him; at first, Nader wasn't sure if he was purposely doing this or if he was nervous and trying to prove himself by acting tough. Nader was also a little nervous, which was not making a good combination. Then, about twenty minutes into the game, Abraham abruptly swung around, kicked him hard, and pushed him from behind, causing him to come down onto his right arm. Nader realized he was trying to force him to fall on this arm which he knew had been broken three times already. Nader had gotten his arm reset by different people each time because the injuries had not been extremely serious, and he wanted to avoid going to the hospital so his brother would not find out he was playing soccer. Nader could not fathom why an old friend would want to do him such harm. They had their past disagreements but nothing worth physical harm. His team was awarded a few free kicks because of this, yet Abraham's aggression did not subside, and it became obvious he was trying to get him out of the game. Nader decided to give him a warning and teach him a lesson. The next time Abraham approached him, Nader ran into him full force, causing him to fall flat down on the field very hard. He knew this made him mad, but when Abraham rose up, he looked up and stared into the stands, his gaze was unusual. Nader realized every few minutes he would glance up at the stands, right where Nader had seen those familiar eyes. Abraham stopped abruptly, staring. Nader followed his gaze, and suddenly it clicked. Those eyes belonged to Abraham's father.

About forty minutes into the first half, Nader's team scored their first goal. Now they were ahead; for those first forty minutes, Abraham could not get anything through him, causing him to become furious. Abraham was distracted, constantly staring towards his father; it was as if he was under harsh pressure that he himself did not understand. The horrible feeling that overcame Nader at different moments throughout the day was about to surface once again. It's funny how a person can feel in their gut that something is just not right, yet they ignore it and keep moving, always fighting nature. Sometimes it is just better to stand still. The ball was kicked by the other goal-keeper toward Abraham. The ball was high and behind Nader, so he turned his back to Abraham to block him with his body as he lifted up about four yards into the air to kick the ball back with a seizer kick. His entire body was in the air, his legs above the rest of his body. Within seconds Abraham was underneath him, pushing Nader's butt up into the air; it made an impact with Nader. Cursing, Nader lost his balance, his legs went into a 90-degree angle in the air, he came down hard onto the moist ground, landing directly on his right arm. The moment he hit the ground, his body went into a roll, trying to shake off the pain. He slowly rose to his feet, grasping his right arm, which was in excruciating pain. It was so intense it was now traveling through all his bones as if someone had slapped his body against the ground like a whip. They were given a free-kick, Abraham a red card, and was removed from the game. Nader made his way over to the ball to go for the free-kick. He gestured to everyone he was OK as he sauntered over, still in shock. He was still holding his right arm tightly; it rested against his chest as he ran to kick the ball. The pain became unbearable. He fell to his knees in intense pain, realizing that there were tears running down his face. He was helped off the field and taken to the locker room. Several people were attending to his injury, but he had practically left his body as his mind put together the sequences of his day once more. As great as his physical pain was, his sadness about this situation was even greater. He couldn't believe he was now out of the game. If anyone touched his arm, he would yell so loudly from the pain, they knew his arm was badly broken.

As the car was traveling through the city streets, the pain still hammered up and down Nader's arm. He asked the driver to turn on the radio so he could hear the game. On the radio, they were discussing the unsportsmanlike choices that Abraham had made; suddenly, his name was all over the radio. He knew that his brother would hear this, and his life would not be the same after this day. This thought saddened him more than anything; he sunk into the leather seats and wished he could disappear into the cracks of its stitching. He beckoned for the driver to take him home even though his friends strongly disagreed. Boloor was the first to see him as he walked into the house in a daze. She immediately realized something was wrong and ran up to his side, looking at his arm,

-God, what has happened to you? Your face is as white as snow! Go inside so mom won't see you like this.

He wanted to die when she touched his hand, but he somehow managed not to scream and asked her never to touch it again. She helped him inside his room and brought him some pain pills. Parry was there too. They agreed to an appointment with their personal physician, Dr. Fatahi, to occur the following day. Besides, they all agreed that his mother and brother should stay out of this. By now, Boloor and Parry were taking care of him and kept his mother occupied enough so that she did not come into his room.

He began doing as much meditation as possible, he could not move his body at all, and the pain was in every bone. After a few hours, he heard his brother call asking if he was OK; they responded that he was fine, just a bad headache. A bit later, he called a second time and was told that he was sleeping. He did not know if he knew about the incident or if someone told him about what has happened to him? So, he asked for the receiver to be removed from the phone, so if he called back again, he would just get a busy signal. Parry and Boloor were concerned about his mother finding out what was going on, but they continued to keep her away from him.

But they were not able to distract her much longer. Just as he was remembering some of the good points of the game, in a bit of delirium, he heard Hussein's family gardener talking to his mother outside. Parry and Boloor could not do anything, both standing in the room with Nader, they squinted knowing what would happen next,

-Hello Hajji Khanoom, how is Nader Khan, is he okay? How is his hand?

The gardener was still talking, but his mother was now standing in his bedroom doorway, yelling,

-What is happening to him? Why didn't you tell me he is at home hurt!? What happened to him!?

Just as she was about to touch his arm, Parry and Boloor stopped her, telling her he had broken his arm but didn't want his brother to know about it. He was going to the hospital tomorrow. He only wants to see Dr, Fathai. This plan was not good enough for his mother, and within a few seconds, she was raising hell. She had her veil on her head and insisted that they go to the hospital right away. She started cursing Parry and Boloor, accusing them of not caring about him. The two looked offended but knew Nader was their mother's baby. The gardener continued to add to the chaos. He came in to bring him some flowers, continuing about how he had heard about his mishap on the radio. Nader's eyes rolled to the back of his head, wishing he could tell the gardener to go away.

The next thing he knew, he was on his way to the hospital, but only Parry was accompanying him. They had made a deal with his mother that he would only go to the hospital if she would stay home, and thank God she agreed. He was resting his head on the back of the car seat with his arm wrapped, hanging from his neck. Tears were running down Parry's face as she was holding him to give him comfort and support. For a moment, he forgot about his pain and the soccer game. He was so overtaken by Parry's kindness and concern for him, and he wanted to just reach out and hug her. This is why he felt that Parry was not just his sister but more like a second mother to him. He could not move, so he just smiled and whispered to her that he was okay and not to worry. He noticed a look of slight relief on her face, but his pain showed once more as the car went over a bump, speeding to the hospital. Not knowing his soccer game outcome, he asked the driver to turn up the radio volume. Maybe it would cause him to focus less on the pain if he could hear the game broadcast. The radio was finishing up commentary on a different game; he waited patiently for the announcer to switch topics.

Half time had started for the game he was currently announcing, and the man quickly began a discussion about Nader's eventful game. The only thing they talked about was that the announcer bellowed that his team had been victorious, one to nothing, and a slight side smile appeared on Nader's face. For a moment, he didn't feel pain and was very glad to hear his team had won. The feeling of some type of accomplishment wouldn't last very long. The car came to a halt in front of Najmiyeh Private Hospital. At that time in Iran, there was medical coverage for all, but privately owned hospitals existed for those who wanted or who could afford to use them; Najmiyeh was one of the top private hospitals in town. Nader tried his best to relax in the car while Parry went to check with their personal doctor, Dr. Fatahi. She returned within minutes and said he was on the way to another hospital close by, a general government-owned hospital called Senna. Their doctor wanted to treat him there, so they took off for Senna Hospital. The second their car pulled up to Senna hospital, a nurse was waiting for them who took them straight to a waiting room.

After a few more minutes, the nurse came back and said Dr. Fatahi was with a patient who needed emergency care and it would be a bit longer. She walked over to Nader and attempted to check his arm. Nader and Parry simultaneously yelled, "Don't touch!" She backed off, a little surprised. After Parry described his pain to the nurse, she returned with some strong pills, and he gladly swallowed them. Nader closed his eyes with Parry at his side. Parry seemed to be feeling the same pain as he was and kept holding on to his shoulder. Nader started to lose consciousness as thoughts and memories were swirling around in his brain at the speed of light. Then, he had a disturbing thought; he remembered he was scheduled to compete in the swimming championship in about four days. How could he participate in this event with his broken arm? This could not be happening to him now. He had worked so hard for a year and a half in preparation for this event. He could feel himself sinking into depression behind the curtain of painkillers. He wouldn't be able to prove he was the youngest record-holder in the country, which would have made his mother and sister very proud. Being just about seventeen years old, he wanted to experience the normal transition from boyhood to becoming a man, and this was a time for a teenager to start to show his own identity. His athletic accomplishments had been a great vehicle to support this natural transition. He was thinking that if he could become a young swimming champion, then maybe his brother would begin to respect him and acknowledge his achievements. Maybe he would let him be the person he wanted to be. But now, there wasn't a damn thing he could do but sit by the pool and watch the others compete, watch the others play soccer. So many memories flowed through his mind like a hurricane. He floated away into a dream state.

    A vision of the wise old man took over his troubled mind. He saw him sitting across from him; he had a soft, peaceful smile on his face. He gently touched his arm, and Nader drifted off into unconsciousness. He was instantly enjoying a beautiful summer afternoon. The sound of music could be heard from one of the houses that overlooked the first soccer field that he had built with Abraham. Classical music rang through the field as he was playing with his team against another team. Then with a strong kick, a player from the other team sent the ball soaring towards Nader's goal. It caught them all by surprise. Nader flew into the air and kicked the ball hard as he crashed onto another man who was going for the ball. They both fell, sending the ball in the opposite direction. The ball traveled down a small hill to the east of the field and down into a large running creek. No one wanted to go get the ball; usually, the closest player to the ball would go retrieve it out of courtesy. After Nader saw that no one was moving, he went after it, even though he was at the other end of the field. Even Hamidi, who used to run after the ball for their team, was not moving.

Everyone just stood there watching him run after the ball like it was his fault for kicking it so hard.

    The music coming from the nearby house was still lingering in his ear as he headed down the small hill. Feeling frustrated, he was standing by the bank of the creek, staring at the ball. Interestingly, the ball was sitting in the middle of the running creek, not moving as the creek was flowing downstream. He found a stick and tried to pull the ball towards him so he wouldn't have to enter the water. But the stick was no help and only served to push the ball away. Then, the ball moved downstream a few yards and seemed to stop traveling with the water once again. It was as if the ball was just sitting on top of the water, challenging him to capture it. He got into the water to grab the ball with his hands, having enough, but the ball just bounced away and traveled a little further downstream. It had a mind of its own. By now, he had completely forgotten about the game that was in progress. He had become absorbed in this new game of chasing the ball down the creek a few yards at a time. The ball continued to move, always just out of his reach. When he got to a long narrow bridge, the elusive ball traveled down and underneath the bridge into its shadowed tunnel. Not wanting to enter the narrow and dark tunnel to get the ball, the only other thing he could do was walk up onto the other side of the bridge and reach down towards the ball on the other side. He then realized that he was in his soccer uniform, and it was not permissible for a man to be seen in public wearing shorts. Also, there was a grocery store on the corner of the bridge owned by some of his relatives, name Ghafory, and he didn't want them to see him either. So, he decided to run quickly over the bridge, hoping that no one would see him. Within a blink of an eye, he was on the other side, and the ball was sitting in the middle of the creek once again. He entered the creek yet again, but this time he stepped into some black, gooey mud that had gathered on the bank of the creek. It didn't stop him, and he went towards the ball again, but the same rotten thing happened again. The ball escaped his grasp, slipping away from his fingertips. He was sure it was playing a game with him. He was quite frustrated by now but didn't think of giving up this inter sting chase.

Finally, he reached a fancy, long and tall wall; the ball continued traveling through a narrow waterway underneath the wall and disappeared. He couldn't see the end of the wall, so he climbed up over to see what was on the other side. He was stunned as he gazed at the other side of the wall. There was a garden full of various trees, beautiful, illuminated flowers, and breathtaking scenery. The river was pearly blue and clean. There were multi-colored marble stones on the river bank. If he had wanted to see heaven, this was it. Yes, this had to be heaven because he had never seen anything like this before. And there was the ball, sitting right in the middle of the river waiting for him. He dove into the water again, but the ball was still playing this perplexing little game with him. He just kept going, knowing that he could not give up, just like heroes in the movies. A hero would never quit until he accomplished his goal. But the strange thing about this all was that he had never really seen any movies. He had not seen any kind of film on TV or even been to a movie theater yet. He had only watched soccer on TV. The fact that he heard "heroes never quit in the movies" echoing in his head made it all even more strange. The game between him and the ball continued and became quickened, in the presence Nader lost all his clothes and now was naked, but still, he would dive into the water going after the ball, and the ball would jump out of his hands, and still play the same game, but Nader exit the water and dive back in after the ball, now he really was tired but still did not give up. Soon the river came to an end at a large muddy and filthy pond. It was here that he finally was able to grasp his hands firmly around this elusive soccer ball. He got out of the water, ball in his hands, and he lifted it high into the air as if to show his victory over the ball. But it did not occur to him, or he did not realize or thought he was completely dressed in a clean cloth, and there was no sign of filth or any spot on him or the ball. He heard the sound of people cheering for him, and he looked up to see the infinity of people of all races, Chinese, Middle Eastern, European, White, Black, and... they were cheering him. He rose the ball in the air, and suddenly the sparkling fireballs of all colors began to shoot out into the air and soon covered him and the mass; it was as beautiful scenery as you could see. He felt incredible jubilation as the cheers for him continued; it was then that his dream was interrupted by the sound of his own screaming.

He was back in reality at the hospital, and Dr. Fatahi was checking his arm, not knowing how badly it had been broken. He saw Parry out of the corner of his eye, and she was tearing up again. The next thing he knew, he was in the operating room, and there was another doctor giving him a shot. They were preparing him for surgery, and he fell under another haze. Six hours later, he awoke, and everything was a blur. Parry was there holding his hand, which was now entirely in a cast. This was an incredible feeling to have his sister there, loving him and caring for him. He could only see the tips of his fingers, and his cast was supported at a 90-degree angle against his chest. Dr. Fatahi entered the room and informed him that he had been in surgery for five hours. His arm had been cracked and badly broken in the area above his wrist. Dr. Fatahi was more than their doctor; he was a family friend. He gave him a speech about life and how people can waste their life by miscalculating the proper time for certain things, and then he left the hospital, leaving a laundry machine of words spinning in Nader's head. His dreams had been crushed by the speech the doctor had just given him. On the drive home, he wanted to cry, but he couldn't. He just stared out the window, thinking about how his life was ending. He imagined that he would be entering into a new time now; he would have to find a new way to maintain his identity with his brother before his ideology was forced down his throat. He didn't know how this challenge was going to come about, but he knew he would have to face whatever it would be. Sadly, in his gut, he felt as if he would be saying goodbye to soccer, and he knew he would not be happy just as a swimmer. He didn't even know if he would be able to swim competitively again yet. The more he thought about this, the more he could see all his plans had been thrown out the window like dust from a rug. It was as if someone had taken his life and rewritten it, slamming the final copy against his forehead. His life officially was taking on a new direction.

Four days later, he was sitting by the pool watching the other boys compete. His coach, Mr. Sorrory, was just as hurt as he was, as he stared at Nader in deep disappointment. After all, he held a national record, and none of the other guys were record-holders. His coach was wondering why he had put himself in the position to be injured when he had such an important competition coming up. He knew that if his arm was not in a cast, he could have competed. He would have been the youngest champion to this day. He just sat there in misery and watched as Bahman ended up in third place. He came up to him afterward and said they would take the championship together next year. But in his heart, he knew there would be no next year. There was an inner voice whispering to him. All he could hear was to wait amd hope for things to change.

*****

Chapter 6

Then Came A Defining Moment In His Young Life...

The moon in Iranian literature has a romantic yet respectful symbolic meaning. Many poets describe their love or their mother to be lighted underneath the moonlight. Maybe it's because the glow of the moon removes the darkness of the night. The moon was also used in traditional horoscopes as the full moon, half, or quarter. Perhaps, at that moment, for Nader, the moon had very little significance in the sense that he was sitting beside the pool thinking about his misfortune and why had it happened to him, not noticing the reflection of light playing with the water. Since the radiance of the moon was the greatest tool to get rid of the dark of night, it was taking some of his sadness away. In his mind, he could see the water clearly, and he could see himself swimming lap after lap back and forth, breaking a new record. The moon illuminated the water for his eyes to see, and he imagined himself being the fish who owns the space underneath the water. The memories clambering around inside his brain kept getting more painful and unbearable. He now was a bit of a loner, spending his late nights beside the pool. By now, he knew beyond a shadow of a doubt that Abraham had purposely harmed him. He was looking for him all over, but it seemed that he had vanished. Surprisingly, his brother did not show up for a long time, and he never asked why his arm was in a cast even when he finally did show up. Nader was told he accepted Parry's explanation that Nader had slipped on a banana peel and fell. In the beginning, he did not give much thought to the fact that Abbass seemed to be withdrawing his intense concern about Nader's life. But as time passed, he was more concerned and perhaps confused about why Abbass did not care so much anymore. In fact, it was as if he was trying to make peace with his little brother. His behavior was getting much softer, and he hardly asked him to study. In fact, he did not after his hand was broken! And he did not give him speeches or orders. He was enjoying this change in Abbass, but at the same time, he did not like it. Deep in his heart, he felt that something was missing, something that did not make any sense. And the more time passed, the more this issue bothered him. But there was nothing he could do about it except approach Abbass and ask, but he worried confrontation might make matters worse. He might change again and start treating him like one of his soldiers. So, he put this concern on hold and began occupying his time by looking for Abraham everywhere. He thought Abraham was the source of all understanding and mystery.

The more he was around the pool, staring at the water, the more he would daydream about competing and winning, and this started to really get to him. He never visited the soccer field or watched his friends play. He just couldn't. It was too painful. He used whatever distractions he could. He visited his old treehouse in between excursions, he thought of a way to find Abraham, and he thought of his mother. He was still very close to his mother and decided he wanted to help her out of her depression instead of worrying about his own; maybe writing her a beautiful poem would help her. He began to talk to the moon and describe his mother to the moon; soon, he had several pages scratched up about his mother and the magnificent moon. But no one ever saw that notebook.

One day Boloor suddenly called for him. She had received a letter for him. First, he did not want to look at the letter thinking it is from the doctor, or Abbass had something to do with it. But he glanced at the letter anyway, and his interest was peaked. He read the return address a few times to be sure he was reading correctly. And yes, it was a letter from his friend Hussein, and it was in a small, teak envelope. It was postmarked from Broojerd, the city where Hussein's family farm was located. It had been a long time with no news from Hussein after a small argument they had had, and he missed him a lot. He had looked toward his window almost every day, but there was no sign of Hussein. He went into the trees to find a quiet location and opened it. It consisted of 26 pages, and he read its entirety a few times. It could not have been better timing for Hussein's letter. The distressing truth of Hussein's family and his relationship with his father had changed his kind demeanor, and he had become filled with anger. His words poured over the pages,

> -I will not be back, I hate my father, I cannot handle this... the belt which is meant to hold up my father's pants is used to slash my butt and back. I cannot accept any more abuse by that mad man who considers himself to be my father. He is supposed to provide love and peace in my family, and I know he killed my mother the same way. I was tired of being punished so that my brothers could be in peace; I cannot stand up for my brothers anymore. I will not come back to Tehran, and I will finish high school here and then leave for America. I do not want to stay here and deal with that mad man. I will never take a beating from him again...

There was much more; Hussein had finally shared his feelings with Nader on the most trusted level. Hussein said that he had more to tell him, and he would mail the rest the following day. And sure enough, the next day, he received the second part, which was about 28 pages. And again, he was at his place, sitting alone, quiet, and reading Hussein's letter. Now that he was gaining more insight into Hussein's personal life, he had more respect for his sad situation and mostly for him. He had been his best friend, and his circumstances always caused him to forget about his own problems, one of the gifts a good friend bestows in such a twisted way. He was thinking that Hussein should be here, and he could help him. He felt Hussein was wrong about some aspects regarding his family. The second letter continued,

-You should thank God you have such a nice and warm family. Your brother is a good man. Your mother, Hajji Khanoom, never disrespect her. You do not know how precious it is to have your mother next to you, and she is one of the best and kindest. She is just like an angel...

He was right about Nader's mother, but about his brother, he was doubtful. Hearing from Hussein was a relief, but he wanted him back as his buddy. He felt better knowing he was okay and that he considered him a good friend. He thought Hussein did not care for him anymore like he had been discarded as a friend. In his ignorance, he could not understand that Hussein was carrying lots of pain in his heart, and he did not want Nader to be worried about him. Or he felt ashamed to disclose it to Nader. How wrong we are most of the time, not knowing what to do, sometimes not wanting to accept the truth. Just lost in our problems, and we do not see or feel others. Husssien's letters opened a new window in Naders's heart and vision.

The cast came off Nader's arm just a few days before school started. He went to Dr. Fatahi, who personally removed it. He was worried if anything was crooked and hoped they did not have to break his arm and readjust the bones because it had been so drastically injured. He had prayed to the moon many nights that this would not occur. First, he was worried because his forearm had become the size of a baby's arm. But the doctor spoke up,

-It will be back to normal size within a few months. It is smaller now because air could not get in.

Then came a defining moment in his young life. Dr. Fatahi went over to his small bookshelf and grabbed a book turning quickly to Nader with a serious expression,

-I want you to read this. This book has changed my life, and it made me who I am today. You should read it and be sure I get it back.

Nader knew what he meant when he said,

-It made me who I am today.

He knew the doctor had come from a very poor family. He worked to put himself and his brother through school while still taking care of their mother. Accomplishing such a thing in Iran is almost impossible; you must be a solid rock and sacrifice almost your entire teenage and college life as well. He promised to bring the book back after he finished it.

Sitting in the car, staring at his arm, thinking of Abraham, of hunting him down, his eyes fixated on the cover. It read *The Old Man and the Sea* by John Steinbeck. After that, he forgot about the book. He forgot he even had the book. Parry mentioned to him a couple of times that doctor Fatahi wanted to know if he had read the book and wanted to be sure that he would get it back. His response was that he was almost through with it, and he will take it back to him when he is done, but really, he didn't even know where the book was. He was thinking that he would buy another copy, and after he read it, he would take it back to him. But soon, he forgot about the book yet again.

School started, and he was registered at one of the private schools. It was a tough one. School studies were the last thing on his mind. By now, he had begun to hate the school and was transforming into a bitter person. He was no longer a kindhearted, polite, shy farm boy. To get to school every day, he had to take the bus, which was right across the street from his house. He would run and jump onto the double-decker bus in an instant. At the time, the buses were all red, and the back with a large, round open entrance with no door and an aluminum post right in the middle for an employee to hold onto. There was an employee who would check your ticket and make sure people were safely inside. It was the first day of school. He got on the bus, and the bus was on its way; as he turned, his eyes landed on Hussein running across the street to get to the next bus. He was so happy to see Hussein and did not know which school Hussein was attending. The bus stopped at the next bus stop, and he jumped down, waiting for Hussein. He knew he was going to take the next bus and could already see it approaching; he would hop on at this stop. Soon the bus stopped, and he jumped in, coming face to face with Hussein standing in the doorway. They stared at each other and smiled. They would not usually hug because they felt that they were big men now, and they needed to show that they were grown up. But at that moment, they did not care, and they reached and hugged each other. They both were happy to see each other, and before they could say anything, it was time for him to exit the bus. He was registered at a different school, Bhaman, than Hussein, who was going to Jam, and he hated that. The reason his mother and brother had registered him at a Bahman was because one of the neighbors used to teach there, and private school was more rigorous than the public one. His brother's plan was for him to study hard, extremely hard. After all, that was how he would become a great doctor, engineer, or attorney. He had to walk an additional ten minutes to get to school after the bus. At the gate, the first thing the guard said was,

> -You are late the first day. Make sure this will not become routine. They will not tolerate that here. This is NOT a public school. They mean business here. Next time if you are late, I cannot let you in.

Surprisingly Nader wanted to punch him before he was even done talking. He almost did but didn't. He had never had such a feeling before. He never thought about disrespecting his elders, not even once. This feeling was new to him, and the worst part was that he just knew it would have felt great. He did not have to wait long before dealing with the guard. Two weeks later, he punched a fellow student knocked him flat down on the pavement, bleeding. And a week after that, another incident occurred, and he was instantly kicked out of school. He didn't understand what had come over him. His actions felt right at the time. He requested to go to the school Hussein attended, but that did not happen, and he was registered at a different school, call Bharam. His new school was farther from the school Hussein was in and about an hour's walk, and this upset him as well. He remembered there was a physics class, and the teacher was a large man, but a great teacher, and he almost had lost his eyesight. His wife used to drive him to the school. Nader was fascinated by him when he was drawing a shape on the blackboard. He would not miss any lines, and his drawings were perfect. With no sight at all, this man just knew.

By now, Nader was used to being the last one to walk in class, and the first one out, he hardly had any books. He would only carry one notebook pretending he knew it all. It was about three weeks into his new school, and he waited for the teacher to come as he would enter just before him. This teacher's rule was that no student could walk in after him, so when he entered the class, he would shut the door behind. But something got to Nader, and he decided to challenge him and walk in after him. He could never have imagined that he would do what he was about to do. His upbringing was all about respect for rules and regulations. The time came to start class, and his teacher entered, grabbing the doorknob to shut it behind him. Nader was behind him pushing to get in, and his teacher would not let him in. He pushed his way in, causing his teacher to fall right on the first row of chairs. He rose up madly, bellowing,

-Who is he!?

First, everyone was quiet, and then one of the students opened his mouth and called his name.

-Nader... Sir...

That was a wrong move for the blabber-mouth student to make, and within a blink of an eye, Nader had him in his hands, and he was traveling through the window with him following. And that was it; Nader was expelled from his second school, so proud that he was no longer attending it. His relationship with Hussein was becoming a bit strained as well, for he was constantly telling Nader to straighten up, and he never wanted to hear it. It was like old times again, a perpetual part of their friendship. Nader did not realize that he was clearly filled with rage. Here was a young man, mad at his brother, mad at the world, mad at himself. He was raising hell to protest what had happened to him, wanting revenge for his failure. He revolted against anything and everything if there was a way to. If something was a standard set by someone else, Nader had something to say about it. The most interesting part of all of this was that his brother never said anything; he was told he did not know anything about what was occurring at Nader's schools. It was his other brother, Bijan, who was making phone calls to register him in another school. But this time was different. The only school that would accept him now was called Ferdossi. Before he was sent there, he hated that school, but now he thought it was cool because he knew it was a school for bad boys. Studying had no great importance at this school, and everyone was just looking to get their diploma or drop out. There were a few, of course, who studied hard, keeping a serious tone. The first thing Nader had to do was set a standard so the big boys would leave him alone. He wanted to show them that he was as tough as anyone. The first thing that captured his attention was the man who was controlling the traffic at the entry to the school. It was not a worker but Mr. Agha Husseini himself. Mr. Agha Husseini was a teacher, the vice-principal of the school, and a well-known goalkeeper for the national team when Nader was a young boy on the farm. He was always wearing dark glasses, and it was told that he had a false eye. The story was that during one championship game against the Russian team, he had stopped the Russians from making any goals. One of the Russian players became livid and kicked him with all his might straight in his eyes. Only one eye survived. He was different than the rest to Nader, who had some respect for an ex-national soccer player, but Nader did not know if Mr. Agha Husseini knew who he was. Soon Nader found out Mr. Agha Husseini had several table tennis set up in the schoolyard and was renting them out. Whoever had the table rented could be excused from class. One of the tables was always rented by Nader, and he wasn't even a fan of table tennis. But as time went on, he became pretty good at it, and it became an outlet for Nader to show the world how big and bad he was. One time one of the other boys did not want to sell his table to Nader. Nader took all four rackets and broke them in half as he bellowed,

-You better not walk out of this school, little boy. I am waiting for you out there.

He honestly did not know how he came up with such a line or idea and really didn't know if he was capable of executing such a threat. At the time, he didn't know the rackets belonged to Mr. Agha Husseini as well, and no one messed with him. So, the boy ran to the office to complain, and calmly Nader walked to his class. Nader was sitting in the class waiting for Mr. Agha Husseini to open the door and inform him he was kicked out of school. He waited and waited, but no one showed up. He was a bit skeptical as to what exactly was happening when class ended. He felt confused yet happy. He thought he had just performed the act that would get him kicked out of school, but that didn't happen. But he was now happy because no one would dare mess with him if Mr. Agha Huessini would not even approach him after such an incident. It became a win-win situation, except for the part about having to stay in school. After a few boring weeks had passed, Nader decided to skip school one day. The next day he was debating if he should go or not but finally decided to go and see what Mr. Agha Husseini's reactions would be. As he walked inside the gate, he was waiting for him, and his first words were,

-What happened yesterday? You did not show up.

For a second, there were millions of ideas that crossed Nader's mind, and he mumbled,

-My uncle died.

And surprisingly, Mr. Agha Husseini did not say a word after that and asked him to go to class. In Nader's eyes, he had gotten away with not coming to school by killing his uncle. Then, he began to imagine how many uncles he could have, as many as five, and it seems he could get away with murdering each one. So, he started fake killing uncles, aunts, friends, even his father, and the only reaction he would get was,

-Okay, go to your class.

And Mr. Agha Husseini was always waiting right at the gate like clockwork to respond. Finally, a moment came that Nader was not expecting. It was a cloudy day, and he was much sadder on those days. He did not go to school the day before, and he knew who would be standing by the gate waiting for him. He was thinking about who he was going to kill now. He had already killed five uncles and several relatives, including his father, so now what? It seemed that the more kind and calm his reactions were, the guiltier and worse he would feel, and sometimes Nader wanted to just hit his head with a rock and ask him why he was so kind to him, why was he so patient with him. Why would he not call him on his lies? He contemplated how he was a damn liar, bad man, and Agha Husseini should not be nice to him. But his little temporary heaven did not last much longer. Nader arrived at the school, and he could see him from a distance. Agha Husseini was waiting for him, and Nader had no one to kill this time, so he was at a loss. Without any reservation, he began to run like he was late for class, and he wanted to get to the class before it started. He never ran to get to class before. Just as he reached the gate, Agha Husseini blocked his way and stared right into his eyes. It was a long stare, eye to eye, and Nader had nothing to say. There were several other students standing around waiting to observe what would happen next, and Nader just stood there like he was deaf and dumb.

-Okay, who is it this time? Let's see, you have killed several uncles, many aunties, and many relatives, even your father. Who was it this time? The only people left to be killed are your brothers and sisters, and I know them all, and I know they are not dead. So maybe, the only one who is left is your mother? Are you going to kill her next?

And that was enough for Nader to pounce like a tiger! You never talk about killing someone's mother! Mothers are like Gods for Iranians. Nader wanted to punch him right in his dark glasses so he would lose his other eye too. Nader's fist crunched into a hardball, so tight his knuckles turned red. He closed his eyes and felt his body getting ready to lunge, but it wouldn't move quite yet. Just then, a honking car blaring, caught his attention, his eyes blinked open, his head swiveled, and his eyes landed right on the passenger in the car. He could not breathe; it was as if he wasn't even there anymore. Some boys were blocking the car to pass by, and as they sauntered over to the side of the road, the car took off with Nader still staring into the passenger window. His fist softened, losing all its power. He stood there motionless for a moment, not even realizing the other students and Mr. Agha Hussein had already gone inside,

-Do you want to play? You could have the table.

One of the boys felt bad for him and offered to play with him. He walked to the table, but he did not play. He just dropped his notebook that he always carried and sat on it while holding his knees. His mind fluttered. He felt as if he was going to throw up. He sat there for hours, on a notebook, staring at concrete. What had happened to him, what happened to the boy from the farm? The one who his mother was so proud of, the one that use to always help whenever possible. His move to Tehran, his beloved violin girl, all played back in his mind. He saw her, sitting in the car with such a kind and beautiful smile watching him. The sound of her violin echoed in his ear once again, and he could not hear anything else. She was the violin-playing girl behind the window, all grown up with long, shiny black hair, big almond eyes, an angelic smile that fit her body frame perfectly. She stared right at him, taking his anger with her down the road as her car flew by as quickly as it had come. It was as if it was a sign from God. She was a messenger, no, an angel, appearing once again to guide him down the right path.

The sudden appearance of his violin girl had shaken him in a way nothing had in a very long time. That night he could not sleep, trying to think of where she could live. The next morning, he found himself standing in the same place, at the same time, waiting for her car to pass again. But it never came. Her distant appearance seemed to take its toll on Nader's life regardless if no words were spoken. He walked onto school and looked up to see Mr. Agha Husseini watching him. Class had already started, yet he walked calmly past Nader, exchanging a kind smile as he stepped into the building.

Starting the next day, he never missed class; he was always there but still had no interest in actually studying. A week passed, and he became really depressed. He had looked everywhere to find his violin girl with no luck. He was quiet and calm, but inside he was a volcano waiting to erupt. Smoke was scattering throughout his entire being, clouding his feelings, vision and pushing him into a world of terrible emptiness. This was a place where no one would wish to be. Sometimes he thought of suicide, but the thought of his mother stopped him. He yearned for the guidance of the older wise man, he found himself begging for him to appear, but nothing happened. As he was going through all this emotional drama, Hussein was paying more and more attention to his studies. He was constantly advising him of doing the same, yet Nader argued that he didn't feel the pain and heartache that he felt, and he was not the one who was being robbed of two championships. He should have realized that Hussein was not much into sports anyway. But Hussein was there for him as, once again, they had both gone down different paths. Hussein was pushing himself very hard to be good in all forms so he could go to America. Later Nader found out that Hussein's father promised to send him to America to study if he graduated with honors. For this, he had to be in Tehran, so Hussein had left Brojered and returned to Tehran permanently.

As time passed, Hussein was seriously getting ready for America and preparing for the dream of leaving his father behind. Hussein's idea was to get to America then slowly bring his brothers over. This goal propelled him forward at all times. Nader really had no other close friends besides Hussein and Bahram, just classmates, and that was about it. Hussein was not fun anymore because he was into his own thing, just as Nader was into his when he was pushing to be the champ, Hussein had completely forgotten about his struggles, and now he had forgotten about Hussein's struggle.

*****

Chapter 7

Mysterious Infatuation With The Violin Girl... Love Connection...

It was a snowy winter day with fluffy snow covering everything. People were walking around in the snow, going about their business as if the trees, cars, streets and, buildings were not disappearing in the snow. Bored and missing Hussein, Nader decided to go to Hussein's school and see if he wanted to do something after school. It seemed as though some voice, something, told him to go see Hussein. This time he decided to ask Mr. Agha Hussieni if he could leave early, so he made up a story that he had a doctor's appointment. Luckily, he let Nader leave. He was waiting for Hussein's school, Jam, to be over. The school was located on a busy street named Jadeh Ghadimeh Sherman, at the area called Gholhak. It is one of the oldest streets that connect the old city of Tehran to the northern part. The school was inside a wide alley, and he knew there was a girl's school farther down the alley as well, and the corner he was standing at was the best place for the boys to gather and look for the perfect girl of their dreams. When the boys would find a girl they liked, the pursuit would begin to get her as their girlfriend. At the time, the boy and girl school were separated. On this day, he was the only one alone while everyone else was pairing up. Generally, you would not be alone. You would be with one friend or more, and then you would wait for your girlfriend to show up. If you were alone, everyone would always notice you, and if you were not from that neighborhood, the local boys would harass you, possibly beat you up for being in their neighborhood and trying to pick up their girls. The girls were protected by the boys, even if you did not know each other closely. So, you would all walk together, or you would walk with your girlfriend. You already knew which direction she was going to be heading, or if she was walking home or taking the bus. At the time, boys and girls could not date openly. It was prohibited. So, all your meetings happened without your parents knowing you were dating; it was especially hidden from the girls' brothers or father. They were very protective of their sisters or daughters. In some areas in the south, you could get killed or stabbed for trying to bring dishonor to a girl and her family.

The bell at Hussein's school began to ring. The school was still about a couple hundred yards away, but he could hear them clearly, and soon the alley was packed with students. Most of them were not in a rush, and they were taking their time for the girls to arrive, so they were securing their place, waiting for their dream girls. Soon the girls began to arrive in different groups, and the fun began for both sides. Everyone began smiling or flirting, and he had no part in this. Nader was barely even aware of what was going on as he patiently searched for Hussein. Finally, he saw Hussein approaching with a couple of his friends; they were carrying on a serious conversation. He was tall, very good-looking, and always serious. He was the girls' dream boyfriend, but he was not yet into girls that much either. He was kind of shy around girls, just like Nader was as well. He finally saw him and approached as he tagged along with them. But after a few quick words acknowledging him, Hussein continued his conversation with the other guy, discussing the English language and how he should learn the language faster to be ready for America. The other guy was giving him advice as well, leaving Nader out of the conversation. They stopped as they finished their conversation because one guy had to take a different direction to get to his house, and they had to take the bus or walk home. Nader was not interested in the conversation, so he was killing time and looking around observing others as Hussein finished up.

It was then that finally, the angel of help arrived for Nader again. He knew it when his eyes glanced at a group of three girls just across the street waiting by the bus stop. He thought he was dreaming. Without hesitation, he began to walk across the street, staring at one of the girls in the group, completely forgetting Husssein. She had not noticed him, even as he almost got run over by oncoming traffic. As he got closer, he could see that she was his lost violin girl. Yes, she was back, and he had found her again. Now, nothing else mattered to him with her in his sight, beautiful and sweeter than ever, "God, she is beautiful." His thoughts were screaming to him inside. She turned towards him with such a holy smile on her face, and for a second, her eyes locked on him, and she froze. He did not know if she could remember who he was, and he had no idea if she even knew that he was the one watching her from his private treehouse many years ago. But for some reason, his reflex was to hide himself behind the tree right in front of the public library. What if she saw him? What if she knows who he is? He did not want her to see him like this. He was a wounded, sad guy who thought he was not alive anymore, and he did not want her to see him the way he looked. He snuck to the other side of the trees and tried to see her from behind the tree without her noticing him. But her eyes landed right on him, and he backed off behind the tree, speechless and motionless. He could never understand why he used to lose control of his emotions and his soul, and he would get so embarrassed and nervous when it came to her. She had some sort of magic, like a mystic power over him, and with just one blink of her gorgeous eyes, she would capture his entire heart and soul, and he was under her spell. This was just the way it was with her and no one else. He was lost behind the tree, trying got blend with the shadows.

> -What the hell happened to you? Why did you leave? He was talking about studying, not like you wasting time chasing balls or girls.

There was Hussein standing in front of him, talking to him, but Nader could not hear him. He could not even see him. He just heard the bus stop, and he knew she would be getting on the bus, and he had to get on to see where she was going to get off. So, he carefully looked to see if she was getting on, and she did get on looking back toward him. As she entered the bus, he ran, and just as the bus was about to take off, he jumped up and held on to the front post and made his way behind the people and adjusted his view to see her. She was standing up, holding onto the post in the bus's aisle. Then, a boy got up and gave his seat to her. Generally, the buses would fill to their capacity, and many passengers would ride standing up when there were not any seats available. There was a game the boys used to play. They would take a seat, and when there was a cute or pretty girl standing by them, they would give their seat to the girl so they could make a connection and perhaps engage in conversation. He wanted to reach out and punch the boy so badly, but he was not close by, and he did not know why he was so jealous. How could he feel that he could claim authority or ownership, like she belongs to him? He had never even had a simple word with her, and he did not know how she felt about him. But that was the way he felt, and no one could change his mind. In his heart and mind, she belonged to him, and he did not care what anyone said or thought. He could see that she was looking to see if he was on the bus, and he didn't know if she saw him getting on the bus. Finally, she rose as the bus was coming to a halt at the next station, and he knew she had to walk past him to exit. He had to choose whether or not to exit before her or hide. The bus stopped, and suddenly, he rushed up onto the second floor and watched to see in which direction she would go.

    He watched her cross the street as the bus sped away and she looked after the bus, he knew that she knew he was on the bus, and he was embarrassed. He sat by the window looking out, lost in thought, and thinking about her and her only. Nothing else had any meaning for him. Now the problem was, how could he see her every day? He knew which bus station she got off at, and it was only four stations before his house. He thought, all this time, she was only four stations away, about a mile from him, and he didn't know. He began to contemplate how he would see her every day; his school was much farther, particularly farther from hers as well. Ideas popped in and out of his mind. He didn't realize he was now about twenty stations away from his house. He looked around, and there was no one left on the second floor. He rose and walked down to exit at the next station and took the bus back to his house. He was now smiling, and his sadness had dissipated. He walked in the door, and there was Boloor,

>   -Hussein stopped by twice. He is looking for you. Call him or go see him.

It was then that Nader realized he had completely ignored Hussein and didn't even say a word to him before jumping on the bus. He went to the phone and dialed his number. A moment later, he was talking to Hussein, explaining the whole story. But when he called her,

>   -my violin girl,

Hussein laughed very loudly,

>   -You don't even know her name, and you are in love with her, and you think you are going to get married to her? Man, you are crazy... I must speak to your brother...

That comment was the wrong one. He angrily yelled at Hussein for the first time ever. Hussein had never seen him like that, completely furious as Nader was in that moment. Hussein waited a few minutes for Nader to calm down. And that was it. Hussein never said anything bad about her again, and Nader knew that she was his soulmate, or at least in his mind she was, until he actually married someone else one day. Nader hung up the phone, and Hussein knew he was not the same Nader anymore. Something in him had changed. There was such a noticeable change in him that his mother, Parry, and Boloor noticed it. They began questioning him as to how he was. But he just calmly smiled, and their interest peaked when they watched him after his shower, preparing nice clothes to wear for the first time. He had never paid attention to his clothing before. He would just throw something on and run out. He asked Boloor if she could press a shirt for him, and that was too much for them to handle. They began to think he was up to some sort of joke or playing a game with them, but they were not sure. At the same time, they were happy to see a smile on his face and did not want to jeopardize anything to change his newfound happiness. So, they went along with him and helped him while they joked all the way through the process; he had everything ready for the next morning. But the problem was that he could not sleep all night, and he was rolling around in bed, waiting for the sun to come up. He was busy planning what to do and what not to do, and how he should plan to transfer to Hussein's school so he would be closer to his Violin Girl. This way, he could see her every day, walk her to school, watch her placing her books on her beautiful chest while carrying them every day. And most importantly, he had to figure out a way to talk to her. He had to somehow get the courage to speak to her, but he was too chicken to go through with any of these plans.

Finally, the morning light came to replace the tense darkness of the night, and he was up and in the shower getting ready to leave. His plan was to go and find a secret place at the bus station where she got off the day before and wait for her, but he didn't want her to see him, and for that, he needed to go early enough to find his place. Besides, he did not know what time she would get to the bus stop or where she lived. All those questions were waiting for him to find answers to, and they were burning questions. He was now experiencing a new life as he was on the way to experience the sweet taste of love. But this time, it was not about soccer or pretending to be a big fish in the water to impress others. It was a strange new feeling, like he was flying high. He was a dreamer dancing among the clouds, and he was lost in time. And there he was, running with his new suit, new shoes, and a new shirt to get to the bus stop. He was an entirely new person running to that bus. He was not just different because he was wearing new clothing, and maybe if she were to see him that day, his clothes would reflect the newness he felt deep within his soul. Then, he started to wonder what he would actually do if she saw him.

He could have taken a bus to get to her bus stop, but he did not. And he was there so early that he did not see any other students walking. He had chosen the location where he was going to be so she would not see him. It was a concrete electrical post next to a large flower bush across the street from the bus stop. Recently the city began to use concrete posts to replace the wooden electric posts, and the beauty of them was that there were holes all the way through up to the top. He could stand behind it and watch through one of the holes, and she would never even know he was there. He had waited for almost an hour, and there was no sign of her. He moved away from his position several times to make sure he covered all directions; there were now students getting on the bus, but still no sign of her. It was getting late, and he had to run back to his school to be on time, and that would have taken him at least a half-hour, if not more, but he was not leaving until he saw her. Sadly, she still had not shown, and he was getting very disappointed. He walked out to check around one more time. Maybe she was hiding somewhere as he had done. He searched the alley where he saw her walking the day before. Then, just as he turned, there she was, riding on the bus passing him, with Hussein standing a few yards away from her, on the same bus. They both stared at him, then at each other, then back on him again, long after the bus drove by him. He did not know how that happened. How could she be on that bus with Hussein? She got off the bus stop he was waiting at. And a sad thought suddenly hit his mind. What if Hussein was dating her or had an interest in her? He almost forgot about school and continued to look toward the bus, even when the bus was long gone from his view. Then, he noticed a student running for his life who attended his school. He remembering he was late and began to run after him, it became a race between the two of them. He got to school just in time before the classroom door was being shut closed. He wished the school would catch on fire, so he did not have to stay there, or he could have a reason to be transferred.

Sitting in class physically but not being there mentally was not something new to him. He was always thinking about anything besides what was going on in class. He thought for the first time in his life that maybe he should go to his older brother and make peace with him, ask for his help to get transferred to Hussein's school. He would agree to follow his wishes and study hard to become a doctor, engineer, or attorney. Then he realized that this would immerse his brother right back into his life, and it was no longer an option. He knew he had to get his grades up to be able to transfer to Hussein's school. He knew he had to figure out how to be with his love without his brother's help, and he was consumed with all these thoughts of planning how he should go about everything. Then, the school bell rang, and all the students walked out for a ten minutes break, but he was still sitting there lost as he tried to concoct a plan, "Nader, you must walk with me to the teacher's lounge. Mr. Agha Husseini wants to see you there." His teacher's voice broke his silence. He walked Nader to the teacher's lounge as though he was worried Nader would run away. He wondered what he could have done wrong this time. What if there was a complaint from his Violin Girl through her parents? But why? He did not have to wait long, and soon he was standing in front of all the teachers. There were about fifteen of them, and even the principal was present with Mr. Agha Hussieni standing by him, smiling at him for the first time. Then, he noticed his lost notebook in the hands of the principal, who was also smiling along with the rest of the teachers.

-Is this your writing?

He handed Nader his notebook, and he saw the pages in which he wrote the notes by the pool, about the moon, and comparing the moon to his mother. Confounded, he bowed his head, yes.

-Would you read it for us?

That was the hard part, reading your thoughts, your personal feelings that were so private, in front of all your teachers who prior to this point have been your enemies. And he, being the shyest boy on the entire planet, how could he possibly do this? His voice was lost, he could not breathe, and he could not even look up. He was just staring at the notes, and he would have paid, or done anything, to walk away from there without opening his mouth.

-You are in for something greater. What if you read it?

It was Mr. Agha Husseini's voice that gave him a bit of confidence to find himself and just to be able to stand there in front of everyone. After all, Nader had a lot of respect for him, and Agha Husseini's way of dealing with him was the main reason he could calm down and begin to act like a normal human. And if it wasn't for his tolerance, he probably would not have been at school anymore, and perhaps he would not have run into his Violin Girl. So, he stared at him, and his smile gave Nader a bit of courage. He began mumbling and kind of whispering what he had written on the pages,

-These are good words.

Then, for just a moment, he checked the cover of the notebook to be sure that this was his notebook. But it was his, and they were his words, and he was reading it for the first time in front of all his teachers. It seemed to be several minutes before he had finished five pages. And after he was done reading it, the sound of clapping rang through the room. Nader could not believe what was happening. For a second, he looked around to see if there was someone else in there that he didn't see, and the clapping was for him. But there was no one else. It was an honor for him. It was about ten minutes into class time, and all the teachers were still in the room, so they all rose to exit, looking at him with admiring expressions. He was still standing there in shock when Mr. Agha Husseini announced,

-We want you to compete at the national composition writing competition. We are all sure that if you did this, you would bring honor to our school.

Now he was a bit less embarrassed and feeling quite happy. He did not know that he had other talents besides playing sports. Later he realized he had left his notebook in the yard, and Mr. Agha Hussieni had discovered it when he was checking his table tennis area after school. He kept it all this time. He was the one who, once again, had opened a new door of hope for him to be someone he never thought he could be, a writer. Running toward the bus stop, thinking about what had just happened at school, he was intent on finding his lost Violin Girl, and it felt like a dream. This was a dream that you would never expect to happen to you and could not have been a better script for someone to write for you. He was flying without strings or wings, not running, not hiding. And in his mind, he was already a well-known writer that was his way to make his violin lady proud and show her something great that he could do.

He remembered the first time he ever saw a movie. It was just a year ago with his older cousin. He guessed he decided to take him to see a movie because he was so depressed. The movie was about World War II, and the Russians were fighting the Germans. He could still remember a certain scene very clearly. A group of Russian commandos had a mission to take out a hill, and several machine guns were shooting right at them from over the cliff. One of them ran and attempted to drop his last bomb inside a small hole that had machine-gun fire coming out, but he missed it. All the other members of his team were killed, and he lost the last chance to stop the machine-gun fire, and he knew the rest of his fellow soldiers would be killed. So, he ran and dropped himself right in front of the hole and covered the hole for his fellow soldiers to escape; they finally captured the rocky hills. This scene never left his mind. Of course, that was the first time he had ever seen a movie, and he did like it tremendously. He took the bits and pieces of the last few years that were stored in his mind and de-constructed it as he walked down the street. By the time he reached the bus stop, he had already written his first movie. He did not know how much time it had taken him to reach the bus stop as he waited for his Violin Girl. His eyes were chasing bus after bus, and finally, there she was, and Hussein was standing a few yards away on the same bus. He was looking patiently, but the bus took off, and she did not get off. Sadness had replaced the happiness in his heart. By now, the only conclusion he could think of was that Hussein had something to do with her, and he had an interest in her. Why did he have to go after someone he would die for, why? He needed to speak with him, but how can he expect his friend to give up his love for him? In their culture, friends die for each other, and they give up their lives for one another. He could not ask such a thing from

Hussein, but he could not stop loving her either. It was a couple hours later that he reached his house, sad and disheartened. Boloor again approached and said,

-Hussein is looking for you.

She added,

-You are sad again?

-I am just tired,

He responded slowly before entering his room. He was looking around, and without noticing what he was doing, he began clearing his paperwork. Somehow, he knew that in order to get closer to his Violin Girl or to become a writer, he needed to get serious right away. There were just three months left in the school year, and that was not much time for someone who did not even have a book, just one simple notebook for the whole year. And the notebook was sitting on his desk. He glanced at it and read it again. He did like it. It wasn't meaning anything to him when he was writing it, but now it was making lots of sense. He kept telling himself he had to get serious. He has to become disciplined. He has to push himself hard, and he meant hard.

As he was sifting through piles of paper, he came across a book, *The Old Man and the Sea*, the one he never read from his doctor. He remembered that he wanted the book back; he had forgotten he ever had it. He looked through it and read a couple of pages, and a month later, he was still reading it again and again. Why? He did not know. The pages began tearing and falling out, and there was no way he could return the book to their doctor, and because of that, he never visited the doctor again. He was lucky he never got sick, or he would have had an earful from the doctor. But just reading over the story and the situation that the old fisherman had to deal with was inspiring. After his entire struggle, just as he thought he had caught the biggest fish, he loses his fish to a shark. But he was not disappointed or sad. He just left for the sea the very next day and the day after, like nothing ever happened. It was like every day was a new and beautiful day for him, no matter if he would catch a fish or not, or less or more. And it was then that he realized he didn't have to let anything bother him or stop him from getting where he wanted to go or who he wanted to be. He could just push for what he wanted to happen, and if it happened, it happened, and if it did not, so what. And he started a new life, a new challenge within him to get what he wanted, and of course, it wouldn't be easy, especially when it came to his Violin Girl.

Several days after he last saw Hussein and the Violin Girl, he walked out to go to school, and there she was at the bus stop waiting for the bus to arrive, right across from his own house. He hid himself behind the bus's ticket booth and watched her as Hussein approached him,

-You are going to waste your damn life because of this girl.

Hussein again was giving him advice. This time he did not mind because now he could pretend that he was talking to him instead of hiding. They began walking across the street, but he did his best not to face her or lock his eyes with her. He didn't want Hussein to see his reaction; he would be too embarrassed. Besides, she was Hussein's girl. And that was why she was using the same bus stop even if she had to walk a mile longer.

-Look at her. She is one fine woman.

He was surprised when he heard Hussein making such a comment. He looked up and saw that a tall girlfriend of the Violin Girl was approaching. Her name was Zarry. They were always together. He knew her. She was the sister of one of his friends.

-You like her?

Curiously Nader asked, feeling the excitement build.

-Yes, if I wanted to have a girlfriend, she would be the one. I like her. She doesn't get on the bus until I do. She likes me. Just watch her.

Then his Zarry approached and joined Violin girl. He was right. A couple of buses arrived and left, and Zarry continued to watch if Hussein was making a move to get on a bus. Both she and the Violin Girl did not get on a bus. It was then that he realized he was wrong about Hussein and his Vilon Girl. Hussein had no interest in her; he liked her friend! He was happier than a mother holding her newborn child. He was in again and had no excuses not to go after his love and marry her. Now the book made more sense. Just go on with your life, and things will fall in place.

-Hey, the friend keeps looking at you. She is cute, man, and classy too.

Nader pretended that he was not interested, but what Hussein said made him a new man with a million-dollar smile. He was ecstatic inside, like he owned the world. He got the courage to turn and look at her, and there she was, looking at him with that golden smile of hers, which was not just a smile. It was a stunning and holy gift, something that could make your bones shake. And the story of him and Violin Girl began a new dimension. Now they both knew they liked each other, but he still did not know if she knew about the treehouse or not, and he still did not know her name. Nor did he know if she knew his name. So, one day, he told Hussein to call his name from across the street so she could clearly hear it. The next few months, Nader was studying day and night to pass his classes so the next year he could go to Hussein's school and be with his love.

*****

Chapter 8

The Unspoken Rule...

Summer was on the way, and Nader hated this. This was the first summer he wished would not arrive. Soon he could not wait for her at the bus stop, and he did not know how he would see her. By now, he knew where she lived, and lucky for him, she was only a couple of houses from one of his friends from grade school. He remembered him as Mohamad Mandeghari, with whom Nader organized the first soccer team Sharzad with, and he was a chubby kid. He also was a shy guy like Nader and did not mix with the crowd much, especially in the neighborhood. But for him to live near her house was a gift and a big blessing because he could easily walk around her house pretending he was there to see his friend Mandeghari, so no one would suspect him. The unspoken rule was that the boys of each neighborhood controlled incoming traffic, and that meant if an unknown boy came around looking to pick up girls or to make friends with them, they would be chased out and punished for their disrespect. This made it risky to venture into other neighborhoods; you had to be really brave and careful. Despite the great risks involved, he didn't care either way and would have gone around her house no matter what. But now Mandeghari was his God; he could have anything he wanted from Nader, maybe even a limb if needed. Whenever he would go to check on his love, for sure, Nader would bring some fresh pastries for him, and every time he visited, Mandeghari was getting fatter and chubbier. He would visit a minimum of once a day during the summer, and soon they started playing chess underneath the light post, right across from her house. They would play for hours into the night, waiting for her to show up in the window. But what was not so great is that Mandeghari did not have an older sister the same age as her, so he couldn't use his sister to send messages or start a line of communication. Also, she was Jewish, and few Muslim families would have established friendships with her family. Her father was very sensitive about the Jewish faith. He, of course, was very protective of her and wanted her to be with a Jewish man, as Nader found out much later. But he did not care if she was Jewish, Muslim, a monk, Christian, or atheist. He wanted to be with her, and nothing could have changed that. It was much later that he had found out she had to fight her father for years to be transferred to the multi-school she now attended from the Jewish-only school. In Iran, they had a multi-school system, and each minority religion had also created its own schools. Her mother named her Fariba because of one of their best friends, who they loved very much, and died at a young age. In the summertime, many things usually changed for families and the makeup of the neighborhood. Many families would travel for summer vacations which were the worst and best for young boys and girls. First of all, traveling was fun and seeing a new city was exciting. Those who did not have a boyfriend or girlfriend were happiest of all. It was the best opportunity to find one when you were vacationing. It was much easier to meet someone during vacation, because generally those families who were vacationing, especially on the Caspian Sea, were very open-minded. At night there were parties and dancing, and during the day, the focus was the ocean and beautiful bikini-clad women all over the beach. Generally, several families would team up together and go on trips together so the younger generations could hang out together and mingle.

The first month of summer was the hardest time because he hardly saw her, and he didn't know her schedule. Unfortunately, his trips to her neighborhood became just about serving Mandeghari his pastries, and his demand was growing. He started ordering certain kinds and requested some for his little sister; soon, Nader was buying pastries for the whole family. He did not mind that much because they were his guardians in the neighborhood, and no one would question it. By now, everyone knew he was with Mandeghari, so he had a safe passage. Part of his time was spent with Hussein as well; they both had to study. He had to take tests for two classes in the second month of summer, which were the two classes he had failed in spring. At the time, if you failed up to two classes, the school used to give you a chance to take the test once again in the summer to pass it. So, if he could not pass those two classes, he could not go to the next grade, and he would be behind Hussein by one year. It was the first time he was facing such a dilemma, and he did not like it. Hussein used to study his English religiously to be ready to explore America when he finished high school. The two courses Nader had failed in the spring were English and Arabic language. He was determined to pass them, and he succeeded, even though most of his studying was done the last fifteen days before the test date.

The painfully slow summer had finally ended, and Nader was ecstatic. He barely saw his love. He caught glimpses of her just a few times and was sure she actually only saw him once. He could not wait for school to open in a few days. On the first day of school, Nader was waiting for her to show up by the bus stop. The bus stop was right across from his house; he conveniently placed a large wooden box behind the wall facing the street in the bushes and stood on it, waiting. As he saw her approaching from the distance, he would walk out of his yard every morning, so they would both reach the bus stop together. This way, he would not appear to be waiting for her, so he would not look like a wimp or un-manly. So, of course, it was always a coincidence that he used to walk out at the same time that she reached the bus stop. And there he would be, waiting on the side pretending he was waiting for his friend. He would not stand in the bus line or take the bus if she would not get on. He would stand on the side and run and jump on the very last second the bus was leaving after she had gotten on the bus while still looking for the invisible friend he was waiting for.

Now when he recalled the fake frustration in his face from the invisible friend not showing up, it was very amusing. More interesting was the fact that he did not find it odd that he had been waiting for the same friend to show up for three years. This was quite funny. Remembering these moments still brought happiness to his heart and soul, a youthful hope that could not be exchanged for anything else in life. One morning she was late, and he was getting worried. In his mind, he was not going to leave without her. At this point, he had been playing games with the Violin Girl for two years now, and it was about time for him to do something. By now, all his family and friends knew about the mystic love affair and either teased or tried to give advice. But he didn't take any; he liked the way things were. Maybe deep inside his heart, he was worried if he got close, what was built up within would vanish. He hesitated and was about to jump on the bus when he heard,

-Fariba? Why are you so late?

Zarri, her tall friend who liked Hussein, was waiting at the bus stop for her. She yelled on purpose to let Nader know he should not leave. He looked over his shoulder, and there she was, Fariba, his Violin Girl rushing to the bus stop. They all rushed onto the bus, and that was the first time the two came face to face. He backed up for her to get in, and she did, but only after she stared straight through his eyes and into his soul for a moment that made time standstill. He was doomed, motionless, speechless, and a bit embarrassed that this was happening. He could not breathe because she had seized hold of his entire being, and he was in her complete control. God, she was so holy and beautiful, and he still to this date will never forget that moment in time. It was in that very moment that he knew she loved him also, and the feeling that she also cared about him was like heaven beyond his wildest dreams. The bus had taken off, and he did not even realize he had forgotten to get on. It seemed he was glued to the pavement. Then, he began to run to reach the bus, but he was too late, and sadly he could see her watching him with her soft smile as the bus traveled into the distance.

This moment was the start of the happiest period of Nader's life. It gave him a reason to be and to do things that he never thought about before. He began to plan the future in his head, thinking about him and her and two kids, a boy and a girl. He wanted the boy first so he could protect his sister when they grew up so she would not be bothered by the bad boys. And the plan was in motion, with him flying high into this magical dream of uncertainty. He now attended Hussein's school, and every day at 7:30 AM, they were all at the bus stop getting on the bus, at 12:15 PM taking the bus back from school, and again at 1:30 PM taking the bus back to school and finally the last trip, 4:30 PM on the way back home. That was the school schedule for the entire year. And they loved it because they had more time to have fun with their girlfriends, even if it was a distance to travel every day, just looking at each other from a distance felt like the ultimate reward. Nader's seat in the classroom was right next to the door so that the minute the school bell would ring, he could be out of the class onto the street, waiting for his soul mate. He was in class physically, but mentally as before, he was somewhere else, and where he was, Nader did not know. Every second, he was thinking of a different plan, which would soon be replaced by the next one. The game of pursuit was on.

Then one day, he recognized a familiar teacher, one from his old school, who was transferred to his new school. He knew him as Mr. Sadaghyanlou. He was his English teacher and knew about Nader's ability to write. At the time, with his long hair and strange starving look, he appeared eccentric to all. Generally, all teachers there were clean-cut with a suit and tie. And there he was -- wearing an outfit like the dervishes but a bit more modern to satisfy the school board. Everyone was always blinded to who he was because of his appearance, even Nader was, to begin with. They all looked at him with their eyes but not with their hearts. But later, Nader had a change of heart; Mr. Sadaghyanlou had secretly introduced him to the world of Sufism. He was a Sufi, a dervish who belonged to a group called "Anghah." The main leader of the group was "Shah Neamatolah Angha, Pear Ovici." Of course, the radical clergy opposed them and perceived them as a threat for their control over the masses. Because the group, like every other Dervish group, would look at Islam the way Rumi, Omar Khayyam, Hafez, Sanai, Saddi, Shakheh Attar, and many other Iranian poets and philosophers would, the clergy labeled them enemies.

Soon Nader was standing in front of a large, heavy-set man who was the head of school activities and art department, and the man was telling him that he wanted him to compete in the writing competition. Nader was happy to hear these words because he had commented before that his class was boring, and he needed something more exciting. Later the man asked him if he could write a play and he said yes. But he had never written a play or read one for that matter. The same afternoon he got hold of a couple of plays and read them all. One was an Iranian play and the other from a German writer, Bertolt Brecht, which he could hardly understand at the time. Then, the same weekend he took a friend to see a play on the street of Lalezar. He did not know at the time it was going to be a commercial, a satire play that was kind of lightweight and mostly geared to average working-class folks who just wanted to have fun. However, it was funny.

A week later, he was starting to find his groove for what it was all about. He wrote a twenty-page play. And then, later, he directed the play with a friend and played a role as well. He played a tough street man with a good heart. That was his first work in the entertainment business. The play was fun, and everyone liked it, so once again, he was popular in school, and his older brother and family did not know anything about his new hobby. His older brother especially didn't know of his new involvement with the arts, and there was no way he would have been notified of his endeavors. He would have destroyed Nader's beautiful new world of artistic fun. His mother was still continuously in gridlock with Abbass, constant power struggles were always occurring, and Nader was always on his mother's side. But his art was now a big distraction from his mother's unhappiness. Nader's world was turned upside down in such a short time. He went from having his body filled with anger and spite to finding his love and a hidden artistic side. By now, everyone knew about his violin girl even though he still had not even held a conversation with her. Maybe it was God's will to keep them from one another because of their families' beliefs. Nader could only plan and wait.

*****

As the year ended and summer arrived again, Nader dreaded the anticipated boredom that would once again befall him. But he could not think of anything to do to change this situation. He would just have to manage the summer. Surprisingly the story of his romance with Fariba had now become a known and most talked-about subject among his friends. Even his family, with the exception of his three brothers and his mother, knew about Fariba. All his nieces and nephews knew, and most of them were a bit shocked. During that summer, the police department started a motorbike police service to observe the area. Before, there were on-duty police on foot that were responsible for certain areas at night time, and the shifts used to change every twelve hours. By now, he knew the two men who were responsible for the ally where Fariba's house was located, and they both had tasted his fresh bakery items many times. Especially the one who used to work at nighttime. They were also the recipients of many fine cigars from him as gifts, and anytime he was around, they would let him do as he pleased. But suddenly, two new officers on motorbikes replaced the old ones, and they toured the area more often. Unfortunately, they did not know him, and since he wasn't from the area, they would question him. His last name would ring a bell, and knowing who his brother was, he would be notified immediately. They would have used it as an opportunity to get close to his brother, pretending to take care of his family. He had to come up with a way to become friendly with the new officers on duty, and he did so with help from his friend Mandeghari.

His friend's family had hired a lady helper, and they bribed her to act a little flirty with the officers and introduce Nader to them. She did a great job, but one of the officers just plain disliked him, and for some reason, he would not pay attention to her. Because of him, most of his activity around Fariba's house had to be done when he was not on shift. What Nader never thought about was why she didn't seem to play the violin anymore. It never crossed his mind until one day, he was passing by an alley, and he heard the sound of a violin being played from inside the house. A few weeks later, she was walking to get ice cream, and there he was with his friend, walking close-by, acting out their plan. Just as he was enjoying the best time of his life with his love, even if it was from a distance, out of nowhere, Fariba's brother showed up, and they ask her and her friend to get into his car, and he took Nader's love away, and he hated him for what he did.

The next day she heard Nader's voice in the alley underneath her window; it was always his voice yelling for his friend Mandeghari instead of ringing the bell. But in reality, he was calling for her to let her know he was around. And then, after a few minutes, there was the sound of her violin again echoing into his ears and overtaking his existence. It was about 9 PM, and he was sitting under the weak light of the electric post in the alley playing chess with Mandeghari. His entire attention was on the music, and he lost every game they played that night. She began to play again from that day on. Every time she would hear his voice, even if it was for a short time, the sound of the violin would again fill the air.

It was in the moonlight of a late summer day, he was sitting by the pool recalling good and bad memories. He thought of the treehouse, Fariba in grade school, the pool, the competitions, the farm, the soccer game, and all. He realized that all these things were a part of his history. He could not have them back or recreate them the same way they had happened. And now he had the choice to create something new, to always create new opportunities. He was walking in circles around the pool losing count of how many times he circled around. Finally, his chest lit up; he had a plan. It was a light of encouragement, and he was ready to do something and no longer just enjoy his love from a distance. He mumbled softly to himself,

-I need to talk to her... I need to talk to her....

Soon, he came across this small and very short boy named Fareed, who used to live right across from Fariba, who also attended his school. It was Reza who broke the news to Nader about Fareed. He was two grades below Nader, so he did not have much contact with him or had ever seen him before. However, several times he thought he should become friends with him to use him to get to Fariba or send a message to her through his sister. His sister happened to be a good friend of Fariba's, but she was going to a different school than her. Within a few days later, Nader got his chance. He was walking toward Friba's house and noticed a few boys trying to rough Fareed up. He was scared and did not know as Nader stepped in, staring them straight down as he growled, asking what the problem was.

Luckily the boys backed up, and nothing happened, but Fareed was so thankful, and from then on, Fareed thought Nader could be his protector at school as well. They walk together to Reza's house, who also was a neighbor of Fareed. This worked well because Fareed also joined their nightly chess game, and soon his messenger to Fariba was established. Nader came up with a plan and decided to go to her room in the middle of the night and speak to her under the moonlight. There was a tree by her house that he could use to climb right over the wall and onto the second-floor balcony, right to her room which opened onto the balcony. His friends thought it was crazy, but he was determined to do something crazy or special to prove to her how much he loved her by risking his life. Fariba had a huge, tall brother; in fact, he was almost three times bigger than Nader. Her father was a large man as well. But Fariba was very small in size. Finally, all his friends decided to cooperate with him deciding his plan would be fun and exciting. So, the time was set, and it was planned to occur during the shift of the officer who was friends with Nader and knew that he wanted to marry Fariba. So, he sent a message about his plan to her through Fareed. An answer came back that she would be waiting for him, which made him extremely happy. The dark night arrived, and he was on his way with four of his friends. Soon they all gathered at Mandeghari's. The night did not start out as calmly as he had planned. Out of Nader's bad luck, on the night he had organized to execute his crazy plan, her family had company, and they were socializing and having fun.

He was wondering why she did not tell Fareed about having guests the night he was going to see her. Then, he thought it might be that they just dropped by, which is not unusual in Iran. It was now 11 PM, and it was a few hours that he was sitting in the tree, overlooking her house, hiding inside its branches, waiting. He could not wait any longer. Fareed also had not shown up; the lights were out in his house. More importantly, the lights had gone out in Fariba's room. Nader was ready to move over the wall. But her brother and a few other guys were hanging out in the yard by their pool. He was several years older than him and believed he was finishing college. They were hidden beside the wall smoking hashish, away from the eyes of their parents. He had no choice but to wait and now could not calm down either. He was worried. What if her brother would notice that he was sitting in the tree? That would not look good. So, he waited and waited, trying his best to blend in. Several times his friend Mandeghari walked underneath the tree, telling Nader to forget about it and come down, but he was not going to give up and couldn't answer anyway.

It was sometime past midnight when all the guests finally left, and he was still waiting. Finally, all the lights in her house were turned off. He sat there for about forty-five more minutes waiting for the family to fall asleep, and then the time arrived. Quietly just like he was a professional thief, he climbed up the wall and up onto the balcony. He really did not know what he was doing. It was crazy. He could have been arrested and put in jail. He could have been beaten up badly, and what an embarrassment if he were to get caught. How would he be able to look his mother in the eyes? It was a bad move, but he was blind and stupid at the time. At any rate, he must have been out of his mind to make such a move, but he could not help himself. Now he could see her through the tall balcony window, sleeping like an angel, with her back toward him. He could smell her, he could feel her in his arms, and there was no way he would go back.

He looked around one last time and then quietly entered the room through the tall balcony window. During summertime, all windows were left open so that cool air could come in. So, there was nothing between him and his love but the soft white curtain. Standing by the window for several minutes, he could hear all his friends talking quietly in the alley, anticipating what was next. After all, nobody had ever attempted such a daring and crazy act, and this was a new adventure for them all. He was confused, and fear began to bombard his thoughts. He did not know what he should do next. What if she yelled when he touched her? What if he got caught, and what if this was truly a bad idea? Why is she not waiting for him even though she knew that he was coming to see her? But it seemed at the time he had no way out, he could not go back, and he had no courage to move forward. He was doubtful and confused, scared and uncertain. Then, a light came on on the second floor of the house right across the street. Someone appeared in the window of the house across the street smoking, and now Nader had no choice but to enter her room. Otherwise, if he just stood there, there was a good chance that the man or someone else would see him from across the street thinking he was a thief or an intruder. Then they will begin yelling, "There is a thief!" and would awaken the entire neighborhood. And there was a great chance he would get cut and arrested as a thief. He knew he had to make his move, go back or get inside. Finally, quietly and carefully, he entered and sat and hide by the bed away from the view. He was so scared that he could not breathe; he could feel all the joints in his body locking. Luckily for him, her back was toward him. He knew he had to hide from the man across the street's view; he sat by the bed behind the wall. For a second, he thought he should just sit there until the daylight, and she would wake up to his smiling face. But this was not a good choice. He was whispering in his mind for God to help him out of such a stupid plan when suddenly she turned in the bed toward him and sleepily adjusted her pillow, closing her eyes again. He could hardly see her face. Then, the cannon broke loose, and God didn't help! She opened her eyes, sat up, and began to yell,

-Thief! Thief!

He moved immediately and covered her mouth while begging,

-It's me, Fariba. Do not yell. It's me, Nader.

Then he realized that another girl, who was sleeping on the other side of her, began to yell. Hell broke loose dazed and confused, almost peeing in his pants. The light in the room came on. After seeing Nader, Fariba was quiet and just was watching him in shock. But she could not do anything about the other girl who jumped up and attacked him with whatever she could get hold of. Frightened and not knowing what to do, she was standing in front of the tall window through which he had entered, so confused he was forced to run out through the door into the upstairs walkway. He did not know where he was heading as the other girl gave him a push, and he felt himself begin to fumble downstairs. He was simultaneously covering himself from her beating on him. He was in trouble now, and things were getting worse by the minute. He rose up to see Fariba's brother and father rushing up, holding sticks; he knew he had to somehow get out immediately. In Iran, windows are made of covered glass all the way from top to bottom on the side of the stairs, going from the first floor to the second floor. He saw the glass and ran like hell, diving into the glass windows, falling over 15 yards, crash landing on an abandoned property outside. The fact that he was covered in bits of glass, bleeding, and limping, did not register. Nader jumped up and ran, and within less than two minutes, he was up and over the wall and running beside a river.

Just the year before, the city had put up a concrete wall on both sides of the river and made it smaller. There was also a new sidewalk on both sides. The river was almost full of water as it was the end of the summer, and the weather was getting a bit cold at night. This caused him to have no way to escape. He pleaded with God as to what to do next as the loud voices of the neighborhood mass were echoing into his ear. By now, the whole neighborhood was out to catch the thief, and every light was on. He could see the beams of flashlights moving all over the walls, buildings, trees, and through the air. Then, he noticed several boys approaching through the narrow walkway. They jumped over a short wall, holding their sticks,

-We will cover this side, and you guys watch the other side, so he cannot escape from the other side.

Not knowing who they were at first, he took a vow to kill them if they touched him. He was so bewildered and lost that he did not know the boys were Mandeghari and his other friends; they were keeping others at bay. They stared for a long second, and suddenly, Mandegharia moved and pushed Nader right into the water. He landed in the river, traveling with the current. Then, he realized they were running beside him on the top and was distracting people from seeing him. At one point, one of the friends pushed him down underneath the water with his stick so that the approaching people across the street could not see him sticking out of the water. The problem now was how he was to exit the river because there was a five-yard high wall on both sides, and the current was fast, and it was pushing him forward. It would take more than the help of his friends to pull out. So, he kept going downstream until he found a safer place to exit. Luckily, he was a good swimmer, like a fish in the water, but he was getting cold, and he could feel pain all over his body. He then heard Mandeghari yell,

-Second Bridge, we will meet you at the second bridge,

It was a long way down to the second bridge. It seemed as if he traveled over ten miles. He was losing strength but still begging God to help him get out of this mess, praying that he would not be killed by the swift current. He was searching for the bridge, but most of the way was dark, and he could not see anything. Then, finally, he saw a part of a bridge that was lit by the light on the top of an electrical post. He pushed himself to the side so he could grab whatever he could get a hold of in order to stop. He knew if he missed the bridge, the next hope would be several miles away, and he would not be able to make it. He was in a crazed state by now, and suddenly his side had impacted with a sharp object inside the water, "Oh my God…" His voice raised out of extreme pain he felt on his side as he managed to get underneath the bridge, but he got hold of a sharp side of concrete and stopped. Before he could think of what to do next, he heard voices talking underneath the bridge on the opposite side from where he was.

-Did you hear anything?

A woman asked with a worried voice.

-No, it is probably some guys up top messing around. Do not play games. I paid for this, and I am going to finish it.

There was this rough voice of a man talking to his prostitute. Half of Nader's body that was still in the water was freezing, and the other half was leaning on the concrete block which was sticking out of the water. He was motionless. It was about an hour later, and several men had come down to have the pleasure of the prostitute. Nader grasped the concrete, not moving. It did not bother him, he just did not want to be caught, and he really did not want the workers who were enjoying the prostitute to see him as well. It was a problem and a big one, but if he could just hang on a bit longer, he would be safe. Whatever it took, he quietly pulled himself out of the water and lay on the concrete block by the side of the bridge in the shadows. Finally, after they were done, the prostitute was pulled up the bridge, and they were gone. Soon Mandeghari and two other friends were climbing down to see if he made it. Mandeghari's flashlight shined on his face, but he was out of it and did not have the strength to answer their call before they found him. Later he realized it was an engineering mistake that had placed concrete a few yards out of the bridge's post but not through the entire river, so the water had washed the dirt from the middle part and created a deep section. The concrete had become like a bed for men to have fun on at night. But he was thankful that it helped him.

The next morning, he was recovering and realized his friends had transferred him to a hospital. They told everyone that he had crashed coming down the mountain into a river—another lie to cover his mess. And again, there was Parry and Boloor, who both knew the true story and covered for him. He still remembered the first time he was in his love's room, looking at her; it was well worth all the unspeakable trouble. However, after that incredible stunt Nader pulled, he was nicknamed and known as Majnoon. Majnoon was the name of a guy in a famous folk story that was in love with Lilly. The title of the book is *Lilly and Majnoon*. Majnoon was so in love that he lost his mind and could not see straight about anything but his love. After that, there would not be any gathering where they would not talk about his love life, and he felt special. Later the truth about Fareed came out. The small little neighbor had never told Fariba that Nader was going to see her. He flat lied to him. And his bad luck that he had chosen a night that her relatives were visiting and it just happened to be her birthday. One of her nieces decided to spend the night with her. She was the one who attacked him like a tiger. Long after that night, he could not forget the beating from the niece. But he could not be happier for the outcome. He again realized she also cared about him and perhaps loved him. Maybe she was not as entranced as he was, but she cared. And that gave him a reason to go on, and this inspired him to be somebody and not give up. He would do it all for love.

However, his actions had farther-reaching implications than he could have realized. The incident made life for Fariba's family much more difficult. It turned out that Fareed's family were religious fanatics. They did not want anyone Jewish in their neighborhood. It was his family that had set Nader up to embarrass Fariba and her family. In fact, they had even begun to spread rumors that someone had tried to rape Fariba. Plus, Jewish families were known to keep large portions of cash in the house, and rumors of a thief trying to find the money spread as well. Nader felt horrible but did not know what he could do. But he knew he had to do something about Fareed and his family, and quietly to shut them down.

*****

Chapter 9

Love Has No Boundaries, But Is Forbidden By Traditions, What Would You Do?

Another summer was ending, and he was filled with anticipation yet again for what was to come. Melancholy set in when the memories of the past few months crossed his mind. He was eager to see his love once again, grateful that fall was gracing them with its presence. Sleepless nights were common during this time because many did not know if their special person would even be returning to the same school for the year. Parents would sometimes change the schools that their sons or daughters would attend, and there was little you could do about this. Decisions about which schools students would attend were strictly based upon education and what each school had to offer. Every night Nader prayed Fariba would not change schools because he would have died if she did. He had reason to be worried; he feared that he, himself, was the very reason. He had pulled such a crazy stunt by trying to have a rendezvous with her that night in her bedroom like he was Romeo or something. All of the serious concerns of his youth had taken their toll on Nader's relationship with his family. For the better part of the year, and the previous one, he had practically forgotten about his mother, who was his life. She meant the world to him, but due to the intensity of his situations, and the constant craziness of his life in general, he was not aware of his mother's troubles. He was so selfish it did not even occur to him that she was falling into a deep depression. His mother was a strong person but very private about her innermost thoughts. Her reason for keeping things to herself was that she wanted to spare everyone from worrying about her, especially Nader. All problems were kept away from him. She also wanted to be a stable source of support for his life; it was him whom she was mainly concerned about. He only saw her smiling, and that was it. This was a common trait to find in Persian mothers. You learn to be strong and reserved.

It was late in the afternoon one day when he came home to change and go meet a friend. Before Nader got to the main house to head to his room, he heard Abbass and his mother yelling at each other. They were arguing very loudly, and Parry and Boloor were begging the two to calm down. He stopped behind a tree, hiding from view, getting mad. He knew the normal way was to walk in and help them to stop, but he also knew there was nothing normal about Abbass and his mother. One must come out the victor. He also knew if he were to walk in, he might attack and insult his older brother. Unfortunately, no one was backing down, and the argument was heating up. He did not like it one bit. He had never seen his brother or anyone yell at his mother like this. Then, his mother's voice broke his heart; he hadn't heard this tone in her voice since he was four years old. She suddenly burst into tears, and that was enough to set fire in Nader's soul. He was pacing back and forth outside, debating what to do. Blood was appearing in his eyes, out of anger. He saw red. His fists were clenched so hard, he could feel the pain through his fingers. Nader didn't even realize he was talking out loud,

> -I should beat the shit out of him. I should put him in his place. He should never yell or disrespect our mother. He should never be acting like this.

The argument was about certain decisions for the future and about what had happened in the past. For the first time, he was hearing some truths about their family that he would never have guessed in his entire life. After listening, one occurrence, in particular, stopped him from defending his mother. Sadly Abbass was right. He felt ashamed, not knowing of the many things that affected his family. The words spewed out of their mouths. The family was almost broke, out of money, not even close to being rich anymore. Abbass was telling their mother that Bijan, their other brother, had wasted a lot of money on failed businesses. He was adamant that she should not give him any more money to throw away; this money came from selling more farm property which was their mother's life. He realized that the money for the property that they were supposed to get from the farmers was not coming in, and this caused a deficit that greatly affected his mother's financial situation. Now she had to depend on Abbass and her other sons' help, and that was not too easy for her to handle being such a proud woman who took care of many all her life. It was too hard for his mother to deal with these circumstances. Her authority was now undermined, but in her eyes, she was still the leader and the one who gave orders. The world of business in the city was unknown to her, and she did not have the knowledge of how to build a successful business. But who could ever take the crown from a queen or the king? In her eyes, they were still children, regardless of if grey hair was now sprouting here and there. Your child is always a child in your eyes, even if he is in his sixties. Now Nader was pacing faster and thinking he must do something about this. He could not have stayed quiet or walked away, pretending that he did not know what was happening. He also forgot that his friends were waiting for him. But it came to the point that he had to do something because things were getting out of hand. Suddenly, it occurred to him that his brother could get so angry that he might lose control and hit his mother. He really would kill him if that happened. Now he was pacing in circles like a madman and went to pick up a big rock. He was going to go in and beat up his brother with this rock. But he stopped in his tracks. For a moment, he felt like a chicken, not having the courage to support his mother. But any actions against his brother would have been as disrespectful as his behavior toward his mother. Besides, Abbass was the head of the family and a very powerful man in a society, which Nader really did not care about. It seemed that whatever action he could have taken, he would end up the loser. His mother was a great woman, and he knew she would have forgiven his brother, and he would be seen as wrong in the end. Also, he had promised his mother to respect his older brother and not insult or talk back to him.

The commotion inside grew louder. Parry and Boloor were yelling at Abbass, who was acting like a mad man. Nader, still holding onto a rock, could not wait any longer and headed toward the house to enter. He was going to kill his brother, but in an instant, the windows in front of him shattered, and glass was flying all over. The fight inside stopped. He looked up to see his sister Parry appear in the broken window looking out. Nader immediately hid behind the bushes so she could not see him.

-You guys should be ashamed of yourself… Nader must be outside; would you guys stop it… get out, Dadash...

She called Abbasss, Dadash, which means brother. She spoke with a powerful, angry tone of voice, demanding Abbass to leave. It was the first time Nader had seen Parry so angry. He never saw this side of her before. And after that, he heard nothing. No one said a word. There was just dead silence. He sat in the bushes, feeling deep pain inside himself by witnessing this side of his family he was not aware of. He was feeling horrible about not knowing how to support his mother. And still, it was a mystery to him who was the one who threw the rock into the window. He heard someone sneaking around in the bushes several yards away from him, and he rose up to see his father. He then sneaked out into the street through the wooden side door. He didn't know if he should feel bad or good. But for the first time, he did admire him for what he had done; he also knew no one could have imagined that it was his father who threw the rock through the window. Parry, Boloor, and his mother, they guessed it was him in their mind; perhaps they thought it was Nader. He was so engaged in thought that he failed to notice that his brother, Abbass walked out of the house and left without looking back. He was followed by Boloor holding a glass of fruit juice, looking around for Nader.

-Nader, Nader, where are you...? Come out...

But he sat in the bushes and said nothing. What could he have said? That he was a chicken hiding in the bushes, or that he wasn't the one who threw the rock and it was his father? Who would have believed him? No one had seen such an act from his father, and besides, he was not supposed to be in Tehran. His father was living on the farm, and he hardly came to the city, and if he did, they had to know of his arrival so Abbass would not be around. If Nader showed his face, he would have been given credit, and he did not want that.

Later, when he asked his father how he happened to be at the city house, his response was,

-I had missed you guys and your mother, I came to see you all, but it was bad timing... I always come and watch you guys... I miss you all, especially your mother.

It was then that he realized his father loved his mother, and he cared for her. Boloor was still calling Nader, and then Parry came out and joined her as the two were looked all through the bushes, calling him confused as could be. The two walked back inside to take care of his mother, assuming he had already left. He sat inside the bushes for a bit longer, then quietly and carefully exited and walked inside, pretending like he did not know that anything had happened. It was almost impossible to hide the sadness he felt. They all knew from his fake smile.

-What is going on?

And the three also played the same fake game that he was playing.

-Nothing. Hajji Khanoom just had some kind of headache. She's resting.

Boloor, still holding a glass of fresh juice, reached over and handed it to him. Inside, Nader was smirking at them, the fact that they were putting on a fake act was eerie to him, and the secret was really not a secret. That day Nader learned a lesson. Sometimes in life, it seemed that it was advantageous to be fake and not truthful in order to save face or keep everyone moving forward, so they did not break down. He grabbed the glass of juice and went over to his mother and Parry, who was trying to convince her to drink a glass of juice also. But what was surprising was that his mother had a smile on her face, and she was trying so hard to get rid of her tears and pretend to him that nothing had happened. She awkwardly reached out and offered him the drink that was being offered to her, even when she could see that he was holding a drink. That moment, looking at his mother, he felt sorry for her for the first time. He never thought he would see her so disappointed and tired. He could see and feel her pain and disappointment of losing control of her life, of being told what to do and what not to do. He had to do something to make her laugh, to help her forget about her pain. In spite of the sadness he was feeling inside, he began to play along with her, and he placed a big smile on his face. Then, he started dancing silly and jumping up and down. He began doing a mock belly dance and a traditional dance called *Baba Karam*. Parry and Boloor joined in the activities. Boloor grabbed a pot and played the drums as Parry was clapping and cheering. At first, his mother thought this was stupid and silly, but soon she gave in, and a smile appeared on her face, but this time a real smile, one from deep within. This was a smile that showed she felt cared for, a moment where the roles were switched. Then, he asked his mother to dance. Despite her resistance, she gave in and began doing a few moves to make Nader happy. The room was now full of joy, but in his heart, he was still burning inside. It was then that he realized that there was more to life than just him and his drama, his needs, and his self-centered desires. Life means family first, and if he does not care about his family now, then how could he care about his family later? He was hit with a bolt of reality right into his heart. He realized how ignorant he had been to not see the truth of his family and to have been too preoccupied to take care of his mother, who meant everything to him. How could he forgive himself for failing to be aware of her pain, and how could he have failed to be concerned? The laughing had captured the room, and it seemed his mother had forgotten about what had happened a few brief minutes ago. She would probably have easily forgiven his brother's harshness and replaced the ill-feeling with love and affection. That is why there is an expression in Iran,

-Heaven is underneath the feet of mothers.

Which means, heaven belongs to all mothers. What his father had done to stop the argument between his brother and mother would not leave his thoughts. It was that day that his father had disappeared. No one knew where he was, and his mother was going crazy. Her reason was that people would talk behind their back, and she did not like that one bit. His family seemed to be so concerned about what others thought of them as if they were only living for the approval of other people. This was a tough tradition to break; it had been passed down through generations. Perception was everything; judgment was handed down by your community in all aspects of your life. The family would not talk about his father being missing, soon it became a sensitive subject, and everyone was blaming each other for the situation. He didn't know if he should have told his mother what his father did. Later he discussed the matter with Parry, and they decided not to talk about it. Of course, things between his father and Abbass were very tense. Abbass had tried to get treatment for their father's opium addiction, but this had been unsuccessful. Nothing ever worked; he was always going back into using it. It was an ongoing struggle between them, and Abbass was pressuring their father. It was increasing to the point that his father was on the edge of losing it.

 Abbass used to have a hideout near the farm where he would party with influential guests. It was a great secret location where they would not be discovered. It had this running well with the best-tasting water you could find. There was a pool, a place for hunting, and plenty of opium that the guests would be offered. His brother was against drugs, so he would not join them. Nader remembers seeing the head of the parliament and other big officials there. But his father was a farmer and also an opium addict and did not care about any of these visitors or guests. The name of these visitors had to be kept secret, but his father did not care, and when he was mad at his brother, he would reveal their names as if to prove that he was not required to follow Abbass's wishes. His father had also become a slob; he had no respect for nice clothing or anything really. So, every time his brother used to have a visitor, he would send a message to his father to leave or go to Tehran, and he wouldn't let his father come back until the visitor was gone. His father had somehow become a prisoner of his own son, just as he was a prisoner of opium. Abbass had someone pursuing his father to get him into rehab, and this pursuit was increasing, so Nader guessed his father wanted to get revenge on his brother. It turned out his father had taken a job as a servant and began working for another family. He lied to them and told them his son Abbass had thrown him out of the house. He really wanted to embarrass Abbass and had done a great job, but he had embarrassed their mother even more. He would have an attitude of not caring about their mother's feelings or family friends. Later his mother placed the holy book, Koran, in front of Abbass and asked him not to retaliate, to leave his father alone. She even went further to say that if he would not leave him alone, she was going to leave Tehran and would go back to the farm. Somehow everyone came to an understanding that it was too late to force his father to get treatment, and somehow, they had to tolerate and accept him even if it was painful.

But for Nader, witnessing the fight with Abbass and his mother, knowing what his father did, became a day that changed his path. Now he could not just think about himself. He had to be thinking about the entire family and mostly about the future. What he still did not understand was why his older brother was completely ignoring him. It was a good couple of years that he had not truly bothered him. Right after his forearm was broken, ending any possible career in sports, Abbass was no longer interested in what was going on with him. It seemed at the time that he was just waiting for him to get out of sports, and he would be happy. But he was wasting his life even more now, so why did he not care. Maybe he knew Nader needed to grow into an adult; he may have felt he needed to find his own way. He knew he could not stop thinking about it until he found an answer. But now he had made a promise, he would pay attention to his mother, and he would be more aware of her situation.

It was the next day that he realized he had completely forgotten to join his friends. However, the opportunity arrived another day, and he managed to ease everyone out of being mad for his no-show. He gathered with few friends at the home of one of their classmates, Ahmad, who used to live close by to him. They were in his second-floor room to help him set up his new telescope, thinking they could search the city for a pretty lady by the pool or something—no such luck. There was a short nightclub dancer right across from his house, and she always used to change in front of her window, and she would keep the window open just enough so they could see her walking back and forth, naked, just to tease the boy. That used to make Ahmad pleasantly frustrated, cursing at her, begging her to please open the curtain a bit more. She knew how to play with Ahmad's nerves. Ahmad's interest in the opposite sex started with this illustrious lady, and at school, he talked about his love affair with the nightclub dancer all the time.

The dancer's teasing had worked, and soon, Ahmad, Nader, and few other friends headed out to "The New City" to get together with few cute young ladies to get rid of their thirst for sex that club dancer had started within them. Of course, the plan started with the boys talking about taking Nader to get him a lady so he may forget about his violin girl. There was always a reason for what they were doing, no matter how stupid or unheard it was. The new city had a few blocks designated for prostitution on its south side. The government did not want prostitutes walking around the city streets, so they made it legal only in this one specific area and called it the "New City." The place was hidden behind a tall wall and was close to the neighborhoods with only one gate to enter and exit. It was the first time visiting for Nader, and for a first-time visitor, it was quite an experience. They knew they would be leaving with a wild story. But before they left for it, they bought a brand-new suit, shirt, and tie, polished off with fancy brown dress shoes that had just hit the market. Then they grabbed a taxi and headed to the unknown. Generally, young boys who used to go there for the first time were shy to tell the taxi driver where they were headed. Besides, you always got out of the taxi on the block before or after, and then you would walk so you would not be embarrassed. It was always amusing to pretend you weren't going there when you really were.

They entered the gate, and the search for your favorite lady had begun. They were walking through the street, entering different houses, watching the prostitutes, looking for pretty ladies. Generally, there were three alleys with houses on both sides. Each house had several ladies seated out in the closed yard wearing sexy clothing. You would choose a lady and then go to a designated room.

It was there that Nader had his first real experience with a woman; it was interesting. He felt warm and hot, enjoying it, of course. But it did not stop him from loving or deeply caring for his Violin Girl. Nader kept debating in his mind if he had, in fact, cheated on his love by having sex with another. The fact that he had not even spoked or kissed his beloved violin girl was irrelevant. In his mind, they were already married with two children and a house next door to his mother's. He became a politician, representing himself, taking logic to make everything sound fine in his mind. But the only real concern he had was what would really happen to Fariba? Would he still see her at the same school? Would he have to hunt her down again like wolf thieving in the night?

*****

Chapter 10

No Advice Or Lecture Would Have The Same Impact As Life Lessons...

Another tumultuous summer came to an end. Nader was waiting to see what fate awaited him. When the memories of the past few months came to life in his mind, he sometimes got depressed; he had not seen Fariba for a long time, he was very eager to see his love again. With his smile, he became drunk and unconscious. But he was a little skeptical that life would be kind to them with his presence. As the fall season approached, sleepless nights were common for students because they did not know if that particular person they were looking for, especially girls, would be coming to the same school this year or not. Now, the first day of school was arriving. Nader was worried and prayed every night, hoping Fariba's school would not be changed. Because if that happened, then Nader would be depressed, and his soul would die. He had reason to worry. Because he was the one who plotted that nonsense stunt, meeting Fariba in his bedroom, as if he were Romeo, looking for his Juliet.

It was the first day of school, yet again. There was nothing more exciting, except the last day of school. You were always ready for the first day, wearing your nicest and perhaps new clothes, shaving if you had new hair on your face. It was the same for everyone, but it was easier for the girls, they had to wear the same color uniforms, it was a different color for each school. You would know which school the girls were attending by the color of their uniforms. But the makeup and hairstyle were an open field, and they were not shy about how they made themselves up. Their skirts were designed way above the knee's contrary to popular belief. The latest fashion in Europe always used to hit Iran at the same time. Nader was really impressed and had even more respect for his Violin Girl because she hardly wore any make-up. It seemed as if she knew that he did not like a lot of makeup on women. He always thought that beauty in a woman came from simplicity, and if they put make-up on, it was better to in private and not in front of everyone's eyes. And even then, in the time of short skirts, moderation was best.

Nader walked out of his house, but this time was much different than before. He did not hide behind the wall waiting for her to come. He just walked out. There are things that can occur in a teenager's life that will serve as a defining moment. It can be a large or small incident, but the effect of it is huge. And that incident will change you. No advice or lectures will have the same impact as this actual life lesson. You grow into maturity from these types of incidents, and his witnessing of the fight between his mother and brother was the very thing that changed him in this manner. This year was different. He felt more mature. He was in a new stage of his life. And now, his first priority was to pay extra attention to his mother because she needed it. For the first time, he had a tie on with a brand new suit. And that had shocked many, including Hussein, with whom he now had a closer relationship. The only thing that hadn't changed was his concern that his violin girl would not show up. As he lingered on the sidewalk, casually scanning the streets, finally, there was a beam of light. She was approaching the bus stop holding her books more beautifully than ever. He suddenly forgot every problem he had had before and was captured again by her beauty as if he was seeing her for the first time. Her being and presence were just so spectacular. But this time was different. He has been crazy enough to go into her room; he was a bit nervous and embarrassed and knew he would have to say something. He did not know if she had told her close friends that the "thief" was him or not. Being that it was common to share your secrets with your best friends, he was sure she had done this. He was worried about how her friends would react.

But the first glance from her eyes fired a flame inside him and burned through to his soul. There was that holy, wonderfully shy smile of hers which gave him a feeling that only God could understand. Then, he was relieved. He felt that she did like his courage; she was also going to the same school she had been and seemed to like him even more than before. Hussein and a couple of other friends were present, and unfortunately, they did not stop joking softly about Nader and his excursion into the night. He could see her friends giggling while they were glancing at him. It seems after what he did by going to Fariba's room at night, it irritated her friend Zarri, who after that started disliking Nader. Maybe she was jealous she had no one or that Hussien would not do the same for her. Nader did not know the reason behind her hate toward him. She always used to dye her hair blond, and now in Nader's eyes, her looks were evil. He could feel bad energy coming from her. Something told Nader that she was going to be a problem, and he was right. Zarri was also interested in Hussein, who would not pay attention to her, which was making matter's worse.

A few months into the school term, Zarri organized a group of senior students to write a complaint against him, and only four girls from her class did not sign this. One was Fariba. They had submitted a written complaint to their school principal that Nader had bothered them on the way to school and back. At the time that this complaint was filed, he was doing a play with the girl's school, which had happened to be Fariba's school. The fine arts teacher came to him and said that the main educational office had decided this year to have a play combined with students from both the boy's and girl's schools, and they would enter into a competition regionally, and the winner of regionals would compete nationally for first place. Nader's school was one of the ones chosen to do a play with the school located next to theirs, which happened to be the school his love was attending, and they would compete at the regional competition. And what could be more delightful news than the fact that he was selected to be the one to organize the play. He was supposed to be the writer and the director, the one who runs the show. And what could be a better situation for him than to be able to spend time at this particular girl's school. He remembered muttering thank you's to God quite a few times after receiving the news. To his disappointment, things did not go as planned, and one of the TV actors was called in, and he took over as director. He changed everything and brought in other schools to participate. Nader did not like this, and he let the director know, which led to the play he wrote getting the ax. Instead of his play, they decided to use a foreign play, and Nader was also demoted to the producer and not the director. He was still expecting to be one of the performers also, but even that got changed. The man's response was that they had to pick an actor from each school so more schools would be able to participate. Nader was also larger than all the other actors, and he would not match the part with the others. He would have been too strong, and he would have overshadowed them. But the reason was not important. He really wanted to perform and especially play the part of the lover who was shy and finally gave up everything to get the girl he loved. That was the theme of the play he had written, and it disappointed him that it was axed. He did not know why he liked the part so much, but it seemed he was telling his own story or something unexpected which might have been on the horizon. But still, all was not lost because he was at the girls' school and he was close to his love, and that was the only happiness he had.

Zarri's complaint came right in the middle of rehearsals, and he was furious. He had never done anything wrong, especially to her. Why would he jeopardize his love thinking badly of him? When he was called by his principal and was told about the complaint letter, he was red as fire. It was very embarrassing to get a complaint from a girl. He was humiliated and worried that they would take him off the play. If that happened, he would not be allowed to go to the girls' school, probably ever again. But in this instance, he was lucky to have his older brother on his side, even if he did not know what he was up to, but his name was an influence on the situation. He had to use his actor's passion and explain to them that Zarri was just nuts. He told the principal the truth, and he told him that the real reason for the complaint was because he liked Fariba, and Zarri was upset because she was just an unhappy person. The principal promised him that this explanation would stay within his office. He left and waited for the decision about whether or not he could go back to the girls' school.

At the bus stop, Fariba could see his anger, but he noticed Fariba, his love, was not talking to Zarri and was standing by herself. At the same time, all of Nader's friends had heard the story and had established a new mission to punish this evil witch, Zarri. But Nader didn't even know about it. Things got really bad for Zarri. Later he felt sorry for her and convinced his friends to leave her alone. She had learned her lesson. The news of his forgiveness had reached Fariba, and she admired him for that. Luckily, a few days later, he was told he could return to the play, and he was happy as hell. His principal had had a phone conversation with the girls' school principal, and he flatly explained Nader's love toward Fariba and that Zarri had done this act out of jealousy. The girls' principal had called Fariba in, and she had backed him up completely. She, in fact, told the principal that he had protected them from other boys. She also told her principal that she had feelings for him, but that they were not boyfriend and girlfriend, and when the principal heard regarding how much they were in love, yet all these years, they had not even spoken a word, she was so impressed and touched about their distance love affair, that she decided to keep it secret as well. Later, the two principals spoke, and after they shared their thoughts, the adults were impressed by the way their relationship was progressing with caution and boundaries. Because of their admiration, they decided to leave them alone. They both ended up becoming the favorites in the two principal's eyes; she even let Nader have free reign at the girl's school. Zarri's plan had backfired, and it ended up helping him in a way he could not have imagined. The play was successful, and every day he was more taken with his love, but they still had not had even one word face to face. Their relationship continued to be a distance never traveled by touch. But it was as beautiful as it could be and blessed by the Holy Spirit.

*****

Just as Hussein was still working hard toward his dream of America, Nader was having his run of fun and fame while he was physically and emotionally fighting on two fronts, his family and his love. It was about this time that suddenly he found out that Boloor, Abbass's wife, was pregnant. He was very happy for her; it was about time for her to have some kind of hope for her marriage to continue. He could see she had changed into a much happier woman; she was no longer the sad person she had been and was full of hope for the future. She carried the idea that things would change with Abbass. Hopefully, he would soften, and the sound of a child laughing could lighten all their hearts. The saddest tragedy of all time was the marriage arrangement between Boloor and Abbass. At the time, Nader was about three or four years old, living at the farm. His brother was lying down one day with his head wrapped in a scarf. He told him he had a horrible headache, and Boloor was sitting inside the room calmly, sadly. Nader was so young and completely unaware that this was their first night of marriage and did not know, Abbass had been forced to marry Boloor. One of his uncle's sons had sent a message to Abbass in Tehran that if he did not marry his sister, he would kill young Nader. In addition, their eldest sister, who was married to his older brother, who was also his cousin, would be forced to divorce, disgracing them all. Abbass, knowing about the violent nature of his cousin, was worried for Nader's life, so he had come to the farm to reason with them, but he was ambushed by many friends and family, and they had persuaded him into marrying her. In fact, he would not sign the marriage document, so they grabbed his thumb and placed it on the document as if he could not read or write. His brother left the next day, and Boloor's sadness began from there. Later, Boloor developed a strong love toward Abbass, but he always thought of her as his sister because they had grown up together. In addition, Abbass was very high in an educated society, and Boloor was just an uneducated farm girl who could not join him at parties or gatherings, unable to fit in and mingle appropriately, so to speak. So Boloor lived with Nader and his mother and ended up like a second mother to Nader.

Several times his brother approached her wanting a divorce, but she did not want one. It seemed the whole family closed its eyes and ignored her situation. Instead of the family supporting them to get a divorce, everyone encouraged her to stay in the marriage. They thought that if she had a child, things would get better. But his brother Abbass would not allow her to have a child, even though this was a natural feeling any woman could dream about. Abbass always thought that someday he was going to be divorced from her, and having a child would make things too difficult and would not be fair to the child either. In reality, he was right. Abbass had no love toward her, and he did not have any husband and wife type of feelings for Boloor. Nader was the only family member who really thought they should divorce and each start their own family. But he was only one voice and the youngest one at that. Even if she would have agreed, the rest of the family each had their own opinions, and the most unjust one was the way society used to look at divorced women at the time. They were seen as no good and were really looked down upon. And the family cared for her, not wanting to see her have to live with that stigma. This is why having a baby was so important for Boloor. And suddenly they were all surprised and happy for her. Nader guessed his mother finally got to his brother and had talked him into having a baby, and now it was on its way, for better or worse.

Soon after Forogh was born, as the new baby, she was just as dear to everyone as Nader was. He remembered he had heard several different stories about how he came about. His mother's version was the one he accepted most. At the time, his mother was living at the farm, and their farming business was very successful. His father used to have a fan. Because they always used to fight, they were sleeping in separate rooms. His grandmother, who was a simple lady, had Nader's mother promise to not have any more children, and that meant she could not have sex with his father. She already had three sons and three daughters, and they were all about two years apart in age. Nader's older sister had children of her own as old as seven before he was born. Since it had been seven years that his mother did not have another child, when she became pregnant, no one suspected. But later, Nader found out that even though his mother and father would fight, they were still madly in love. She did love him through all the turmoil of their marriage. So, when she discovered she was pregnant with Nader, she kept this hidden from everyone, including her husband and her mother. His grandmother used to live on the farm next to them, and she rarely visited them, and his grandfather had died at an early age. The only one who possibly might have known about his mother's pregnancy was their helper lady, Beby, and she was sure to keep quiet. His mother had later told the story of how she wore loose-fitting long dresses and a veil during the last five months of her pregnancy, and towards the end, she would not go out and proclaimed to be sick most of the time, and she washed herself at one of the stables with the help of Beby in secret. The only other one who knew about her pregnancy was Parry, who was young and the only daughter who was not married yet. But her lips were sealed.

Then, the day came that his mother was about to give birth, and this became a surprising moment of truth for all. They called a birth nurse to help with the delivery, and his older sister was called. Thinking that Beby was joking, his sister did not go to help his mother right away because she didn't believe this story could be possible. But when the birth nurse arrives, and Nader's older sister, who was living next door, saw her, she rushed over to her mother. Upon going to see her mother, his sister became shockingly aware that their mother was, in fact, about to give birth, and she then sent for their grandmother. Soon the entire village was aware of the news. When the messenger reached his grandmother to tell her the story, she began to yell, "Why are you joking with me?" Then, as she watched many family members and villagers walking to her daughter's house, confusion set in. She was mad when some of them came to her and congratulated her on "the news." The next thing that his grandmother witnessed was the schools closing; all the teachers were heading to her daughter's house. Still doubtful and baffled, his grandmother took off and went towards her daughter's house. On the way, she didn't know how to respond to everyone congratulating her. Arriving, she was greeted by a gathering of all the farmers; they were celebrating, with Nader's father leading the celebration. And the story goes that he was the only child at whose birth his father danced. His grandmother finally reached the room full of women where his mother was as someone was cleaning Baby Nader up. The birth nurse then handed him over to his grandmother and exclaimed,

-It's a boy and the biggest one I have ever seen.

As his grandmother was holding Nader, even then, she still could not believe what was happening and began to look at his mother in disbelief. But his mother was feeling a bit exhausted and also ashamed about having had another baby in secret and was covered with blankets from head to toe. She did not know how to look her mother in the eyes. Everything would end up in happiness, and that is why he was cherished and protected by all.

But Forogh's birth was a much happier occasion than Nader's, especially for Boloor. He and Parry were overly excited and began to get everything ready for the incoming child. But during this period, they hardly saw Abbass. If he would show up, he used to leave right away. But when Forogh was born, he was happy. You could see the smile of happiness on his face. Finally, they had a new family member, and for some time, she kept everyone content. But Forogh, who Nader named and somehow had become so close to, did not help the marriage as planned.

*****

The school year was half over, and Nader had the challenge of balancing his time between his family and his own lifestyle. When you are in the last year of school, the only issue with your family is how to get you into university and what major you must choose. Nothing else matters, nothing. As usual, the top three majors that all parents desired for their children, without exception, were to be a doctor, an engineer, or an attorney. He hated all three and could not see himself in any of these professions. The dilemma was how can you tell your parents what your real wishes are when they really didn't matter. When you're young, you didn't know what life is all about, and your parents had experienced life. So, they know better about what would be good or not good for you and your future. In their mind, they had already chosen your wife and even where you should live. But Nader was not going to follow their wishes, and he was sure about what he wanted, and he was determined to get it. One of the things he wanted was to get married to his Fariba. He was a little confused about the job issue, and he would change his mind every so often, but the school projects had a lot to do with his interest in learning to be a writer.

It was a rainy afternoon one winter day when Nader entered the office to speak to one of his fine arts teachers asking him for some tickets to the movie, "The Sound of Music." They were showing it in one particular movie theater, and tickets were sold out for four straight months. Nader heard that Fariba wanted to see the movie and he was going to surprise her and send her a ticket. It was overheard in her conversations at the bus stop. Usually, that was one of the ways to tell your boyfriend or girlfriend indirectly what you like or want. Then, Nader noticed a couple of suitcases, and standing there was one of his classmates, Ali. He was from the state of Mazandaran and the city of Sarri. He did not look good and was almost in tears. He knew their chemistry teacher was Ali's uncle, and Ali was staying with him. He stopped and listened and realized he had gotten kicked out by his uncle's wife into the street, and he had no place to go or money to get a place to stay to finish school. He was leaving to go back to his hometown of Sarri. The Principle was trying to give him hope and understanding that life is full of both sad and happy experiences and that he should not take it seriously. Nader did not know what came over him, but he just walked over to his suitcases and asked, "Are these your suitcases?" The two stared at him, just realizing that Nader was in the office.

-Yes,

Ali answered. Nader grabbed them, and as he was walking away, he said,

-Then, let's go, you can stay at our house, you cannot go, you must finish your school.

The two just stared at him for a long time. The principal did not know what to say. For him, it was very unusual for a young boy to just invite a guest to stay at his house, especially if the guest was a young boy. This was mainly due to the privacy needs of female family members and the protective feeling that men felt for them that was required by the Islamic religion.

At the time, it was not advised or allowed for any unknown man to live with you. But the principal did not say anything, he was worried that Nader might change his mind, and for now, he was happy that Ali had found a place to stay. They walked out of the office, and Nader had forgotten to ask for the movie tickets. But then the next day, Ali had gone to the principal and told him why Nader was at his office. The principal handed the tickets to Ali to give to Nader. He was surprised to see he got five tickets instead of two, and Nader delivered them to Fariba at the bus stop through a six years old boy; a message was attached, "God sends you the ticket..." It cost him a few dollars to buy the boy ice cream. But she knew who the God was and where the tickets came from, and she was impressed, and he heard they were talking about it at the bus stop many days. Of course, Ali, who now was living at his house and naturally was taking the bus with him, had become his speaker and promoter. He didn't need to do anything because Ali was doing it all for him. What he had done for Ali was news at the school, and everyone now hated Ali's uncle. But these types of things were natural at Nader's house. His mother always used to bring home the mentally handicapped people from the farm. They were taken care of at their house. They had their own place to sit, right next to the entry door, and they had their own food that his mother used to cook for them. She always used to say if she takes care of these needy people, God will take care of her family. And Nader quickly learned to be unselfish.

However, they were now busy, completely immersed in their final year, and he was behind. At the time, before you graduated, you were required to take a national test, and that was the only way you could receive your high school diploma. The test was especially hard in mathematics, physics, geometry, and chemistry. High school in Iran was like college in the US. You learned more in the last 3 years of high school than you did in all of college in the US. So it was not an easy exam, especially for Nader because he had never completely concentrated in school. School had been so boring to him. But in order to get what he wanted out of life, to leave the family, and be who he wanted to be, he had to pass the test, and the deadline was closing in. So, his mother was happy to have Ali with him, and she was treating him like her own son. Watching over them both, making sure they were on top of things. She now had new responsibilities, and she loved it. If there was a night Ali would not show up, she would nag Nader all night about it. She would think he had said something to bother him, or she would worry that something else may have happened to cause his disappearance. She would worry that he didn't have food to eat or a place to stay and worry that he was freezing to death. But at the same time, she used to nag at Nader that he was wasting his time with friends and trying to use him. He knew his mother was struggling with her own being, with her own existence, and she was dealing with the disappointment of not being in charge. But deep down, she was a giver. He remembers that at the farm, she used to have people spy on the families for her to see who was not doing well or who needed help, and she used to send them supplies at night. She would have her helper leave the food by their door, knock and leave, so they would not be embarrassed. There was storage in the back of the second-floor house that was the supply room. All food supplies were stored there, and his mother had the only key to the room. Nader would watch when she used to leave the room open if she was distracted, and he used to take supplies from the room to hide. Then, later at night, he would sneak out of the house with few friends, and they leave it behind people's doors. He had his own spies to find the needy, and they were a couple of farm kids. Later his mother realized there were supplies missing, and he heard her talking to Beby,

> -I do not know if I am going crazy or nuts, but I feel I am missing things from the storage room.

Later on, Nader heard that the man who used to deliver the supplies came to his mother and asked her why she had asked someone else to take the supplies to the people, and he was concerned that his mother no longer trusted him. It was then that his mother realized she truly was missing things from the storage room, and she was not crazy. But who could be doing this? Then, the two decided that it was probably his father. He may have gotten ahold of the key. Nader realized he could not continue what he was doing anymore, but he had some supplies left. He had to put them back in the room or give them away. Finally, he decided to give them away, and it was then that he was caught by his mother as he was sneaking out at night. He was embarrassed, but his question to her was,

-If what I have done is wrong, then why are you doing it?

What could she say to this six-year-old brat? One day Nader returned home from studying hard and received the worse news of his life. There were about four months left in the school year, Forogh was just a few months old, and he was told that they had to move from their house. The property had been sold, and they would be moving within a few weeks. The place they were moving to was not that far, and it was almost the same distance to Fariba's house but very far from the bus stop, and he would no longer be able to see her there. Besides, he was leaving Hussein and his other friends and being with them. He would have to travel back and forth; he would not be close to them like before. But the new location was nice and very upscale, and that was what his brother was always talking about. They had bought a smaller piece of property, but it was still quite large, and there was a four-bedroom house on one side and a two-bedroom house on the other side for the gardener to stay in. There was also a large store on the corner facing the street where his brother Bijan opened his flower shop. Within a half-mile, there were four ministers, four different foreign counselors, and the previous prime minister.

The rest were a mix of foreign immigrants working in Iran; they were mostly Americans and Germans. But he still did not like the move. He used to take the bus with Fariba to the bus stop at his previous house and spend some time with his friends in the area, and later at night, walk back home tired and bored. He remembers one of the friends used to get his brother's VW bug, and they used to cruise around looking for his Violin Girl. They would always pretend they were not waiting for the girls so as to not lose respect or appear to be foolish. So sometimes they used to park the car and pretend that it was broken and they were trying to fix the car. Just imagine, they were wearing ties and high-class suits, and now they had their sleeves up and a couple of dark spots on their clothing to show that they were working hard. And always the minute the girls would pass them, they suddenly had the problem solved, and they got in the car and drove past them feeling like big shots. They had many of these tricks up their sleeves and were coming up with new ones every day. After their move, Ali was placed with one of the gardeners, so they knew there was a roof over his head, and he was fine. But he used to come and visit them, and at school, Nader was always with him. His mother was always worried about Ali, and he had to call her almost every day and chat with her to assure her he was okay. He always had to take food with him to take to Ali, but the food used to go to the workers at the flower shop instead. Everything was kept secret from his mother until she walked right into him, bringing food to the workers one day. She saw that the food container that he was supposed to take to Ali was left on the desk at the flower shop. Of course, later, he played that he had forgotten the food, and as usual, he would have the speech from his mother.

*****

Chapter 11

There Is A Magic That Can Be Derived From Nature...

Sitting in his room, eyes out the window, staring at a line of tulips, sitting perfectly even and crisp, was breathtaking. And it wasn't just the tulips, the mass of colorful violets, different roses, and all other kinds scattered around him. Other people had to pay to enjoy the beauty of tulips or could dream about it, but for him, this was free. Bijan was a gardener, and their entire property was covered with all kinds of flowers, and their large shops on the street side were full of plants and flowers. The tulips, one by one, seemed to be whispering a story into Nader's ears. If you really listen quietly and block out the distractions of the outside world, you can hear the song of flowers. Flowers have the innate ability to feel, to absorb the energy that is around them, and apply it to their beauty. There is nothing more peaceful than what you can gain from a flower. There is a magic that can be derived from nature with its spring blooming flowers, and especially from the nut and fruit trees. To watch the process of the leaves forming and then the transformation of the flowers into nuts or fruits is fascinating. Watching this phenomenon every day until you get the chance to pick the fruit from the trees with your own hand and eat them cannot be replaced with any experience. Or watching the flower grow and bloom into a beautiful flower and then die in front of your eyes. He was one of the few lucky ones to have had the chance to experience such joy regularly.

Nader had the ability to enjoy this for many years at the farm, and now he was fortunate enough to see a wide array of flowers being grown right around his living space. There were also a few sections of mint that were being farmed just because of Nader. He had to have his fresh vegetables for breakfast, lunch, and dinner, or food had no taste for him. His mother was always sure that there was a plate of freshly washed vegetables from the garden with every meal, just for Nader.

The mass blooming of tulips and sombul signifies the arrival of the Persian New Year called "Norooz." The celebration of Norooz begins with the last Wednesday of the year known as "Chahar Shanbeh Suri." On the eve of the last Wednesday of the year, bonfires are lit in public places. Fire and light signify the hope for enlightenment and happiness throughout the coming year. People leap over the flames, shouting,

> -Give me your healthy, beautiful, red color and take back my sickly paleness!

Norooz ceremonies are symbolic representations of two ancient concepts - the End and Rebirth in conjunction with the eternal battle for the balance of Good and Evil. The rebirth of nature represents the beginning of harmony, always beginning on the first day of spring. The exact historical formation of Norooz is unknown; it goes back several thousand years, predating the Achaemenian Dynasty. The ancient Iranians had a festival called "Farvardgan," which lasted ten days and took place at the end of the solar year. It appears that this was a festival of sorrow and mourning, signifying the end of life, while the festival of Norooz, at the beginning of spring signified rebirth, and was a time of great joy and celebration of new life. The second symbolic representation of Norooz is based around the idea of the triumph of good over evil, according to the Shah-nameh (The Book of Kings), the national Iranian epic by Ferdosi. Norooz came into being during the reign of the mythical King Jamshid, when he defeated the evil demons (divs), seizing their treasures, becoming master of everything but the heavens, and bringing prosperity to his people. In addition, the arrival of Norooz was a time of happiness and excitement for all. During those thirteen days of celebration, the school was closed, and students had the rare chance to have fun and party. The tradition calls for the elders to give out gifts to the younger people, just like Christmas. Everyone would get new clothes and shoes. All households would replace old furniture with new furniture if they could afford this. There was also a major clean up, sometimes houses would get painted. It was about the renewal of everything around you. And finally, the thirteenth day of celebration calls for all family members to get out of the house and go out into nature. There are huge picnics; some areas will be filled with people, food, and music. The custom called to grow greens before the arrival of Norooz, and they give the greens they'd grown specifically for the New Year to the water to take the sadness and sickness away and bring health and happiness to all on the thirteenth days of Norooz. The entire day was a time for partying for all, dancing, singing and playing ball. It was the best time for the younger people to make connections, gaining girlfriends or boyfriends in the perfect spring sun. It is a celebration that freshens the mind, body, and spirit, reminding all of the joy of simply being alive.

It was the last day of Norooz, and Nader joined his family and friends besides one of the rivers, which was already packed with several other families. Just as everything began going great, his eyes landed on Abraham. He was with some of his friends, and they were about to start a soccer game for fun. He was looking right at Nader holding a soccer ball. They stared for a long time, and neither of them knew how to react or what to do next. Nader had looked for him for a long time, with no luck in finding him, and now he was there looking at him. He wanted to punch him so hard that he would not see the light anymore. His presence brought to mind all the past painful memories, and he did not know how to handle him now. Nader was sure if he would have seen him right before or during his hard time, he would have harmed him, and there was no question about that. But now, a few years had passed, and Nader could see he had changed too. He was still looking at Nader, but it seemed that he wanted to say he was sorry for what he had done. Then, he raised the soccer ball into the air and gestured to Nader as if to ask if he would like to join them. Within a few minutes, Nader was playing soccer with them and was on the opposite team, just like the day when Abraham injured him, and this was the only thing he was thinking about. They were losing the ball every which way to the amateur players. And each time they would approach to pass each other, it seems there was some kind of invisible force that would stop them from meeting face to face. The game did not last much longer, and they were all tired. Nader then realized he was not the same soccer player he used to be, and he was not as sharp either. He knew he had not played the game for a long time; otherwise, he would not be as tired as he was. It was later that Abraham came and sat next to Nader, handing him some hot kabob still on the metal holder along with a drink. Then, came the moment of truth, the moment for which Nader had waited more than two years to have, the truth that had changed his life completely, and sent him into a different direction, the moment to finally divulge to him why he did such an unjust and unsportsmanlike act,

-I am sorry for what happened to you. It wasn't me. I was following his orders to do what I did to you.

And then he was silent. Nader waited for him to continue and waited for a long time, but he was quiet and did not want to continue. Nader could feel and see the sorrow in Abraham. But he had created a disturbing question in his head, and now he was dying of curiosity to know who had ordered him to inflict such a painful and unfair punishment upon him and why? In the next few minutes, many people and many reasons came to mind, but none made any sense. He looked into Abrahim's eyes and whispered,

-By whose order?

-I work for Savak, like my father.

Then, he shut up again and did not say anything as he rose up to leave. But Nader was not about to let him leave until he knew who gave him the order. So, he rose up and stared him down, and Abraham knew what he wanted to know. He could see the pain and suffering that Nader had gone through, and now all the pain had come back into his soul and bones. For some reason, for a moment, he became a human. After all, he was a soccer player and a good one, and more than that, they had been good friends, very close friends. And now something was telling him that maybe it would be better not to know the answer. Maybe it would be more peaceful for him, and after all, it was long past, and he could not change anything about what had happened. Knowing the answer to this burning question could not help him get back to playing soccer. So why should he push the matter, and why should he know? But he saw the change on Abraham's face as he stared back at him... a look of fear, a look of sadness and frustration. It was a grim expression that he had on his face. He turned and noticed Abraham's father had just arrived on the same motorcycle as years ago. Then, suddenly it clicked that he had seen his father at the game on that fateful day, and he was not wrong about that. Nader was bombarded with the challenge to put the pieces together, and he did not have to wait long, as Abraham was staring at his father as he stated,

> -Him... The mad man works for your brother. I am sure he would not issue such an order on his own. Maybe you should ask your brother Abbass if he placed the order.

Abraham walked away, leaving Nader with many unanswered questions. He walked away, ruining Nader's New Year. Now the past memories were back, interfering with his sanity. What could have possibly possessed his own brother to issue such a cruel order? In those moments, he hated Abbass, he must kill him, and he must do something. He must tell his mother, so everyone knew who he was.

All night and for the next few days, he could not release the thoughts of why that terrible thing had to happen and what he should do to his brother. But there was no answer to satisfy him. What if Abraham had lied to him and what he said was not really true? How could he or should he trust him? Even if he would confront his brother, for sure, he would deny it. Then whom should he trust, Abraham or his brother? He had no resolutions, and the uncertainty was driving him crazy, pushing him into insanity. Everyone knew he was sad, he was not himself, and he could see it in the face of his love, the Violin Girl. She was also sad and concerned and wanted to know what was going on with him. He really wished he was able to hug her, burying the pain, he wanted to feel her and speak to her and tell her how he felt, but he knew he could not have such a gift. But there was Ali to help him. He was giving her the news by carrying loud conversations close by her, between himself and Ali, and she used to inform him the same way. Somehow their new way of play-acting communication worked every time. But Nader could not get the sick feeling for his brother out of his system, and he knew he had to do something to let him know how wrong he was; but what to do? Every moment brought a new idea into his head, and he didn't get anywhere with any of them. Most importantly, if he brings this up and his mother finds out, he would have to deal with his mother's reaction. She probably would be in total disbelief, and if she did believe this, she would get extremely upset, and that was the hardest part. He wanted to look Abbass in his eyes and ask him how he could permit himself to take a dream of a man away from him. He thought maybe Abbass was feeling guilty after causing such a horrible act, and that was the reason he had left him alone. Maybe he just didn't like sports. What if he approached him for an answer and he started to interfere in his life again? But Nader still had no answer to any of his questions. He only knew he should take a stand and maybe remain silent for a while. He wanted to execute a plan the right way, but he had to be patient. He was whispering to himself.

    It was not very long that he had to wait. There was a month left in the school year, and he was already sad because he did not know what would happen after they graduated from high school. Generally, some leave the country and continue their studies outside of Iran, and that was customary for the richest people. And some, with hard work and luck, would get selected among the ten percent of one hundred thousand or more applicants in the national test, and they would enter university and continue their studies. Some would end up in the military, and some would study hard the entire year to try their chances for next year. A few would just end up getting a job and forget about being educated. Either way, he would not have the chance to see his love like he had been able to every day. Who knew if she would leave the country, and that was a big possibility. Maybe she would get admitted to a university outside of Tehran, or he would. He only knew he must work hard to achieve the goal of first graduating high school and second to do something to his brother for what he had done to him. But at the same time, he tried to see his Violin Girl as much as he could.

*****

Chapter 12

Vultures On The Loose...

It was a sunny spring morning, and as usual, Nader escorted his love Fariba to her school and ran back to his not to be late. But he could see the girls were looking at one of the magazines and reading an article, and they were all giggling with Fariba. He did not know what was going on, and the more time passed, the more curious he was getting. But he did not have time to go and get the magazine before school; he knew it was the popular Javanan magazine. Sitting in class, he only had one thought, and that was what could have been in that magazine. He did not have to wait to buy one. During the break, Hussein, who was in another class, approached him with a big smile on his face holding the magazine congratulating him. Nader looked inside, and there was a group of beautiful young girls competing for Miss Iran, and sitting in the middle was his violin lady, Fariba, more beautiful than all. He was so happy at the time and very proud of her and himself. He wanted to yell to everyone how she was his, his future woman. He thought how they all might laugh at him. How could she possibly be your future wife if you guys have never even spoken a word to each other after three years? He was sure this is what would be on everyone's mind. So, he shut up and yelled to himself privately so he would not have any protesters or opposition, or perhaps an undesirable comment to ruin his happiness at the time. Fariba getting into the magazine was great for her, but for him, it was a disaster. For now, she had attracted all the boys, and everyone wanted to be with her. The race to compete for

Miss Iran to capture her as a girlfriend began, and he was in the middle of a mess. He could do nothing except protect her from the vultures. There would not be a day that passed that he would not get into an argument or fight with someone, and now he was known among the vultures, and they all wanted to punish him. They wanted mostly to prove they could get her, and he could not do a damn thing about it. But he was not going to let such a thing happen, so he prepared many types of weapons to defend himself, and he was ready to go all the way. Then, a day came when a skinny gigolo boy chased her onto the bus, got off with her, and began to follow her. He was alone at the time, but everyone in the area knew he was not from the neighborhood. Nader approached him and asked him to back off, and then he did what he should not have done. He slapped Nader right in front of his lady and pushed him away just as she was watching. Then he noticed before he bounced back that two larger boys were approaching. His new enemy acted like the two were coming to back him up. But it was too late. Nader was already on fire and crazy. He rebounded back and punched him so hard he fell right on his back, laying there motionless. Within a few minutes of blows between them all, a group of bystanders came to Nader's aid and broke up the fight. By then, the three of them were covered in blood, and everyone's shirts were ripped off, including Nader's but not as bad as the other three boys. Immediately the three boys took off running as they noticed that the whole neighborhood was backing Nader. He looked up to see if his Fariba, his love, had seen whom he had fought for her, but she was gone. He only knew that she had seen the beginning of the fight and how much more, he did not know. For the next few weeks at the bus stop and around the school Hussein, Ali, and few other friends were guarding him in case they wanted to retaliate and ambush him. The news of his fight became the most talked-about subject. They called him a tiger, a lion that no one should mess with, and he was pleasantly happy about this.

But the story of his protecting her didn't help the situation. Things got worse. Now the area gangs got into it, and they began to chase her, he was always there, and that was why she loved him. But facing the area gangs was not easy; they were big boys, who carried big chains and knives, many of them had been in jail. They were in it for fun and satisfaction. It was Hussein who approached Nader, showing him a photo of his lady; he had bought it on the street from a man called Bahman Reesh, which means Bahman with the beard that was his nickname. He was so mad and angry that if you had stuck a knife into his heart, he would not have bled. He knew he had to do something about this. So, he sent a message to Bahman Reesh asking to see him. That day, he put on a nice large tie and suit so he would realize Nader was from an important family and he had money to pay him off for all photos he had. The meeting was set in the back alley of his school, and no one knew about this. He also took a knife with him, and he was going to use it if he had to. He knew the alley very well. Many times, he would use the alley to pose just like a movie star and take photos dreaming of actually being one. It was about three o'clock in the afternoon; he did not go to school so he could meet Bahman Reesh. He did not want people around to see what was going on. He appeared by himself. Nader noticed that he was a very skinny, tall man with big red eyes, balding in his thirties. He stared at Nader as if he was up to something. He made sure Nader saw his chain and his knife on his waist. The first thing he asked was if he had the money. They had already worked out a deal for him to bring all the photos and negatives. Nader had found out that one of Bahman's friends had a photo studio; Fariba had taken some photos for the Miss Iran pageant and also for her passport. This guy had given the photos to Bahman Reesh. He assured him he had the money, but he had to see the photos and negatives. He handed Nader the photos, but there were no negatives, and he said he would get him the negatives later; they had to negotiate a different deal, and he wanted to know if he was for real. Nader began to talk loudly as he was holding the photos accusing him of breaking the deal. He would not pay him for anything until he got him the negatives. Bahman Reesh laughed and went for his chain, and Nader did not wait. He hit Bahman so hard on his forehead that he went flat down, and before he could make his next move, he noticed that several of Bahman's gang members were running towards them. So, Nader took off with the photos, running for his life with five big guys chasing him. As he was running, he pushed all the photos, one by one, into his tie, so if they were to catch up with him, they would not find the photos. He wanted to return the photos to her and show her how far he had gone for her.

The chase took them all the way from his school towards her house about three to four miles away, going alley to alley, and street after street; finally, Nader was standing over a hill close to her house. He was dead tired with absolutely no strength left. He was sure that he had lost them and thought he would wait for her because she would be there within a short while. He knew that if he was not on the bus, she would exit two stations before his old house and walk straight to her house. She had to pass the road at the bottom of the hill, and he would clearly see her, and she could see him. He was just getting comfortable with the soft breeze hitting his face when he suddenly heard a car screech to a halt behind him, and five men exited, rushing towards him. He was sitting on top of the hill, feeling proud of what he had done for his love, feeling the glow of victory cooling off, and waiting for his love. They did not wait for Nader to move. Within a few minutes, he was bombarded with kicks and punches, being punished, and slashed by a painful chain. He could not even move his hands or feet to do anything. He could not even rise up to run or defend. He was punished for supporting his love from a bunch of vultures. The hill also overlooked a horse training stable and a few houses, but no one was home at the time, or if they were, they were mostly older people who were taking naps or watching TV. It did not take the guys much time to have him covered with blood. Punches and kicks kept coming, and he was just trying his hardest to cover his face, so their kicks which were aiming toward his face, landed on his hand. But his nose was already broken, and he was worried about his broken forearm. He was sure Bahman Reesh and his gang did not know who he was; otherwise, they would be wise enough not to mess with him. But it was too late; they had gone too far, so far that he could hardly move, and worse than the punishment was that they began cursing his mother and sister. And if you have any kind of brain, you do not curse an Iranian man's mother or sister. This means you want blood, and you want it very badly.

Then, finally, he heard a weak scream of an older woman yelling at them. They stopped, and Bahman searched all Nader's pockets and found nothing but some money which he took. Bahman was still on fire; he kicked Nader a few more times in his face and back and then pushed him down the edge of the hill he was laying on. Nader began to roll down the hill, which actually felt much better to him. He could not see or hear them leaving but knew they were gone or else they would still be attacking. He finally stopped rolling right at the bottom of the hill on the side of a small dirt road. It took him a few long minutes to open his eyes, but the blood covered his view. With much difficulty, he wiped his eyes, and he could see a faint view of where he was. Now he realized he was right on Fariba's path home. He knew she would walk past him any second, and he did not want her to see him like that. On the other hand, he thought if she would see him, maybe she would finally get worried and get enough courage to break the silence. He contemplated what to do as if he had the power to rise up and walk away. He was a man, and she must trust and feel his power and confidence, which is what most women want from a man. And this image was a weak one. No, he would not let her see him like this. So, he looked around and noticed a couple of wild street dogs running out of an opening about ten yards to the side of the road. The decision was made, and he pushed himself into this space. After a few minutes of debate about whether or not he should fall into the hole, he completely pushed himself into the large opening just as she was turning the corner. But he knew there was no way he could reach out from the large deep hole in the condition he was in. He could hear Fariba walking past him with her friend, he could hear giggling, but he could not see her face. What if she knew what he had just gone through on her behalf? What if she would have seen him, and would she still smile?

Soon, she was gone, and he was lying down in the large hole. He pushed himself up and leaned against the side, and began to think about what to do. What if some wild dog attacked him? What if something else happened to him. No one knew where he was and what had happened to him, or if he died, no one would know who had inflicted such a punishment upon him. But with many attempts, he could not move himself one inch. He began calling for help every time he heard a noise or a car passing, but no luck. It was getting dark, and he was getting weaker, and still, he had no luck. Then, he heard sounds coming from the top of the hill. People were talking, and he could see the police car's flashing lights on the houses on the other side, but they did not have any view of him. Then, he heard an older woman yelling at them,

-Don't you guys see the blood? I think they killed him.

He was glad they were there to find him but also upset because now his brother would know everything. He contemplated this and, for a slight moment, decided to stay in the hole. But it was spring, and the weather was very chilly at night. He could freeze to death or catch pneumonia. He was consumed with all kinds of thoughts and then realized several flashlight beams were dancing around the building on the opposite side and getting close. Finally, they were all shining on him. A few officers had followed the trail of blood, and the blood led them to the hole.

Soon he was in the hospital, and despite his begging that they should not get in touch with his family, they ignored his will, and without his knowledge, a phone call had been made. Lucky for him, as usual, Abbass was not home, and Bijan was notified instead. When he heard Bijan's voice, he knew hell was going to break loose. In fact, he was much closer to him than Abbass, and their personalities were similar. They were both crazy and wild. If he wanted to describe his family, Bijan was like the Godfather and had his own men to punish people he didn't like or who disrespected the family, and Abbass was the politician, controlling everything, but no one knew he was doing it. He was always outside of the mess but knew everything that was happening. And Nader was like Michael's character in The Godfather, a family peacemaker. One time he dated girls from a family that Bijan supposedly considered enemies, and he did not like him for that, but he knew he loved her. Bijan was informed, and for the first time, he wanted to prove to Nader and the family that he could be in charge, that he is not less powerful than their older brother. But he could do anything, Nader told them he was hit by a car. Despite Bijan knowing he was lying, he could not do anything. He had no leader who had done such harm to Nader. Based on the description Bijan had gotten from the older woman, it got him nowhere. But Nader did not open his mouth, and he wanted to punish Bahman Reesh himself. Even if they had found them, he would not say anything.

Bijan got a hold of Ali and asked him about who may have done such a thing to him. Ali did not know Nader did not want anyone to know, sales out it might be Fariba's brother who did this to him, and he did not like it. And that was the worst thing Ali could have done. But it was too late. Bijan had Nader in the car, and a few others were on their way to Fariba's home. No matter how much Nader begged Bijan not to go over there, it did not work. But Bijan was in charge now, and he guessed he had the perfect opportunity to prove his worth. Bijan picked up the older lady to help him to identify the men so that everyone knew he was in charge and they must cooperate or get hurt. Then, the worse came for Nader. He was watching Fariba, who had walked out of her house with her brother, father, and her mother, looking into the car to see who was the one that had been hurt and why. He was hiding in the back seat, and it was then that Fariba looked inside, and her eyes glanced at Nader. He had covered his face, not knowing if she had recognized him or not. He peeked through the small opening in his fingers and could see her looking at him filled with sadness, and then she walked away heading toward her house; she stopped to look back for a while, he guessed she was trying to decide what to do, and he was hoping, begging, for her not to get involved. Finally, she just walked inside. And Nader could not forgive Bijan for that. He did not want Fariba to see him like that.

For the next few days, Nader did not go to school and was treated by Parry at her house. Bijan was smart enough not to take him to his house, and he knew that his mother should not see him in such a way. So, when he was resting at his sister's house, Bijan continued looking for the men. He was so mad that Nader was weak enough to let people beat him up so badly. But his search did not get anywhere; Nader did not talk. Two weeks later, Nader visited the photographer who took the photos of Fariba; he gave up the negatives to Nader, he said he was threatened to give up the photos by Bahman Reesh. So, he should leave him and his family alone and keep him out of this mess. He knew he had no fault, and he gave him his word but asked him if he could locate Bahman Reesh or his gang; he must let him know of their whereabouts. He gave his word to do so and left. But, Nader's visit to the photographer alerted Bahman Reesh, and Bahman Reesh and his gang had vanished. By now, they realized they had messed with the wrong family. Nader was going to seek revenge for what they had done to him without the family's interference.

Several times a couple of friends came to Parry's and drove Nader around in their car so he could see Fariba from a distance. He did not want her to see him wrapped up in bandages. There was not much time left in school, and he still did not have any studying done. If he did not make a move right away, he would not graduate, and that was an unthinkable embarrassment for his love to know about. He was concerned, but so much thought had paralyzed his brain he could not think straight.

One day Parry came to the room and asked him if he knew someone named Abraham. Of course, his answer was,

-Yes, I do.

He was told that Abraham was asking to see him. Nader was surprised, very much surprised, and he did not know what to think about it. First, how in the hell did Abraham know where he was? And what does he want from him? In about five minutes, he was sitting on the front stairs facing the large beautiful front yard of his sister's house, talking to Abraham. In Iran, there is always a wall about six feet high around all houses. This provides complete privacy to the front and the back yard of your house. Abraham was holding a box of fresh pastries that he had brought for him. His sister, according to tradition, walked out holding a tray with tea and placed it next to them, with some grapes in a green bowl as well. Nader did not care about tea or grapes. He wanted to hear from Abraham why he was there and how he knew where he was. As usual, he did not wait long and began to speak, but he noticed that most of his attention was on the next-door neighbors to their right. They were sitting on the top stairs leading to the building and could see the next-door neighbor's yard from over the wall between the two houses clearly. At first, he did not think about it much, but as time passed, he was getting curious,

-I know where Bahman Reesh is, and I will take care of him for what he did to you.

For a moment, Nader could not react to what he heard from him,

-They did not find the photos.

He was mostly shocked about how he could have known about Bahman Reesh, how he knew about his whereabouts, and also that they did not find the photos. He knew too much, even about the photos, like Abraham was with him. Abraham continued,

-I already thought about a plan of what we were going to do to him. It is bad.

Nader was silent for a moment before speaking up,

-How did you know about him and his location?

-I said that I do not work for my father anymore, but I did not say I left Savak! We know everything we want to know. Besides, he owes it to you after what he had done to you. But as I said, it was your brother's orders, and he had to follow. If you wish to get back at them, he will help you.

Then, he noticed Abraham's eyes were locked on a black Cadillac that had just entered the neighbor's yard. Nader knew the house was the residence of Iraqi's head counselor in Iran. He and his friends always had discussions about him; every time they would see him, he would have a different lady, and they were all beautiful. Suddenly it clicked in his mind that Abraham is working for the Savak, and he was observing the Iraqi counselor's house. He was not there just for him or to help him find Bahman Reesh.

> -What if you tell me why you really are here?

Nader put the question straight to him as he still observed the counselor with a beautiful girl walking into his building. Abraham looked at his watch, and at the same time, the girl turned and glanced at him before she entered. The counselor turned to see what she was glancing at. Abraham immediately turned and began to play with his hair to cover his face as he looked at Nader, searching for words. Finally, he came up with a few.

> -I think you do have an opportunity to prove to your brother that you are as good as him, and he doesn't need to protect you.

Nader knew he was leading to some kind of a plan he already had thought of in his mind, and he just waited in silence to see what that would be.

> -We need to plant a bug in the counselor's bedroom, in his lights and phones. It will be a problem to get inside his house. I thought maybe you could do that.

Then, Abraham turned to the counselor's house and continued,

> -Right from there, over that wall from inside this yard. They would not expect anyone to go over this wall.

It was too much for Nader to digest, and he did not know what to say or how to react to his offer. He thought he was nuts. He needed some time to absorb what Abraham had to say, and now he knew why he was there and how he knew where he was. But how did he know about Bahman Reesh? And if he does know, then Abbass must know about Bahman Reesh.

Abraham was gone, but not until he had given him a full pitch about the Iranian and Arab conflict many centuries back. He wanted to remind

Nader and encourage his nationalism. So, he reminded him of the Arab invasion, which was led by Omar many centuries ago. In fact, this was one of the hottest subjects to learn in the history books and a sensitive subject to all Iranians. Abraham reminded Nader that the Arab invasion in the seventh century had resulted in the destruction of one of the richest, culturally developed societies at the time. Sadly, when they invaded, they burned some of the largest and most unique book collections, including the libraries they were located in. They completely destroyed a country that offered a complex understanding of agriculture, the founding of the first postal system, the first governmental structure, minister, and minster. There were Persians who found copper and bronze, learned how to melt and shape swords for the army very early on in history. It was Iranian's who built the first earthquake-proof building. The first human rights laws were written by King Cyrus the great, and the first labor laws were offered up by King Darius when he was building Persepolis. He ordered the creation of a coin that was used later for trade, paying all workers one coin a day. These workers were not allowed to work longer than ten hours a day and had every Sunday off. There was also an Iranian who created a calendar, invented the medicinal uses of alcohol, and much more. But the Arab invasion had destroyed it all, creating a melting pot of Persians and Arabs. It is a topic that will be sore in the mouths of Iranians forever. So sad it all was, it led to Persians finding ways to separate themselves, those claiming Arab ancestry and those claiming true Persian ancestry. Thus, you had the creation of the Sunni and the Shiite. In Iran is where you will find the concentration of Sunni, the Muslim world that exists throughout the world is known as Shiite. This re-invention was helped with the passion and influence of Persian leaders such as **Rumi, Omar Khayyam, Hafez, Sanai, Saddi, Zackary Razy, Abolghasem Firdausi**, and many more who began to describe the spiritual part of Islam and combined it with many important elements of Persian life and beliefs. Persians constantly try to let everyone know that they are of the Aryan race, like Italians, Germans, and the Irish. So, from the beginning, our ancestors taught children the history of invasion and used it as a platform to build nationalism within them. This goes for the Arab nation as well. The Arabs followed the same path of mistakes and went much further. This is why both groups have been pitted against each other; some probably don't even know why anymore.

The reason Abraham wanted to remind him about the Arab invasion with passion in his voice was that the same strategy had worked on him in his youth. He used to have lots of hate and hard feelings toward Arabs. They used to make a large cloth mock-up effigy of Omer, the leader of the Arab army, who made the decision to attack Iran. They burned it and ran around as a group killing the burned effigy. Nader quickly spoke his mind,

> -What can be more awful than such wrongdoing and misunderstanding? It seems we never learned from our past mistakes and disasters that unfolded because of hate. Why do we constantly try to make more mistakes and create more disaster for our children and children's children, who we claim we love as if we have no way to bring peace and love into the hearts of our people? Why does generation after generation have to pay for the mistakes of one mistake or wrongdoing of a leader from many centuries ago? Why should we not forget, forgive, and replace hate with respect and love? Why should we not understand that Islam is one religion and it isn't up to men to divide it into Shiite and Sunni? Why shouldn't we understand that this is the business of the men who are changing the religion to benefit their own greed and power? Will we all never learn and then change?

The only thing Nader thought about all night was his conversation with Abraham. He thought of his brother, Bahman Reesh, and revenge. By morning he was anticipating speaking with Abraham wanting to know about this plan he had. Two days later, Nader was notified that Bahman Reesh was found, and he was in the hands of Nader. Nader had learned that this man, who almost beat him to death for defending his love, was also a pedophile. He had a particular interest in little boys. Nader knew an example had to be made. Early the next morning, when people walked out of their doors to work, they saw a man hanging from a tree, by his hands and feet, naked, with a small branch covering his front. His body was painted with the words,

-Pretty boy chaser, I feed on the young.

He was Bahman Reesh. And then the people took care of him, beat him close to death, and he ended up at the hospital. During this time, people did not take well to a man exhibiting such behavior. Not that it is accepted now, but then, this punishment was not considered inhumane.

Phone call after phone call was coming in from those wanting to tell Nader they were proud of him. He was the subject of talk among all who knew him. In fact, that act brought attention to Bahman Reesh and his gang, and about a month later, his photo, along with his gang, appeared in the paper. He was arrested for bank robberies, and he went to jail for a very long time. But Nader's immediate family, such as his mother and sister, did not know anything about the story; many would not even dare discuss it with them. But Bijan wasn't happy with what happened to Bahman Reesh, and when he was told what Nader had done to him, he was furious. Not because he was punished, but because he was not able to punish Bahman Reesh himself.

Just as Nader was enjoying the attention, and decided it was time for him to step outside of the house. He would not be embarrassed because he already had answered and retaliated for the beating he received. He was about one hundred yards away when Abraham stopped near him in a car that he knew belonged to Savak. They looked at each other a bit, and he could tell by his smile that he was indicating to Nader he had done what he said he would do, and now it was his turn to help him. He got in, and soon they were driving into the hills to the north of Tehran, and before he knew it, three hours had gone by. He knew about the plan and the reason he was chosen. He reasoned that the purpose of him wanting Nader to assist in this undertaking was to prove to his brother, Abbass, that he was as tough as him. But something was telling him that there was more to this that he couldn't yet see. At the same time, he was also thinking about what he could possibly have to lose. He would be doing something good and of value for his country. This kind of adventure was going to be challenging, and to top things off, he now knew what Abraham had done for him by giving him Bahman Reesh. So, he decided to go along with the plan, and the time was set. But later, Abraham contacted him and said that they had already found an alternative way to do the job and that his service was not needed. For a second, he was disappointed and sad since he really wanted to prove to his brother that he was as good as him. But he did not get a chance. Later he realized that maybe it was for the best. He was falling into a trap that Abbass had organized for him once again; he would have become one of his pawns in his chess game. Besides, what if something would have happened and he could not attend the national test to receive his high school diploma.

*****

Chapter 13

The Search Is On For Bahman Reesh...

There was about one week left in school for the twelfth graders, and then they would get ten days off to prepare for the national exams to get their high school diploma. Nader had to come face to face with his Violin Girl. What if he did not see her again? He showed up at the bus stop and was visible. He was sure she would see him. Of course, Hussein and Ali, and a couple other friends, were there to see what her reaction would be. He still had a couple unhealed cuts on his face, and he probably looked a bit banged up. She appeared from the back of an alley along with the rest of the schoolgirls. She was looking around, sad, as the rest of her friends were giggling, then her friends noticed Nader, and they began to speak to her, pointing to Nader, her eyes cut to his face and eyes. For a second, she was surprised and did not know what to do or how to react. He was sure she was wondering what had happened to him and his face. Besides, she had seen Bahman Reesh had been tied to the tree on the south corner of her street; she had to know about it. Then, her look changed into a smile stretching her cheeks. He did not know if it was fake or not, but he wanted to see the smile, and when he did, he was happy. The girls crossed the street and stopped by the end of the line. Nader and his friend did the same, as usual; most of the boys, like Nader, never used the line; they would always wait until the last moment when the bus was leaving and run and jump on the double-decker bus. Since the bus had no doors, it made it easy for them to play at being macho, big shots. Ali and his other friend started the play, this time, Hussein was in it as well. Speaking loudly, pretending they are joking with him, but in fact, they were giving Fariba the report of his heroism, about Bahman Reesh and what they did to him, and what he had done to him,

> -This Majnoon almost got killed trying to collect the photos of his love from the street gang.

These comments had caused the look on Fariba's face to change into curiosity and concern. But at least now, she knew why he did not show up for a week. Then, glance after glance began to come from her, as she was getting the report of what he has done for her and also to Bahman Reesh, each glance with more admiration, and the feeling between them was mutual. And, of course, this was all happening by hiding it from the rest of their friends. The bus stopped, and she got on the bus, he waited to be the last, but unlucky Nader could not jump and do his stunt this time, there were too many people in the bus and hanging all over the front gate, and there was no room for him to jump and hang on. And again, the bus drove away and took his heart away into the distance, and he could not do anything about it but just look after the bus. He was standing among a couple more of his friends, but now with deep sadness inside. It was not a good feeling. He never had such an uncertain feeling, staring at the bus thinking it is taking his heart away; he was helpless. He had missed the bus before, but he had never experienced such a gloomy feeling. Hussein began talking to Nader, but he could not hear him. Ali waved his hand in front of his face to get his attention. As another bus arrived, Ali got in the front of the line and gestured for him to get on, but he had no strength to move. Hussein reached and grabbed him, pulling him onto the bus without a word. Ali still was living with the people Nader had placed him; His mother was still paying them as well for keeping Ali. He would visit Nader three to four times a week as well, which led to Nader spending less time with Hussein. After tenth grade, Hussein took on a major in math which had him in many different classes in school than Nader and Ali. In many ways, Ali had become Nader's partner in crime, the most loyal friend he had. The bus stopped, and they got off, walking toward her house with Ali leading the way. But Hussein did not tag along and went to his house. They thought maybe she would have stopped on her way somewhere so he could see her. Ali was telling him if he sees her this time, he would go and talk to her, placing her hand into his. He was sworn he would. But he was not completely listening to Ali; he was worried that sadness would take over his entire being. They walked; there was no sign of her. Now his heart was beating in his throat. He did not even realize they were now home; his mother was ready with two large iced glasses of fruit juice. She brought a bowl full of pomegranates next. She knew he loved this healthy fruit. Then he noticed, at the end of the yard, there was a line of large plants, set beside each other, they created a wall with complete privacy from the other side. He did not know why this new addition was there,

> -Mr. Ali, you should not go back to the other house. You should stay here with Nader and study together. I had the workers make a private place for you two, and I already told everyone there would be no visitors to this house until your final exam is over. You can stay in Nader's room. And you guys do not need to be worried about food, fruit, or drinks… just studying… I want you both to get your high school diplomas.

Hearing his mother's sad and concerned voice, reality slammed into the side of Nader's face like a semi-truck, he only had fourteen days to pass the final national exam, and passing was the only way to follow his heart. In addition, he was not going to let his mother down. The last thing he wanted to see was a look of disappointment all over her face. If that happened, he would be the only one in the entire family who had failed the exam, an embarrassment he truly did not want. So, he just stared at the place his mother had prepared as tunnel vision took over his mind. The only thing he was going to think about was passing the national exam, they began to study. Nader was pacing back and forth at the end of the yard, down the row of plants, for the next fourteen days. He and Ali would study together a part of the time, then separate and take turns rotating from indoors to outdoors. Every couple of hours, they were served with everything you could think of by his mother, sweet honeydew blended with ice and honey, fresh flatbread and mint with feta cheese, kabob, Salad Shirazi, and on and on. A few times, he would sneak off for a short time, take a late-night walk under the street lights reciting what he put to memory, and pass by Fariba's house. There was never any sign of her.

Exam day came and passed. He felt confident with his performance. He knew he had passed. And when the results came, he had received fourteen points out of twenty totals for the whole test. He was surprised his composition grade was the worst, and he had done well in the other subjects. His attempts to see Fariba has all failed. There was no sign of her, as well as Hussein. He felt a nervous anticipation filling his gut as each day passed. It was as if she had completely vanished.

*****

Chapter 14

The Way He Wanted To Be, But Couldn't Change The Course Of Nature And Century Of Traditions...

It was summertime in Tehran, very hot, and Nader was finally out of high school forever. Everyone thought he had accomplished something impossible. He had managed to pass the national exam with only two weeks of studying. Now his mother was going on and on about his talent and intelligence and that he could do anything he wanted if he would put his mind and heart to it. She thought he had been lazy and that he had been distracted by other things that were not supporting his scholastic success. His mother was talking to others about the difficulty of getting into University, and they were discussing the fact that now he would really have to study hard. It turned out that his family did not accept any other major for him than to become a doctor. Nothing less would be satisfactory for them; they had their hearts set on him being the first one in the family to become a physician. This would give them such prestige; they would be assured bragging rights. By having the title of doctor or engineer, you had it made in Iranian society. Then, your real name given to you by your parents would be completely forgotten, and your name would become Mr. Doctor or Mr. Mohandes. Mohandes in Farsi means Engineer. Then, it did not matter if you had any creative talent or any humanitarian inclinations at all, but you would gain total respect. They would not stop there. If a doctor or engineer would marry a lady, their wife's given name also would be forgotten, and they go by Khanoom Doctor; Khanoom is a respected nickname for women or Khanoom Mohandace. But Nader thought there was always a double standard when it comes to this nickname. If the man married a doctor or an engineer, they would keep their real name and not be given a nickname?! That was why Nader just could not fit into this cultural stereotype. The title of doctor or engineer had little meaning in his heart. Something about this way of thinking greatly bothered him. It didn't sit right with him to give up his name for a title that meant nothing to him as if he were to give up his identity. For him to become a doctor was just plain out of the question, along with practically everything else that his family wanted for him. So, in his mind, these professions were written off.

It was a few weeks after school had let out, and all new graduates were preparing to take the biggest test of their life; this was the test that would permit them into the university. This test was a must for whoever wanted to be accepted, and it was not easy. From over a hundred thousand applicants who took the test, only about the top ten thousand would get accepted. You had to be good and talented, and it was not a joke. Life for a young graduate like him at this time consisted of private classes, tutors, and books, which left no time for anything else, and having fun certainly was out of the picture. He wasn't totally clear on what his career path would be, and there was just one thing he was unsure of, he wanted to know where his love, Fariba, was going to college and what her major was. However, he had not seen her at all or heard anything about her. It seemed she had vanished from the face of the earth. Everyone was preparing to go their separate ways. Hussein was getting ready to leave for America, Ali left for his hometown Sarri, Nader never saw him after that. Years later, he heard he could not get into the university, and his family sent him to Turkey. He later became a dentist and married a Turkish girl. Hassan, his other classmate, left for India. Bharaam was lost studying for the test. The rest of his friends and fellow classmates were deeply involved in their studies, except him. He was lost and a bit confused, and he was pacing the streets. He began going to movies a lot, which began to spark his interest in the world of entertainment. The entertainment field was something that greatly interested him, he had studied drama and creative writing in high school, and he had a flair for acting and writing. It seemed only fitting that dramatic arts would be something that would suit his personality. But he had not yet considered dramatic arts to be a legitimate major to study at university, and he knew that being an actor was not a profession that his family would accept. In fact, this would be the biggest insult to them, going against their ideas and beliefs. At the time, being an actor or pursuing the field of entertainment went against almost every family's traditions and religious beliefs. Being from a farm in a small village, this was not something his family could understand. His mother would have probably been heartbroken about his pursuing dramatic arts, but he had a feeling that Parry and Boloor would have supported his career choice. Even little Forogh, who was only age three at the time, would have grown up to accept his "vision."

Nader was wandering around Pahlavi Avenue in the north part of the town by the national TV stations. He was going to meet a man who had helped him learn about playwriting and the art of acting, who he met by accident through a friend Kamran Noorad when he was in high school. Mr. Nosrat Karimi, who really was a genius in his work, was one of the theater's founding members in Iran. He was one of the teachers at the college of Dramatic Arts at the time and had finished his studies in Italy. He later had become Nader's mentor, and he thanks him for that. He wanted to get his advice, and he was gracious enough to meet with him. As he was crossing the street to get to their meeting place, he spotted his older brother Abbass sitting in a restaurant with a lady. He didn't give it much thought at first, but then he remembered that Abbass was supposed to be out of town. What was he doing here with a lady eating and laughing? From the moment his eyes glanced at them, he knew this was not a business-related meeting, or if it was, it must be deeper than that. He was careful for Abbass not to see him, so he walked behind one of the large trees and situated himself so he could observe them. Pahlavi Avenue is a beautiful street with a line of tall large green trees on both sides. Running alongside the trees is a small creek that you would think belonged in the countryside yet was trickling over stones right by your feet. It was a relaxing walk, a place for high-end shops and restaurants where average men could not offer to spend their time.

Just as he was engaged in his thoughts, he noticed Abraham approach Abbass's table and whisper something in his ear. Then, Abbass looked up toward the direction where Nader was hiding. That told him that they were talking about him and he had been spotted. How in the hell did Abraham know he was there? He could not figure it out. How he got inside that Nader did not see him? Where had he been hiding to know where he was hiding? But now he was in trouble, and he did not know what to do. He didn't know whether or not to leave and pretend that he did not see Abbass or stay there until he left and pretend he did not see or know about him. It was about the same time that Mr. Karimi, the man he was meeting, walked up to the front of the restaurant and looked around for Nader as he entered. He did not know what to do, so he just stood behind the tree for a bit longer, uncertain about making any move. Then, luck came to his help, his brother got up to leave, and the lady walked out alone. Abraham already had a taxi waiting for her outside, sending the lady off in a taxicab by herself. Then, a car pulled up, and his brother exited the restaurant and got in the back with Abraham in front, and they took off. His brother never looked toward his direction, but Abraham stopped to turn and look back towards him with a smile on his face. Then, the car took off, speeding into the traffic. He immediately jumped over the creek onto the sidewalk and entered the restaurant approaching Mr. Karimi. It was later that he had to explain the story and his family situation, and why he was late, he understood, and it was a great help for him to decide what he really wanted to do,

> -Is your family going to be with you your entire life? Will your family have to live with the sadness and suffering you are going to face by not following your heart? We as artists are gifted by God to just explain the truth of life to our people as we see it through our eyes and let them make their own decisions. This is the time that your people need artists like you more than doctors. Doctor healing is something

known; they only heal the pain body suffers... but you are healing a sickness that is unknown to them, you are healing their soul, the old traditions which are wrong and cause suffering to us all. By not following your heart, you are betraying yourself, your people, and God.

Nader sensed Mr. Karimi made sure to mention God, knowing he came from a religious family. But they were the words he needed to hear. He knew he had to do what felt right to him no matter what happened; that way, he would never look back and wonder what could have been in sorrow.

*****

A week later, he was still trying to see if he could get some kind of information about Fariba, but the more he searched, the more disappointed he would get. Still, he was not about to give up hope. Again, he had run into Abraham, and he made it seem like an accident, but by now, Nader knew anytime he showed up, there would be a reason behind it. Then, they were sitting at a tea house packed with younger boys and girls, all trying their best to follow the western influence, from hairstyles to miniskirts. Nader could strongly admit that they were way ahead of the western world when it came to style. Abraham opened up,

-I really have to do something for you so you may forgive me for what I did to you. I am still feeling guilty.

The routine was the same, and Nader knew he was going to lead into something else. He was not totally sincere in only wanting to help. There was going to be something else that he wanted from him. So, Nader turned to him and decided to put him right to the test.

-What do you really want this time? What if you just spell it out and get it over with?

But Abraham was not going to give in, he was trained well, and his actions were perfectly thought out. His dream was to go to America and be trained by the CIA, and become the best in his field. He had disclosed this during their conversations. However, he went on to say,

> -No, I really want to do something nice for you, for example, maybe you were to look at the morning paper when they announce the names of those who were admitted to the university, and your name was listed. The only thing you would have to do is show up and takes the test.

Nader stopped reacting for a second and thought about what he was saying. How could he do such a thing? He is not in a position to pull such strings; he was delivering someone else's message. Who else than his brother, Abbass! Abbass! Abbass! Abbass! Now he was sure they had seen him at Pahlavi Avenue. His brother wanted to bribe him not to speak about it to anyone, including him. Abbass knew Nader was extremely sensitive about Boloor and Forogh, but Nader considered him weak not to speak with him straight to his face. He was sitting there quietly, in dead silence, just staring at Abraham, and he did not like it. Being that Abraham was well-trained in how to overcome any situation, he put his fake smile on and began to brag about their old friendship. He spoke of playing together and all the fun times they had, then slowly came back to what he wanted to talk about like a slippery snake,

> -We were good friends, you and me. Our soccer team was the greatest. I am truly sorry for what I did to you, no matter what the situation may be. But I want to correct my mistake. I will tell you the truth, no matter if I lose my job. Yes, I am here because of your brother. Yes, everything I have done to you, and for you, was his idea.

Nader was staring at him quietly, burning inside. He was on fire, flames were scattered out, and Abraham felt it as he continued,

-But you must understand that Abbass did everything for you because you are his brother, wrong or right, he did it with good intention, he thought he was helping you, doing what he could to help in his own twisted way. How can you hate or be willing to punish someone who wanted to help you, even if he executed his intentions in the wrong way? How could you hate him, especially if he is your older brother, wanting the best for you just like your mother?

Nader knew he brought his mother's name up to get to him. But by now, he could not sit and carry on the conversation any longer. He had to get out and get some fresh air. But Abraham was not about to leave him alone. He really did not know how horrible Nader felt by knowing his brother had manipulated and controlled his life from a distance, all along. It was sickening. It was as if Nader was meant to be a robot, with his brother inputting his desired actions. He jumped up and started walking but did not know where to go; Abraham was not about to let Nader leave until he convinced him about what he was there for. But he knew it was bad timing and silently walked with him. They walked down several streets, and finally, Nader whispered,

-If I do not go to the medical school, perhaps he is going to order you to break my feet this time.

-I do not believe that is an option because he wants to help you to be better in life; I would not even be worried about that. Besides, he has his own problems now to be worried about, and perhaps he needs your help. But going to med school is your mother's wish, along with everyone in your family. I wish somebody would help me to get into med school without any problems; it's a gift, not a curse. Nader, it will make your life so much easier and open the doors to worlds you haven't seen.

Abraham lamented as if to coax him into feeling a sense of reverence for his brother. Then, he walked away, leaving Nader standing alone on the sidewalk. As he walked away, he turned and yelled to Nader,

-Maybe this is the last time you'll see me?

And then smiled at him before disappearing into the distance. He was gone, but he had left Nader with lots of thoughts and unanswered questions, which he had no clue of how to deal with. This information caused him to feel even more lost and alone. God, how complicated life can be, sometimes there is more emptiness than happiness. Where is the sweetness of life? Then he realized, almost every other family he knew of operated the same way. There was no one to turn to console him. He was caught between a rock and a hard place, the hard place being another rock. It did not matter what he did. It would either be wrong in the eyes of his family or wrong for him. If he were to act for his heart, his mother would be sad; her heart would sink and worry. And if he were to follow their wishes, he would be a prisoner within his own soul, unhappy all his life. He knew in his heart, sooner or later, he had to take a stand and make a decision that would alter his whole life.

He was so confused about his future that for some time, Fariba was forgotten in his mind. There was not much time left, and the national test for getting admitted to the university was on the way, and he was registered for med school. He knew if he registered and took the test, he would be admitted regardless of what his score was. He would be accepted into a prestigious school which he had no desire to be in. He would take up the space that lawfully and ethically belonged to someone who really wanted to be there, someone who worked hard all their life. He knew in his heart that even if he attended, he would probably drop out and not complete the course. He did not open a page of any book to study. He was hoping maybe things would not go the way his brother planned for him, and he would be free to do what he wanted. Then, one late afternoon, he was walking along a quiet street holding a piece of delicious hot bread called sangak. This bread is so good, you cannot wait to get it home, you have to eat it while it's hot, and thus at least one piece disappears on the walk home. He was absorbed in this fabulous bread when a car pulled up and stopped by him. It was one of his friends, Kamran Norad. He was the one who introduced him to Mr. Nosrat Karimi. He got out of the car, glad to see Nader, and they began to catch up on this and that. Then, he asked him if he had registered for drama school, informing him that tomorrow was going to be the deadline. Mr. Karimi was concerned if he had registered or not. When Nader said he hadn't, a surprised look crossed his face, and he began to encourage him to apply,

-Mr. Karimi has sent me to talk to you. He wanted to be sure that you followed your heart or you will regret it for the rest of your life.

He could tell from his message that Mr. Karimi believed that drama should be his major. They chatted for another few minutes, and then Kamran was gone as quick as he had come. This left him with a new challenge, maybe a new way out of his misery, a new way to follow his passion. The next morning before the college of drama opened, he was waiting at the front door. He registered to take the admissions test to get into the School of Dramatic Arts and film. But this time, he did it for himself. The test was a day after the national test, which he was registered for, and he already knew he was going to be admitted to med school. He was actually relieved now and could focus on studying hard for his drama school test, which he only had a few weeks to prepare for. While he was studying, his poor mother thought he was studying for the med school exam. He didn't tell anyone he was registered for drama school and could not tell a soul in case it led to his brother finding out.

The day of his first test came; he attended and handed in his med school exam in blank. Then, he ran to a secret hideout he had chosen and started studying for the drama school test. The next day he was again one of the first ones in front of the Dramatic Art School; he took the test without anyone's influence, helping him pass. After the test, he had a strong feeling that he did well, but it did not stop him from praying numerous times to be accepted. Now all he could do was waiting for the results, and the wait was hard. He did his best to look for Fariba and spend his time with Hussein, who was leaving in just a few days. He was not lucky enough to find or see Fariba. It was now the last night before Hussein's departure, and all their friends were gathered at Hussein's house to say goodbye. Hussein's father had become the most respected man among everyone by fulfilling the promise he had made to Hussein. And now, the father and son were friends; it seemed as though there were no more hard feelings. Nader approached Hussein's father and said that if he needed anything, he was there for him; Hussein is like a brother to him. He saw the tears in his eyes, and he did not want Nader to see his tear, so he went into the bathroom quickly. Nader never forgot that moment and realized he loved Hussein even if he was extremely hard on him.

Hussein was leaving for his journey to America, and they had all gathered at the airport. Nader was wearing a hand-woven designer sweater that his niece had made for him; he had designed the pattern himself. He wanted to show Hussein how talented he was, and it sure was getting lots of attention at the airport. While they were waiting for Hussein to depart, all were chatting with joy and a bit of envy. It would suffice to say that it was a dream of anyone to leave for America, and if anyone said otherwise, they were lying. They all took a group photo together as a special memory. It may be the last time they were all together. A couple hours later, Hussein was gone; the plane was up in the air, disappearing into the sky towards America, taking away one of the dearest friends Nader ever had. He missed him terribly already, and it started to sink in that he was really gone. This would be a difficult adjustment for Nader because even during times when they were both busy and didn't see each other, he could easily go to his house or see him. But now, he would be located on a different continent, and if he were to knock on his door, he would not be there. He would not be able to hear his voice; they could no longer get into arguments and then make up to chase their dream girls. He was gone, and he had to accept the fact that they were both going towards their own destiny. This was part of growing up and building a future. Hassan left for India to study a few days later as well. Now Nader was down to one friend, Bahram, and with no signs of Fariba.

It was one week after Hussein had left and the night before the results of the national test was supposed to be announced. This was a nightmare night for those who had taken the test. It was the night of waiting for your future, and the following day would be a deciding moment for many students. Some would be delighted to see their name on the acceptance list to enter university or college, and the others whose names would not appear would suffer a huge let-down. The names were announced in the national newspaper called *Kyhan*. The morning soon arrived to replace the long night of ambiguity, but the waiting was still on. He was standing by the newsstand, staring at the paper. He did not want to look as he watched others rushing to get a copy of what they had waited forever for. He was not completely sure if his name would be listed; he felt like the only one who wished it wouldn't be. Finally, every paper was gone from the newsstand. You could tell by the expressions on their faces if they made it in or not.

    He was walking home without a paper in hand, thinking about the next day when the test results for drama school were supposed to be released. These results would not be in the paper, it would be posted on the board at the school. All in all, they did not take many students, only about two hundred in total. Then it crossed his mind; even if his name was there, how could he break the news to his brother and mother and tell them he would not med school but drama? It was a hard task to swallow to convince them. He knew it would be a world war too! He thought if his name were not listed, he would go crazy. Hussein was gone, Ali was gone, Hassan was gone, Fariba had vanished, and it was just him and Bharam and his brother. This was not a pleasant feeling, and anxiety began to creep through his whole body. As he entered his house, Parry and Boloor ran to him, both hugging him while planting kisses all over his face. His mother came in with smoking incense and tears of happiness in her eyes. She could hardly speak; this appeared to be the proudest moment of her life. She began hugging him so tightly, and he had never felt his mother's strength like this before. He did not know what to do or say. He believed they must have seen his name in the paper that he was accepted into med school. This was something he really was not proud of, it made him sick to his stomach, and he hated himself for not having the guts to open his mouth and tell her he was not the one whose name should be in the paper. He had nothing to be proud of, and his mother had a fake son. But how could he open his mouth when her tears were touching his face and falling on his neck, bursting with joy? How could he be so callous as to rob her of her happiness in this moment? Soon the house was packed, a party was on, and the saddest soul of everyone was Nader. He had the fake smile on just for his mother's happiness, even if it was for a short time. But he knew he would not go to med school no matter what, and he was crying inside just like a clown. Then, suddenly and unexpectedly, Abbass arrived with flowers for him. This was the worst insult. He reached and hugged him as happy as one could be when he wanted to stick a knife into his heart and kill him. He was motionless and speechless. He wanted to die, and the longer the night went on, the sicker he was getting. Finally, he began to throw up; that was the best gift he could have received that night. He could hear voices commenting from the living room,

-That it is because he is too happy.

-It is because he is too excited.

But ignoring all, he went into the bathroom and then to his room and locked the door. He asked Parry and his mother to ask everyone to please leave him alone. It was not an exaggeration to confess that he had cried that night and felt like dying. As he sulked in his own misery, contemplating what he would do if he did not get into the drama program, Parry's voice grabbed his attention. He really loved Parry, and she was always there for him, and he was there for her.

-You must at least call Mr. Karimi and thank him for his kindness. He personally called to give us the news. He thought because your name was not in the paper, Mom would have a hard time, so he called personally and spoke to Mom and gave her the good news himself. You know you were accepted into the College of Dramatic Arts… that is why everyone was here to support you. They did not want you to be worried or about you did not get to med school…

Confusion took over Nader, a feeling he was coming to know well, and he just stared as Parry continued,

> -Everyone is happy for you. It was Mr. Karimi who had personally called Mom and Abbass and convinced them it would be an injustice if you would not go to the drama school, and you see they all accepted his opinion and are happy for you. You will be the first writer in the family. Who wants more doctors and engineers? We have plenty of them.

Parry stared at him with a smirk on her face as Nader realized his name didn't appear in the paper, and it hit his mind that Abraham just flat lied to him. He wanted the credit if Nader did get into med school. But Nader did not care; as long as he was not getting into med school, he was happy. But he was delighted that he was officially accepted into drama school. He got up, walked out of his room, and joined his family, still in shock but with laughter within his soul and mind. He was thinking the next twenty-four hours would be the longest, most drawn-out time he could ever remember in his life. The next morning was the day that all the names of accepted students were to be posted on the window. He wanted to see it with his own eyes; he was one of the first ones waiting. It was about 11 AM when the papers went up. His name was on the list, it was true; he was accepted for drama and playwriting. When he saw his name, he could not stand up, and he just sat for a long time and breathed in the comfort and peace that filled the air. Nader felt more grateful than ever.

Later Nader arrived at home and was going to hug his mother and sister in happiness, but this time for him and not for them. But before he could do that, he noticed a new white Fiat sitting in the alley. After he entered the house, they all walked him to the Fiat; it was Bijan who handed him the key and gave him a big bear hug. He was ecstatic and could tell he felt proud to be his brother; this new car was his gift to him for being accepted into a university. It was the happiest time for Nader, and he owed it all to Mr. Karimi, who somehow reached Abbass in his heart. Something Nader thought he had lost years ago. He sat down and relaxed. Forogh ran to him and gave him a great, big hug. He loved her so much, she was close to his heart, and now her smile of happiness for him made the day a great one.

*****

Chapter 15

You Need It, You Little Writer You...

Forogh was moving around Nader's room amusing herself. He could have sat and watched her forever; she always made him smile. She truly was the light of the house and a joy to have around. But he had to go. He was getting ready to experience the first day of college. His mother was ready with incense smoking, hoping to bring luck and success to his life. And then it was Boloor who handed him a glass of fruit juice,

-You need it, you little writer you.

He was ready to leave, and soon he was cruising in his new Fiat toward college, feeling like the man of all men. Traffic was bad, and he did not want to be late the first day, and he finally pulled into the small building of his school. It was a much smaller campus than the University of Tehran, which he was supposed to attend; it was kind of like a drop of water to the ocean. But he was happy. He had not forgotten about Fariba, and now that his life was situated a bit, she became the main thing on his mind. He now had to find her. He began the search again. He had already contacted everyone he could think of and was getting nowhere. Then, on one of his visits to check her house, he noticed her mother talking to a neighbor at the door, which he had never seen. It was the first time he had seen her, and he was sure this lady was her mother because she looked just like her. The first thing that hit his mind was if Fariba looked the same as her mother when she was older, what else could he ask for? Her eyes had landed on him. First, he thought he was mistaken but soon realized all her attention was focused on him. It seemed she wanted to say something or talk to him. Her look was very friendly and peaceful, he could feel it from the smile on her face, and she was talking to him with her smile. That day he walked away; he noticed that even after the neighbor had left her door, she was still standing at the door observing him like she was beckoning for him to come back as if she wanted to have a word with him.

A few weekdays went by. He was sitting in his room, looking out at Boloor through the open door, Boloor was the best friend he had, just like Parry, but now Parry and her husband had moved to their own new house. So now he only had Boloor with whom to sit and talk with at home. He was playing with Forogh as Boloor watched them. He could see the sadness on her face, and he realized she had been a bit different for the last few months. She had seemed to be a bit lost in thought and very reserved, but she would try to hide her sadness. She tried her best to hide it, but he could tell she was not aware of how she was showing her deep sorrow. Several times he wanted to ask her if there was something wrong, but he gathered that if she wanted to talk to him about it, she would come to him. Then, he thought he should open up the conversation about his problem. Maybe she would feel more at ease and would talk to him. So, he asked about Fariba and what he should do. She knew everything about Fariba and always used to tease him. Then she said he should take a bouquet of flowers and go talk to her mother when no one was at her house. Mothers are usually calm, and they have much more understanding, especially when it comes to their daughters.

He took her advice, and it was a beautiful fall morning with the sun shining brightly; yellow leaves were falling underneath the trees when he set out on his way. He picked out the most beautiful bouquet and drove to Fariba's house. He got there and waited for a long time for her father and brother to leave. Then, he rang the doorbell, nervously, shaking like he never had. He practiced his lines a million times and prepared what to say and what not to say, but the moment the door opened, and Fariba's mother appeared in the door, he forgot everything. He went blank like he was deaf and dumb. They looked at each other for a long moment, then, smiling, she stepped aside and invited him to come in. For a moment, he felt worried. How could she invite him in when she did not even know who he was? He might have been a murderer or a thief or some kind of crook. She closed the door, and the thought occurred to him that she might have people inside that would beat him up. He expelled that stupid thought from his mind. While following her through the beautiful garden, he was trying so hard to get the words out,

-I am here to talk about your daughter.

-I know that. Come in.

By hearing her reply, he was more confused and at the same time relieved. Soon he was sitting in their guest room, which was so beautifully decorated with stylish Italian furniture. She entered with pastries and tea and placed it on the table, then grabbed a plate and placed it in front of him with a knife and fork. As she so graciously offered him the pastry, he did not know what to do, but he took one even though he had abolished pastries from his diet. Then, she put the pastry plate down and sat on the other side. They both stared for a long moment while they were each waiting for the other one to speak. He felt they both did not know where to start, and then he whispered in a shy tone,

-I want to marry your daughter, Fariba.

She sat there looking for a long time, he could see the sadness in her eyes, and he was sorry he had said what he said. Why had he come here in the first place? Generally, the custom called for the eldest members of your family, your parents, or the eldest brother and sister if the parents are not around. They would go to the girl's house and ask permission from her parents. And there he was, sitting in their home by himself, playing a role that wasn't made for him.

-I am afraid it is a bit late for that.

She said softly with sadness in her voice and carefully addressed him. Then, he noticed her eyes fixed on a wall behind him, and he felt she was asking him to look, so he did. And he wished he had never turned to look. It was Fariba in a wedding dress. Shocked, he could not take his eyes off the photo. He did not know what to do or what to say. He was numbed, lost, and suddenly died. He didn't even know if he could bear to hear how that had happened. Who is the husband? There was no husband showing in the photo, just her in a wedding dress. He was not even listening when she was explaining everything to him. It was a few days later that it hit him. Her family knew it was Nader who had gone to her room that night. They knew about their distant love affair and attraction. And it was her father and his brother Abbass who got together and decided what would be best for both of them. What he hated the most was that they thought this marriage would never work. A Jewish girl marrying a Muslim boy would be the biggest headache for both families. He felt better when he heard that her mother accused her husband and his brother of only thinking about their positions and how wrong they were.

> -Your brother was worried how he would face the fanatic clergy, those who are in important positions in the government. What if they found out that his brother was married to a Jewish girl? And my husband is in a similar situation. He is a high-ranking officer in the army and did not want any problems.

So, her father had chosen a Jewish boy who happened to live in Los Angeles at the time, they arranged a marriage between Fariba and him. Fariba did not know until school was over. Everything was set and planned out for her. They told her she was going on vacation to America, but the reality was that a new husband and life awaited her. She continued with sadness and grim, "They showed an image of you next to a bride in a wedding dress and told her you had got married. I also believed it at first, and then it was later that I found out it was your niece sitting next to you in a wedding dress. They lied to my child. When she arrived in Los Angeles, the wedding was already planned. She was married and left in the States." He could not ask if she was happy or not, if she had agreed or not, and as much as he wanted to sit and to hear what she had to say, he needed to get out. He was suffocating and needed fresh air. He was about to exit the yard when he heard her voice, "Wait."

He stopped and turned as she walked towards him, holding a violin. She sadly looked at the violin and him and then handed it to him,

-She did not know she was not coming back; however, she would not play if you were not around. I am sure she would love for you to have this. And I do not care what my husband or your brother thinks. This is her heart, and it belongs to you.

Nader left her house, carrying her heart with him. It was many years later before he would even walk by her house again.

*****

The light in everyone's hearts now was little Forogh. She was the soul and the spirit which blessed them all. There could be no better time for her to distract everyone. She was helpful in the way no adult could be, by simply making him laugh and giggle in a way only a child can. As he and Forogh were involved in play activities one afternoon after his classes, Boloor was sitting close by quietly watching; it seemed as if she was not mentally there. She always used to participate, taking her turn with Forogh, but now she sat silently, staring endlessly at the stitching of the Persian rug that covered the entire floor. He knew something was really wrong yet had no idea of what to do. It seemed as if the more fun he had with Forogh, the sadder she became. Then he noticed tears in her eyes. He had never seen her cry before. Nader stopped and gently turned to her with a smile so she would not be embarrassed.

-Are you crazy? Why are you crying?

He pretended that she was crying out of happiness, but he knew she was sad. He knew there was something important bothering her.
She wiped the tears from her face to clear her eyes and turned to him,

>-If something should happen to me would you promise to take care of Forogh?"

He was silent, and he did not know what to make of her request. He remembered seeing his brother with the woman at the restaurant but didn't think she knew anything about that. Something else must have happened. He did not have any chance to respond before she began to disclose her feelings,

>-I do not want him to divorce me. He is asking me for a divorce. How can I keep my head up among the family, among the people? I would be embarrassed. Why suddenly he is asking for a divorce, I do not know. I was told they have seen him with a tall lady. I told them it is a lie, even when I knew it was true. But what can I say, yes… it is true, my husband is having an affair? Does he not want me? Nor respects me? I am no good, not worthy of being his wife. Why now, when I have a little baby and am just starting to have a life with his baby, could he go and marry someone else? Please tell him not to bring her here to Tehran. What is different now? He has never been a husband to me. I hardly see him. You guys are my family. He should let me just be his wife on paper, so I can save my face. He could marry anyone he wants. You have to reason with him. You are the only one I trust that this will not get out. Besides, he really thinks highly of you.

She had not yet finished when Nader heard his brother Bijan's voice from outside calling for his mother. The way he was calling, he knew Bijan was up to something. They both did not want Bijan to see her crying. That would be a disaster, and he would start a war. And his war would not be against Nader or her, but against Abbass; this would be the best reason for him to prove he is a man who could lead the family. He was forever competing with Abbass. It was more important to him than what really should have been done to help Boloor's problem. She immediately cleaned her face and headed to the bathroom with Forogh sporting a fake, strained smile.

Nader was sitting there motionless and speechless, not knowing what to do. She had just asked him to talk to Abbass, to a man whose stifling influence over him was what he had been struggling to get rid of his whole life, a man he avoided talking to at all costs. He was already mad as hell at him for running his life. If he could not reason with Abbass about his own life, then how could he influence him about theirs? He also knew that if he got involved and this problem got out, it would be bad for everyone. He heard Bijan dancing and playing with his mother and talking behind his back,

> -Guess what, your son has gone to ask permission of a parent for their daughter's hand, to get married... and guess from whom? From a Jewish family who used to be our neighbor at the old house... as if he has no mother or older brother. No respect these days.

As those words pierced his ears, Nader swore to the heavens if he was close to Bijan, he would have punched him across the room. He had had it with his brother. What kind of sins had he committed in his past life to have such brothers and no father for him now? He no longer cared how old they were, nor lines of respect; he would say what he felt. Bijan and his mother entered his room, and Bijan did not wait. He began to speak, making sure their mother completely understood,

> -I just spoke to the lady who was supposed to be your mother-in-law. She came to buy some flowers for her house and told me you had gone to her house to ask to marry her daughter. I guess you did not count us as older members of your family and have no respect. What about your mother?

The two were getting heated and started an inquisition on Nader, and for some reason, Nader just to stared at them, saying nothing. He had plenty to say but didn't want to take his anger out on his mother. He thought the silence was the best strategy and most powerful answer and was working, so he began to grab some of his stuff and made his way out,

> -I am moving out of this family. I'd rather live on the street than here. At least I will be able to do what I want and have my peace. I do not need your support.

Nader was out the door as his mother was yelling after him with concern, but he was gone, leaving his mother with Bijan. This was a situation that Bijan did not expect or either did not want to be in with his mother. His strategy did not work, and his mother began to yell at Bijan,

> -See what you have done! He is not married, is he? Go find him! You just drove your younger brother out into the street. Is that what you wanted? This is my house while I am alive. Why are you so mean to your brother? Go find him!

She began to cry. This was the last thing Bijan wanted.

*****

Chapter 16

When Unfair And Unjust Traditions Become Intertwined...

Nader had now been gone from home for few weeks and was staying with a friend. His mother had managed to make life miserable for everyone, so they all were looking for him. He needed this time away from everyone. He knew that sooner or later, his brother and Boloor's divorce will become known to all, and it will be World War III among the family and had no doubt a fire would break out in the family, and its heat would make life hell for everyone. And most importantly, his mother, Boloor, and Forogh needed his support, so it would be selfish of him if he did not return home. So, he had no choice but to return. As usual, his mother was more worried about him than he was about her. Less than a day or two later, a woman was talking to him on the phone. She asked him to visit his brother Abbass outside the house. While Nader was on his way to see Abbass, he was lost in thought along the way. He did not know what Abbass was going to talk about that made him so private? Wondering what would happen between them? Thoughts came to life and died in his mind until finally, Nader was walking in a park with his brother Abbass. Before their meeting, he did not know what would come about between them, but he found him very polite and kind on the phone, just like he was talking to a friend. His voice was not carrying a tone of authority like before. He was surprised that the last thing he wanted to speak to him about was his school;

he never even questioned why or how he was in drama school and not med school. This was mind-boggling because to be an actor was a million times more disrespectful to societal traditions than being a professional athlete. Then, for the first time in their lives, he opened up to him. What he said made Nader feel just as sorry for him as he felt for Boloor. He was speaking like someone who was afraid, hurt. He began to tell Nader the story of his life, the version Nader did not know, and he made Nader forget about all his problems. He was asking for Nader's help. He wanted him to reason with Boloor about the divorce. The whole time Abbass was talking, all Nader could see was Boloor's tears running down her face.

Now, sitting in front of Nader was a man who, all his life, controlled him and everyone he knew, a man who was thought of asking. He was a man who believed he knew more than all, and his way was the only way, the right way of living, and the only way to achieve success. And now, unable to move on with his own life, he was uncertain with his own situation. He was so confused about his own destiny, a victim also of the same customs and traditions which he enforced on others for years. He was feeling bad for the man who happened to be his older brother, and for the first time, he needed his help. He never thought such a day would come, but it was here and as he was facing it. He was uncertain and unable to do anything that would please both people. What can you possibly do when you are watching the suffering and agony of your loved ones, and you cannot do anything to stop it? Now he could see clearly how unfair and unjust traditions destroyed people who advocated them, and in this case, the members of his family were perfect examples. His brother, his wife, and their beautiful little baby girl Forogh were now victims of an archaic tradition. Nader was witnessing his brother finally giving up. He could not pretend to be in a lie of a marriage that was arranged and forced on him. In fact, it was surprising that he had gone as far with it as he did. He had fallen in love with someone else, and the news finally got to his wife. At the time, Nader was doing his first film, "Chine." Between works, he ended up being their arbitrator, without the knowledge of anyone in his family. The most painful part for Nader was that he was used to forcing such a marriage upon him. So, even it was his cousin that threatened Abbass that if he would not marry Boloor that he would kill Nader, who was at the time just four years old, but somehow, Nader still felt responsible for what had happened. And now he had a chance to do something about it? But what could he do? It was so funny to see, and the family used to agonize about the situation, but the minute Nader showed up, they would drop the conversation; their thinking was that they didn't want his mind to be corrupted with the problem. They thought he did not know of the problem rising so deeply between them. But the main reason was they knew he was against every thought they had, and it was his nature to discuss and express his feelings openly and not talk behind people's back.

His brother wanted him to convince Boloor to get a divorce, and Abbass would support her financially until she died. But she absolutely was against the idea and wanted him to convince his brother to stay married and take another wife but not to bring her around. Otherwise, she would kill herself. The saddest part of this was when one looked at their innocent child Forogh. She was about three years old, and all along, Nader used to change her diaper, change her clothes, and all that comes with cleaning up after a 3-year-old. She was much closer to him than her own father. The timing was also bad for him because he was shooting his first film, and he wanted to do the best job he possibly could. He already had a couple successful plays on his resume, and he wanted to keep things moving. But his mind and heart were mostly with them, especially Forogh. It seemed she was aware of everything that was happening, even being as little as she was.

Two weeks into the shoot, he was working fifteen hours a day, then he would be on the phone with his brother and Boloor to help negotiate their terms while carefully trying to keep them both calm. This was not what he needed at the time. So, he had to begin to focus more on his work and pull back from his family's problems a bit. He was deeply saddened and lacking in energy, wishing the problems would end on their own. He felt helpless. He remembered one night they came back from shooting and wanted to rest. But the loud voice of the speakers playing from the nearby mosque would not let them sleep. The weight of Abbass and Boloor were making rest at all hard to begin with. Nader and the director Zyya decided to wander out to visit the mosque, thinking maybe it would help them relax. But it was the absolute wrong move. First, the speaker's name was Hejazi. He lived a few blocks from him in a high-class neighborhood; Nader knew he used to charge a lot of money to speak for one hour. Over a thousand dollars was the expense for a family of three at the time. Secondly, the way he used to speak in the mosque, people could not understand a word, and it was a waste of time. If the topic was religious, it was wrong to charge money for the talk. In Islam, it is unethical and immoral to charge money to give religious advice. But the most upsetting part was when he saw people walking in and reaches behind a curtain to drop money or whatever items of value they had. He was curious, so they walked in and pretended that they wished to do the same, and he lifted up the curtain and noticed a large box filled with money and jewelry. Then, he noticed a man standing by overlooking the box as a couple of other people were taking the donations and separating the money from the jewelry. For some reason, he could not forget the man's face and expression. They called him Hajji Mohammad Zadeh.

Three months later, he was surprised to see the same man in his room in Tehran talking to Abbass, trying to bribe him for something he wanted to be done, and Abbass seemed to be agreeing to help. Later he found out there were two large areas of land in the same city, Saveh, with many acres, which he and a couple of very high influential people wanted to take for themselves. But rightfully, the land belonged to the city and the national forestry. The people had opposed the matter and filed a complaint, and the matter had reached the Shah's attention. The Shah had Abbass give him a report. Abbass's report was supposed to tell the Shah who really deserved to have the land, the people, or the group of blood-sucking greedy men. So, they sent the same man Hajji Mohammad Zadeh, to bribe Abaass with large amounts of money, which Nader saw with his own eyes, piles of money on the table. Abbass used to meet people in Nader's room when he was not supposed to be home, it was a place no one would think of to look, but this day he came in accidentally.

For a while, Nader was sad, and he lost all faith and respect for Abbass, he began to think that he was really one of the crooked government officials, but he wondered why he was so trusted and respected; maybe people are scared of him. This debate ran through his head until a couple of days later when he was approached by the father of a friend, Zyya Dorry, who was the director of the film "The Chine" in the city of Saveh on his return from Tehran to continue the film. This man was living in the same town of Saveh where the transaction was supposed to occur, which also happened to be the same town where he was shooting his film. Zyya's father used to own a nice restaurant just as you were about to enter the city, just as Nader entered to meet Zyya, he was approached by Zyya, and he informed Nader that his father wanted to speak with him, it was odd and surprised for both of them. Though he did not know Zyya's father, soon he was sitting with him, and the man opened up,

-I want you to take that box of pomegranates to your mother....

Now, this seemed odder because he didn't even know his mother, so why is he sending a gift to her. Clearly, he wanted to show his appreciation when he responded,

-...because of the man she had raised.

In the beginning, Nader was confused, wondering what he has done to deserve such appreciation, but soon he realized he was talking about his brother Abbass. As he continued, he told Nader that Abbass brought the money which was given to him by Mohammad Zadeh and gave it to the court, asking the court to arrest Mohammed Zadeh for bribery; he reported that the land belonged to the people. Of course, Mohammed Zadeh was released within a day and never saw any jail time. The land was finally given back to the people by the Shah's order based on Abbass's report. But Abbass had to pay a big price for it, for the people involved with the scandal were very powerful, and twice they tried to kill him. Once, they tampered with an airplane on which he was flying, but it landed safely. Another time they had disconnected the brakes on his car when he was traveling with friends and their family, and they were badly injured. However, this was why he remembered the man who was controlling the donations. It was there that he realized Mohamed Zadeh was a mediator for every side, government, and religious groups.

The film Nader was a part of was also being shot secretly because of the content of the film, and he did not need to ask Abbass for help. Just being his brother was a great influence with the locals; they did not bother or check on him or his crew. After all, Abbass had a high position in the government, but he was very kind and helpful to people, and they did love him very much. The worst part about the situation with Abbass and Boloor was that Nader felt responsible in a weird, twisted way. He was just a child, but if his cousin had not threatened Nader's life, Abbass would never have married Boloor. He wanted to do the right thing, but what that was lost, the situation was so complicated with no one wanting to compromise. Nader felt that Boloor needed to say the hell with the world, accept her divorce and move on with her life. By now, Boloor was very sick, and Nader believed she was so depressed when she finally accepted that Abbass was serious that it manifested physically. It was verified for her that he had been seeing another woman in a different city. This began fighting, words, arguments, and threats involving everyone in their family regarding the matter. The strangest part was that, as always, the second Nader was present, everything stopped like they had an unspoken agreement. They all thought he was ignorant, not aware of the family matter, or maybe that he did not care.

However, they came back from the local mosque to rest and get ready for the next day's shoot, he could not sleep as a feeling of urgency filled his body. It was about 5 AM; he woke up Zyya and told him he had to head to Tehran. Regardless of what Zyya said, he was leaving. He was not happy, but Zyya had no choice but to shoot other scenes until he came back. He was also the writer and the producer of the film, but shooting could not stop because they had a very limited budget. So, Nader took off from the city of Saveh to Tehran. At the time, he was still living with his mother, and his brother Bijan used to live in the same private, dead-end alley. His mother and the family had bought a large piece of property in a very expensive area. One section was the flower shop which his brother Bijan was still running and living there.

Nader reached his house and parked a block away, walking home so no one would see his car and try to bother him. He wanted to be left alone. He got to the house and could barely keep his eyes open he was so exhausted. His mother's reaction surprised him because, for the first time, she was not happy to see him returning from a long trip. Since he was her favorite son, she usually could not go a day without speaking to him, and if she didn't hear from him for awhile, she would be worried and go crazy. Nader was curious and concerned about his mother's demeanor, but he did not say anything and went into his room. He was about to get into the shower and go see Boloor, who was now staying at her brother's house. Boloor was very ill now, and they were taking care of her. No one really knew the magnitude of her illness, or they did not want to accept it. They had come to believe she was faking it to gain Abbass's attention. In reality, they were all so caught up in her situation with Abbass, trying to prove who was right and who was wrong, they forgot that she actually had a heart problem and could pass very easily. Nader was about to undo his pants when he heard Bijan's footsteps entering the yard. He always knew when Bijan was coming because he used to walk a bit fast and made a lot of noise when his feet hit the ground. Bijan entered the main room, and before his mother had any chance to let him know Nader was in the second room, his voice echoed,

> -They called. I am guessing she is dead, or she is dying. Do not tell anyone. Get ready. We have to go. We have to keep it quiet; they may create embarrassment for Abbass. It is good Nader is out of town.

The sudden dead silence let Nader know his mother had just gestured to Bijan that he was in his room. He knew Bijan was coming to find him, and before Bijan entered his room, he was in the alley running. He had grabbed his shirt and ran out through a tall window as he was putting his shoes on. He was long gone before he put either back on. He ran as fast and as hard he could. For some reason unknown to him, he had left his car keys in the room and did not want to go back and face Bijan or his mother. He had a feeling something tragic was about to happen, and his feeling was right.

The streets in his area were very familiar to him, and he could have run through them with his eyes closed. He had walked to his high school through the same streets for two years, every day, four times. By now, he had run past the Fariba's' old school and reached his old school. He ran through Old Shemran Avenue without looking for oncoming traffic; he was lucky there wasn't any. It was one of the busiest streets in town. He was just running and beginning to feel a sense of panic. He did not even know people were observing him in concern as he passed them, as he reached a small hill and ran up several sets of stairs over the hill facing his sister's house. It was about noon and a hot, sunny day. He headed down towards the house and could clearly see the house with people gathered outside and inside. The new two-story house was built in the middle of a hill with a good size yard in front and a balcony in front overlooking the yard with entrances to all the second-floor rooms. As he got closer, he started to go numb. He saw many relatives gathered on the balcony, and they were all wearing some form of black clothing. People were moving in and out of the hallway, and they were occupied with tasks. In this moment, he recognized the grim reality of what was going on, but he didn't want to believe it. Then, he saw Bijan's cars approach and pull in, and right behind his car was the hearse, both stopped in front of his sister's house. The empty casket approached passed Nader and was carried up into the house. That moment Nader could not kid himself any longer. He nearly collapsed. His mother noticed him and stopped. She wanted to come to him, but she was stopped by Bijan; as people watching, they both might break down. She turned to a couple of people and pointed to Nader. Bijan waited until Nader was standing in front of the house, he grabbed him with a few other men and tried to comfort him. But Nader pushed past them and entered the house. He had run over three miles to get there, and he was not going to stop. He did not know how fast he had run, but he got there in the same amount of time it took Bijan to drive. As people saw Nader, many were worried, and they almost seemed to forget about Boloor. As he walked up the stairs, he had to use the railing to pull himself up. He had no strength left and could not feel the presence of the people moving all around him. He was speechless, his voice gone, sound from all around him had dissipated. By the time Nader reached the entrance to the main room, he had fallen onto his knee. Kneeling down, he watched the casket being taken out with Boloor inside with their loud voice praying. If there was a woman inside, only family members and close friends could carry the casket. By now, the casket had reached Nader, and it was carried over him. Right after it had passed, he could see tears flooding the faces around him. A few relatives approached him, trying to pull him up, as they debated whether or not he should go to the cemetery. Bijan put his foot down and voiced he would be going. Nader could not express a single thought. His mouth was numb, his breath was short, and the only thing he looked for now was little Forogh. He loved her more than anything and needed to be with her. He hoped she was not hurting. He guessed that she had been taken away to another house.

The caravan of cars was following the casket as it traveled through the streets of Tehran, taking away one more victim of wrong traditions and bad judgment by parents. Nader was sitting in the car by the window with others, still speechless. By now, the concern about him was growing, and a couple of people were guarding him closely. They knew he was very close to Boloor and they were concerned about him doing something drastic. They also knew he did not like what they had done to her and that he held his uncle and father responsible.

He was staring at the streets, watching people briskly walking and staring numbly at traffic. But for him, everything was slow-motion, nothing was moving, just dead silence. As the car stopped at a traffic light, he did not even notice that a young boy was staring at him and trying to sell him something. So, the boy gave up and walked to the next car. He could see people crying, but he could not hear them.

The casket entered the cemetery of Tehran Beheshte Zahra, which translates into The Heaven of Zahra. And finally, it stopped by a building followed by the caravan of cars, serenely; they all exited and joined the casket to carry it in preparation for burial. Traditionally the body is washed and cleaned, and then it is tightly wrapped inside a plain, clean, white sheet. Sometimes the relatives decide to wash the body of their loved one themselves. But when the dead body is a woman, no men are allowed to wash except the husband. Generally, there is more than one body being washed at the same time in preparation for burial, so there are lots of people waiting outside for their loved ones. Nader was still sitting in the car and did not exit or say a word yet; relatives were still standing by watching him closely. His heart was now with Forogh. He so desperately wished he could be with her and takes care of her in this solemn moment. As he watched people escorting their loved ones' dead bodies into their final resting place, there were mostly women crying loudly. A group of people walked past him, then a group he recognized was approaching; his relatives were carrying someone he had grown up with, his second mother. His beloved Boloor was lifeless. Bijan broke the silence,

-Maybe you should get out and go with us…

He kindly suggested this as he opened the car door. Nader exited with great burden in his heart, and they followed the casket through the graveyard. As they walked, he could see people praying and saying goodbye to their loved ones, but it all seemed so surreal to even be there.

The casket finally reached the grave, and the worker had already finished preparing the grave. He was standing close by, watching, but he was still far away. The clergy began to speak and followed with prayer. He could see Parry, who was so close to Boloor, who was her best friend, and she was crying to the point her body was convulsing. His mother, as to be expected, was crying hysterically too. Nader wanted to do something so that Parry would not be so overcome with grief, but he could not make a move. Someone else did and took her close by to calm down. He was standing there watching everything without a single reaction or expression on his face, which made everyone uncomfortable, especially his mother. He noticed Parry grabbed his arm. He turned, and her eyes landed on him. Crying still, she reached and hugged him tightly, whispering about the good memories they had and how they would have more with Forogh. She continued,

-Now you are the one who has to take care of Forogh. She asked me to ask you to promise you would. She did not trust anyone but you...

By then, Nader could feel her warm tears running on his bare arm and soon becoming ice cold. He hugged her back, still numb. Then, he heard the loud voice calling the prayer, which meant that the body was being placed in the grave. Parry turned and walked away to the grave to say her last goodbye. She approached the grave and wanted to touch and kiss the body, but someone stopped her, and now the crying was very loud. The body was placed into the grave, and as a custom, the relatives and friends, one by one, dropped some dirt on the body, taking turns with a single shovel. Some did not wait for the shovel and used their bare hands. Then, the worker took over and leveled the grave, and there was no more Boloor. She was gone. That was the first moment that Nader had a genuine sense of what was happening; there would be no more Boloor for him to confide in. It hit him, smack in the face, man came from dirt, and man will return to dirt no matter who they were, rich or poor, king or pauper. Boloor and Nader had never fought, not even once, and they never ever talked behind each others' back. There was a bond between them, they just loved one another, and that was it. A mass of flowers was placed on her grave, and soon you could not see the freshly laid dirt. Funerals were also a weird and twisted show, a show to see who would bring the biggest flower arrangement. This would show how much you cared or felt for the family's loss. Soon they were escorting Parry away from the grave. She asked Nader to go with her; he knew in the midst of her deep sadness she was worried about him. The mass began to disperse and say goodbye, and they all finally left the graveyard, leaving Boloor all alone.

On the way back, Nader was sitting with his sister Parry; she held onto his arm, not once letting go. He noticed his mother sitting in his brother's car, staring at him through the window and motioning for his sister to watch for him. Nader knew she had forced his brother to slow down for her to see him. The custom called for the family to take all participants to eat, and usually, shish kabab was served. Nader did not attend the gathering at the restaurant, and a friend drove him to his older sister's house to see Forogh. Somehow, they knew he wanted to see her. A few workers and relatives were getting ready for the family and friends to come back, and someone handed him a cold drink and fruit to comfort him. He took the drink and walked into the bathroom without thinking. For a long time, he sat on in there, doing nothing at all. Several people would knock, asking if he was okay; they wanted to be sure he didn't do anything stupid. He just needed to be by himself. By hearing Frogh's voice, he finally felt ready to face the world and quickly stood up. Before he could figure out what happened, blood was rushing down his back. It seemed that the new toilet handle, which was installed right behind him and too low, had cut his back. The second he saw the blood, it was like an awakening for him. It made life real once again, and for the first time, he broke down to cry. He had not said a word since he had seen Forogh's mother after he returned home, until then. Soon he was covered with blood, and so was the bathroom; his fists were penetrating the wall to relieve his anger; he was trying to do it quietly. But those on the outside knew something was wrong. They broke the lock and entered, taking a firm grasp on him. They calmed him down enough to clean him up without causing a commotion.

Later Forogh was back; the second she saw Nader, she leaned over from the lady friend who was holding her, and she was in his arms. The embrace immediately brought a flood of memories of Boloor. He took her home with him before anyone could question him or return. From then, he knew he had a responsibility toward her; she was as much his daughter as his brother's. He promised himself that he would always speak up when tradition was plaguing those around him. He would fight with more determination than ever, and he would start with his own family. The memory of Boloor led Nader into a new stage of life and a new play named Over the Bridge.

*****

Chapter 17

Certain Events In Life Will Shape And Alter Your Existence...

The birth of his new life, but could he forget the past and adopt a new life he was not expecting to come? Certain events in life will shape and alter your existence. A life path can seem to be going in one direction, and then something catastrophic can occur that will transform your behavior, your values, and your beliefs. It is guaranteed that all do experience transformation in some form or another when you are faced with situations that appear disastrous or out of your control. This was the case with Nader's own growth and development. As a young man, he had encountered so many experiences that reshaped his ideology as well as his destiny, and these experiences covered a wide range of emotions. By the time he had reached college, he had experienced such heartbreak and regret, most of which he believed to have been afflicted upon his life because of the harmful and insidious beliefs of others. Born into a place he loved but seemed alien in so many ways. But the transformative aspect of all the pain and adversity he had undergone would show up in the form of artistic expression. Thus, he poured his heart into writing, acting, and filmmaking. He had been given a vast array of life experiences to pull from, and the memories were numerous and lamentable. But the most devastating event above everything was the death of Boloor, an irreplaceable friend and confidant. The timing of her death was especially difficult, being that this happened as he was facing one regrettable event after another. Besides, two women who meant the world to him were taken out of his life. But whatever the reason was, her death had changed his life. It gave Nader a new direction and a new goal. He was now on a new mission to fight injustice, unfairness, and blindness that existed in traditions and customs. The pain of Boloor's death would hit him every time he hugged her little daughter Forogh; it was with a saddened heart that he would look into her eyes. After many months he was not completely living in his body; he was disconnected from his physical self. He had become disengaged from his family, very quiet and reserved. He was even fired from his first real acting job in the middle of shooting because he did not agree with the way things were being done. He especially became disconnected from Abbass, even though he considered him a victim as well. But Nader truly thought that he stood have stood strong to begin with, all those years back, putting his foot down, wreaking havoc if necessary to protect them all.

He tried to create a solid trust and friendship with the younger family members so he could help them go through the difficulties they may encounter with their parents and elders. But he never recovered from the sadness of Boloor's death; he was like a wanderer, looking for a way out or a way to find answers. At the time, he was still at the Dramatic Art School, studying drama and film, and would sometimes try acting to get away from his thoughts and memories. Sometimes he would create a monologue in private, in the car, or in the house. He constantly thought about Boloor. It plagued him, but what was done was done. But what if he could prevent the same thing from happening to someone else? What if there was a way to positively affect the lives of a few. He knew he couldn't single-handedly change the entire familial and social structure, but if he could help enlighten the thinking of a few, then slowly, it would trickle down.

Nader began discussing the tragedy of Boloor with his heart and mind and created a monologue starting with their forced marriage. He created a question and answer routine playing himself, his uncle, his father, and a few others. He thought it may help him to leave the sad thought of Boloor behind him. He started recording himself to see how he sounded, it became like a cathartic practice, and he began to enjoy it. It was his therapy, his own artistic expression to release what his world had bottled up inside. The more he was recording, the more relief from his pain he experienced. Tears used to pop into the corner of his eyes and soon would run down his cheeks as he spoke. Sometimes, he used to have Forogh with him and would get her involved. She was still a bit over three years old, but when tears were running down his cheeks, she would feel it and hug him tight, crying. Those were the sweetest moment of his life. This game he created was going on for a month, and each time he performed the one-man play, it was getting more interesting and powerful. Finally, one night, he recorded the entire full dialogue, which consisted of two and a half hours, and he was playing over ten different characters. When he was done, his face was completely wet from his tears. And after that, it became an old game for him, he completely stopped; he even left his last tape inside the portable recorder to gather dust.

Later, after a few months had passed, there was a friend of his, Kamran, who came to his house to visit. Kamran was a bit chubby, intelligent, and funny with tick glass. When Nader had to leave Kamran alone in his room for a while to take his mother and Forogh to his sister's house, Kamran decided to play few songs to kill time till Nader was back. At the time, cassettes were the newest way of playing music. So, he decided to put on a tape and enjoy his time, but for some reason, he decided to play the tape that was already inside the player; as the tape began playing, Kamran was a bit surprised by hearing what he was hearing.

When Nader returned, Kamran was gone. Even for two weeks, Kamran was not found and did not answer any calls. Until one night, about two in the morning, the phone rang. Nader was jolted from his sleep and didn't want to answer it. But it would not stop, so he finally gave in,

-You have a masterpiece on your hands. When in the hell did you write this? Do you have the manuscript?

It was Kamran's voice stammering into his ear, and he did not know what he was talking about. Nader thought he was up to playing a game with him as they always did to one another, so he hung up the phone without any response. But the phone rang again, and when Nader answered, Kamran yelled,

-Listen, dummy, I am talking about the one-man act you have recorded. I just listened to the entire 10 tapes, and you really do not know what you have done. This is your ticket to becoming a well-known artist.

Nader realized he was not playing, and embarrassed he responded,

-Please, that is private, and I do not have a manuscript, do not play it for anyone.

They were on the phone a bit longer, finishing up with drowsy responses from Nader. He knew Kamran, and he knew he had a great sense for art, he was one of the best critics Nader knew, so there must have been something there. Otherwise, he would not have called him in the middle of the night or even taken the time to listen. Nader remembered when he used to give him the material he was working on in class, Kamran would sometimes get to only the second page, and he would throw it into the garbage and yell at him,

-This is junk, trash!

Nader didn't hear from Kamran for several weeks. He remembered that night, and he hardly slept after Kamran's phone call. Boloor came flooding back to his mind. Then one day, Nader heard the doorbell, then his voice speaking with his mother. Kamran was a sharp and funny man, very likable. He was always polite and knew how to speak with everyone, he could joke with even the most serious person, and they would not get offended.

-Where is our next soon-to-be most talked-about writer?

Kamran asked. Hajji Khanoom did not understand what he was talking about as she escorted him up to the second floor. And there he was, holding a folder. They walked into his room, and before Nader could say a word, Kamran began talking loudly with the passion of a mad man,

> -Hajji Khanoom, I want you to be our witness. I transcribed whatever you, Nader, said on the tape, exactly as you recorded it, word for word. Some sections I did not understand because you were crying, so I marked those sections. You are going to read and do this play or forget about our friendship. Goodbye. I will see you or talk to you when you have started producing the play. And please do not star in it yourself. Just direct it. Goodbye again, and I mean what I said. Hajji Khanoom is our witness…

Kamran dropped the manuscript on Nader's desk and took off. Hajji Khanoom walked after him to stop him, offering him tea or pastry. But did not worked. Kamran was a long gown.

Nader was kind of baffled but not surprised by Kamran's behavior; he was just like that. He sat upright in bed, staring at the manuscript for about three hours; he did not touch it for a couple of days. His mother would sometimes come and clean his room. She was the only one he permitted to do so. She would always move everything around, jumble papers together in a way Nader could not control, but she could not read. He knew she would never be snooping. One morning Nader walked out of his bathroom and found her in cleaning mode in his room. He grabbed few items from her arms and placed them back on his desk as he tried to escort her out. She kept on cleaning, grabbing the manuscript Kamran left behind. Next, she was asking where she should put it. He took the manuscript from her and politely escorted her out, and he left for class, taking the manuscript with him. The manuscript stayed in his car for a few weeks. Later, one of his female classmates, who later became a famous actress, Farymah Farjami, came to him and said she wanted to have a serious talk with him. He used to give her rides to school. They sat in a coffee shop one afternoon; she placed the manuscript on the table and asked if he had written it. She said, after glancing at a few pages of it in the car, she took it and read it. She loved it and wanted to be in it. She was adamant he needed to produce and direct it. Nader was scolding himself for leaving it in the car. He remembered he had gotten into an accident that day and completely forgot about it. He was always in some kind of fender bender; if only he had better luck. From that moment on, Nader began to take the manuscript seriously. A few months later, he had put a team together, and the play was in production. He did the play in an unusual style that generally would not have been done. First, he searched outside of his school throughout other schools and selected unknown actors to play the parts. Second, he selected each character to look like the original character that they would portray. He took each individual actor who was portraying a member of his family to his family's house as a guest, and there they learned to mimic the characteristics of his family members. He had his actors imitate their predominant movements and even learn how to talk like them using their accents. And all of this was happening in secret, and none of them knew they were being set up and what was going on. Also, Kamran did not know about it until he heard the play had opened in the city of Tabriz. The day after the opening, Ferdosi Magazine ran an article. Ferdosi was one of the most prestigious intellectual magazines in the country, headed by Mr. Abbass Pahlevan at the time, and the article compared him to one of the forward-thinking activists, Samad Behrangi, who was rumored to have drowned in Tabriz's river by Savak Iranian secret police during the Shah. Kamran was so happy that he took some pastries and visited Nader's mother, telling her about it. His mother was surprised and asked him not to speak with his older brother Abbass yet. Nader decided to open the play in smaller cities and tour the country rather than do a run in the capital city of Tehran. Completely happy and optimistic from the first performance, they were getting ready to go to the city of Rezaeyeh for the next. But right in full view of the public, a bystander attempt to shoot the leading lady of the play right in her eyes with his slingshot from across the street then ran away. Luckily, he missed it. It was because of the character she played. Her character had driven the hero to believe he was crazy. The reason for this terrible incident was thought to be because the people identified the hero "Mr. Azady" aka "Mr. Freedom" with Samad Behrangi, the known writer and political activist who was from Tabriz. Samad was a teacher as well, and the rumor that Samad was drowned in the river by the Savak was still fresh on people's lips. Incidentally, the hero in the play also was a teacher, fighting for freedom. In the end, he too drowned in the river. No one revealed the attack to the female actor because there was concern she may not appear on the stage again, and the tour would be canceled. The incident was extremely sad, and Nader had her in his prayers that she would suffer no harm, but the incident and especially Ferdosi's article gave the play more exposure.

Nader was playing a good-hearted butcher who was trusted by the people. He gets tricked by the leader of the village to get Mr. Freedom, the play's hero, in trouble. He finally could not handle what he had done to Mr. Freedom and decides to rise against the aggressor, and they poison him to death. The outfits were long with wide pants; the more material you used at the time for your pants showed how wealthy you were. Men did not wear underwear, so Nader told the actors not to wear underwear, and they didn't. In the middle of the play, in the most dramatic moment, the audience members were laughing, including several American tourists who were sitting in the front row. One of the actors, Mehdi, who was performing the scene with Nader, began yelling at him to cover himself up. Nader was so into the character that he did not understand what he meant. He thought Mehdi had forgotten his words and was adding something to the play to get back to his dialog. Mehdi was standing right on the edge of the stage with his back to the people. Finally, he walked over to Nader and kicked him in his legs, telling him to cover himself. Totally surprised, Nader jumped and hit the table, causing the table to hit a tree which was installed in the corner behind the table, and the tree fell on him. Nader grabbed the tree and placed it back into its place, adding in a monologue to pretend this was part of the play. He did not know his pants had fallen to his knees with his equipment showing seemed as if it was meant to happen as well. The audience thought it was phenomenal, and that was the reason people were laughing so loud. After the play, there were so many people gathered outside that it concerned the city, and they were asked to leave town that same night. But the real problems started when, unknown to Nader, government opposition, who were mostly leftist, began to follow them city to city. Their group had increased as time passed. They arrived in the city of Sarri, where Ali, Nader's high school friend, was from. There was a theatrical festival taking place, and the organizers were worried that what happened in the city of Tabriz and Rezai may be repeated in some form in Sarri. They decided to invite the governor of the state a night before the festival's last day that Nader's play was supposed to go on stage and present him with an orchid. They wanted people to think the festival was drawing to an end to minimize the crowds and any chaos that could occur. This idea actually backfired; protest starting from the same night and brought more attention to the play, and more people showed up, particularly because they were irritated that the city was trying to pull a fast on them. The governor left, and protesting began. The next day more people had attended than the previous days combined. A couple of hundred people were standing outside waiting to get in. Finally, things got rough. And again, Nader and his team had to leave the town right away.

The tour continued to the city of Kermaan to attend another festival. It was there that things got out of hand. The audience got so emotionally into Nader's play, and the activists took advantage of the situation. Chaos began. The Shah's pictures were pulled down and broken, while some attempted to start a fire, but it was put out. Nader and his entire team had to take sanctuary outside at the theater, a large backyard. Within a few minutes, the police arrived, and of course, the Savak got involved. Nader was not ready for such a massive problem, nor did he intend to attract this political attention type. Nader did not know the leftist and the radical religious were following him and were creating the problem. But this time, the problem had gotten so bad, and out of control, outside, the people began to form a line around them, supporting them by creating a wall around their group; they stood in the yard of the theater so they would not be taken away by the police. In fact, no one could leave the theater. The problem continued, and no one knew what would happen next. Nader was talking to his cast, trying to calm them down, and at the same time, he was negotiating with the representative of law enforcement to get them out of this jam. He was trying to convince them that his team had nothing to do with the commotion. They informed him there were three trouble makers in his group, and they had to arrest them, but he was not intending to let them arrest any of his team. And he did not let any of his team know about this matter. Of course, they knew who he was, and if it was not for his older brother Abbass, things might have turned out differently. It was about 2 AM in the morning; Nader heard that the governor had just arrived. He assumed the people had walked out of their houses and gathered around; the government did not want things to get out of hand. Soon he was talking to the governor one on one, explaining the situation. The governor informed him that he knew who Nader was and that he said he knew who the troublemaker was. But Nader reasoned with him and convinced him to help them get out without any arrests. The governor ordered two buses to come as Nader promised his team that they would be OK. Nader decided to get onto the second bus after everyone had boarded. He was anxious; something about the situation did not sit right with him. He paced back and forth on the bus, talking and checking on everyone. He kept cracking jokes as if nothing was going to happen, but inside he was worried, and he knew in his heart that he would be dealing with something very shortly, and Abbass. Then, Nader realized he didn't recognize a couple of people on the bus. He had never seen them before. The more he glanced at them and exchanged a few words with them, the more he realized something was not right. He asked a few of his people, and no one knew anything about them. So, he approached them and put a question to them,

-Who are your friends?

-No one, we just wanted to be with you to support and protect you and be sure you are safe.

They went on to say they were students who were following his tour to support the play. They thought this to be one of the most exclusive plays being performed for their cause. One of them spoke in a very passionate yet soft tone,

-We need such courage like yours to write and perform such an act; it is a perfect way to let our troubles be known not only to our people but to the world.

The more they were praising Nader, the more he was getting worried and upset. He was the only one who knew he never intended to write anything to promote any cause or promote democracy or any political stance. He was completely against violence and the way the leftist and the radical religious groups were behaving. In fact, he had stated his opposition to violence many times. To him, all it was doing was getting uneducated, innocent young boys and girls killed. Nader felt that nothing was going to get accomplished with violent protesting; it would just end in bloodshed with the Savak showing up. He also did not believe in the actions of the communist or radical religious groups, and he was completely against the mixing of religion and state. Power always ended up in the hands of the radical-minded who acted out of selfish reasons, and the goodwill and ideas of the religious masses get distorted. Besides, religion to him was respect, peace, love, and truth. Politics were all lies and manipulation, so how then could the two mix? He was strongly against both groups and decided to be his own man, walk his own path. Nader continued to believe that when you join a group, you must follow all the principles of the group, no matter if the group is supporting the interest of all or just themselves. And more often than not, the group followed their own interests. But what plagued his mind, the problems of his family were intricately woven into how the system was set up. He never realized he would be unable to avoid it. That main character he had, Mr. Azady, really got blood pumping in people's veins.

Nader immediately yelled to the driver to stop. He politely asked the uninvited men to get off the bus, knowing who the troublemaker on his team was and what kind of problems could follow them if this situation continued. Akbar exited the bus and joined Nader. Akbar was playing one of his main characters, a teacher. Nader took a stroll with Akbar a few yards down as he explained the situation to Akbar. Akbar suggested that the right thing to do would be to drop them off in the next city. Nader had a great amount of respect for Akbar and really liked him. Akbar was his confidant and most trusted friend, the person with whom he would discuss dialogues in-depth with or the symbolic meaning of scenes. After the revolution, his name was in the paper as a member of the Savak. It was then that Nader realized why Akbar's photo had never been published in any paper. Even when Ferdosi Magazine had published individual photos of the entire team, they had someone else's photo instead of him. The bus took off with all men back on. But they were dropped off at the next city. The next performance was finally in Tehran; Nader was biased and brought many of the farmers into the theater to watch the play. And for the first time invited his own family as well, it was clear they were not happy to see themselves with their own name on the stage. Especially to be credited for their wrongdoing. Tehran's performance was also very much successful. Nader was surprised many of the well-known film, and stage stars were attending, many of them without invitations. They were there to support Nader. Among them was Mohmad Ali Fardian, who later became Nader's good friend. And Saeed Rad, Fany zadh, and…

However, Nader knew what those incidents meant, and it was good and bad. It was good because he knew he wrote a great play. It was bad because now he was under a microscope by the government. Now, he could not breathe on his own, and he could not live; everything he does will be under the microscope by the government and people as well. And if he took one wrong step and with doubt, he would pay the price. So, he decided to stop the performance for a while, but he began to play it only at the orphanages to do something nice for them. This intense period passed slowly, but the article about Nader and the play kept appearing in every paper. The last performance they did needed no publicity. The audience was filled with enthusiastic supporters, as well as with several famous actors and performers. Later on, the play was accepted to be broadcasted on national TV, but he realized the soul of it would be cut out by censorship; he backed out and did not go on with the deal. This made many people unhappy because this was their opportunity to shine, but Nader was taking away from them. But the articles kept coming, and some of the clergies were very unhappy because of the extreme criticism in the play regarding traditional religious customs. The customs and traditions which had been set by the clergy over the course of history really had nothing to do with the Islamic religion; those in power always add their own side notes. He was told one of the clergies had placed fatva fatwa on his head, which was not good; he knew if this was true anytime one of those blind and brainwashed religious fanatics could walk up to him and shot him to death. So, Nader was cornered on all sides and alienated from his brother at the same time. Finally, the film he had started a good while earlier was completed. He had put everything he had in the film and had borrowed from everyone he could think of. Just one day before he could watch the final cut, in the middle of one night, the film mysteriously disappeared from the studio. It was never recovered, and no one knew what had happened to the film. He was sad, frustrated, furious, and in a position he did not intend to be in. He was now utterly confused about what to with his life. He had made the film in secrecy with a new advertising company he had organized, and now he owed everyone money and had no film. At the same time, he became marked. He was unable to function in the field he loved. He had created his own prison with no options to move forward.

*****

Chapter 18

Do You Believe In Dreams?

If your unkind mind is used and always try to practice it, surely a new window will open for you to another unknown world that ordinary people may not be familiar with. It was around this time that the window to this unknown new world opened for Nader. It was about this time that Nader started dreaming about events and seeing images before they actually happened. In the beginning, he did not give this much thought, or he did not take them seriously. But little by little, he realized that seeing these dreams were not coincidences, and in fact, he dreamed of everything that was going to happen in his life in the future and before it happened, which certainly had an impact on his life. The impact of these events was both pleasant and as well as sad and heartbreaking. But after a specific incident that happened in college, he began to pay more attention to the visions and images which appeared to him in his sleep, sometimes even when he was awake. He remembers he was walking around the main building coming from the small restaurant; he was approaching one of his classmates, he realized a brick was traveling down from the top of the building, and it could have fallen on him. He ran to him and pushed him away to save him. It was embarrassing because there were no bricks falling. Nader explained to him what he had seen, but he started laughing. A few other students had seen what had happened and were chuckling as well. But it was a week later that the same man was walking the same path and a brick really came down, it hit him on his foot and broke one of his toes. This created more problems for Nader. The dean questioned him, asking if he had done such a thing on purpose. The dean thought that maybe Nader had set up the whole incident to get attention. But luckily, at the time of the incident, Nader was working on a script with Mr. Karimi and who could be a better witness. Mr. Karimi was teaching at the college at the time. So, the dean and the school kept everything quiet, and not too many knew about this incident. But that did not stop Nader from becoming alienated from the other students who heard the story.

Soon the news was out; because of this incident and his play, everyone knew who his brother was, and they also thought Nader was a member of the Savak. He had become a loner, a wanderer, looking for answers to how he could change his destiny. It was then that he realized he needed a new hobby, a new friend. He needed to pay attention to his dreams, the visions, and the images which began to come to him. It was then that the memory of the older wise man that used to visit him as a child began flooding back to his mind. He began to study the art of being, just being; the discovery of self, meditations, and attended gatherings with dervishes. Dervishes follow the spiritual part of Islam, which is really what Islam is based on; to begin with, materialism had no place. Examples of this can be found in the words and lives of great philosophers such as Rumi, Hafez, Omar Khayyam, Sanai, Saddi, and many more. But his favorite poet and philosopher were Omar Khayyam.

It was about this time that Nader fell into loneliness. At the same time, Hussein's letters that every so often used to come suddenly stopped coming. In the beginning, it was once a week, then once a month, and then once every few months. Now he had hardly heard from him, but he was suddenly always in Nader's mind. Then out of the blue, after a long time, Nader suddenly received one of his letters; Hussein surprised him by writing about Fariba, his Violin Girl. He had come across her at UCLA in Los Angeles, but they did not talk. They just stared at each other, and when he described that she was with her husband, Nader was saddened and more frustrated. Then, he remembered her violin that her mother gave him. He still had it hidden in a safe place. He thought maybe he should begin to learn how to play, he tried, but it did not go very well. He dropped the idea a few weeks later. By this time, Nader could not find inspiration in anything, and he did not want to do anything. It was as though he was mad at himself like he felt he was responsible for all that had happened to him. He began to feel bad, blaming himself and asking why he had done such an injustice to himself. He had to search for more answers. And he was not going to give in to his brother and do what he had planned for him. He was not going to do what his mother wanted him to do and take a job as a simple employee of the government, no matter what the pay would be. He was just not a man who could work a nine to five. He had graduated from college and had nothing to do. He would just sit and watch the wall in his room, get nagged by his mother and others that he should do something with his life. One day Nader met an American man named Peter the Priest. They became great friends and opened up a small shish kabob house together. But no one knew Nader was Peter's partner. Peter was an interesting man. He was more Iranian than Nader in some ways and was familiar with the works of Rumi and Omar Khayyam, especially Omar Khayyam. The cafe ended up becoming the new hip place for intellectuals to gather and discuss politics, poetry, and lectures.

Around this time, one of Nader and Hussein's old high school friends, Abbdi, came back into the picture. He showed up at the cafe with an American girl. Nader soon learned she was Hussein's girlfriend; she came from America to look for her family. He was told her father was Iranian and left them when she was young, and now she was set on finding him. Meeting Fariba set Nader's mind in motion. Perhaps if he helped Hussein's girlfriend in Iran, she could help him get to the states. But he didn't know Hussein was now involved in the underground movement to overthrow the government. He had sent this naive girl to Iran as a tool to be used for their mission. She truly did want to find her father, not knowing Hussein's underlying motives; no one would be suspicious of this innocent-looking beauty. Several times the Savak had asked Nader to join them, to provide them with info about his friend's actions. But Nader did not want to have anything to do with such work. He would never betray his friend who trusted him. Yet, even if he had wanted to, Nader had no clue two of his close friends were leaders of the underground opposition. He had no idea about their secret activities. Nader also did not realize they were using him for cover to get around. But the Savak had found out about them; they always found out one way or another. They all did not know that Nader was being watched by Savak as well. Otherwise, they would not have gotten close to him. Their thinking was that because of his brother, they were safe with him; no one would even suspect or dare to mess with him. They trusted this belief so much that they were even manipulating Nader to do their work for them, thinking he was not being watched. Blinded, Nader was dumb enough to fall for their traps. They had him involved in little activities that fit into a bigger puzzle, making all seem innocent. The Savak never fully explained what they had used him for. However, things turned out badly for both sides, they were arrested, and Nader ended up under house arrest. It was Nader who used Abbass's influence to get their American girl Faruba out of trouble. Nader had developed an interest in the American girl who swiftly came into their lives, but soon she joined her family in another city.

Once again, Nader was bored and devoid of any ambition. He suddenly decided to go to the farm and stay with his father for awhile. He did not tell anyone where he was going. The idea came to him in the middle of the night, and it happened that he had a car that belonged to a new friend who, unbeknown to Nader, was involved with secret activities against the government. He quietly got into the car in the dark night and took off. It was in the very cold winter bombarded with fierce rain and snow that pelted your skin. The heater in the old convertible fiat did not work. He was freezing, but he had to continue. After a few hours into the drive, it began raining. He was not going to stop being only a few hours away from the farmhouse. But the top of the car was not safe and could not resist the strong wind; it began to leak inside, the heavier the rain fell, the more water began to accumulate. By the time he reached the small mountain top, the storm was overtaken with the most confident wind ever. Visibility was very limited, but he was almost to his destination. Finally, he could see the weak light coming from the top of the mountain; he knew that was their private guest house situated on the mountainside a few miles from the farm and overlooking the farm, with a miraculous view. It was used for city guests. The house was built like a fort for protection, so no one could enter during the nighttime. His father lived in this charming guest house now.

It was about three in the morning when he got to the large, heavy door. It was still windy and pumping rain. He did not know how to get his father's attention. He could see the light and smoke coming out of the fireplace. He tried everything, honking, banging, and yelling. But there was no answer. He began to throw small rocks at the tall window facing him. After several rocks hit the window, there still was no response. His father thought all the noise was from the storm; he actually gave the wind a few curse words for making such a ruckus. Nader was mad and on fire. He began yelling and cursing at him from the bottom of his lungs, but he was getting nowhere, and the rain was hitting him hard. He got back in the little car, which was coming apart in the storm. He decided to take off and go to the village to get help and warm up. He took off but could not see where he was going, angry and frustrated beyond belief. He could not think straight, and to say he was furious would have been an understatement. He was yelling out loud at those he did not know. Suddenly the top came loose as he was turning a sharp corner, he lost control of the car, and it slipped to the side and down the sharp valley. He was now flying in the air. He only remembered that he was thrown out of the car and traveled down through crisscrossed tree branches. Somehow, he got stuck between the branches for a few seconds; he grabbed firmly a hold of a branch and secured himself. He did not know where he was. He only knew he had to hold on. Otherwise, he would begin to fall down the mountain and would be dead. He knew there was a deep valley underneath with rocks and rough trees. The car was gone; he slowly twisted and tangled, maneuvering himself onto stronger branches. He did not know how long he would have to wait for the sun to come up so he could see where he was. The rain was pouring down.

The branches he was holding on to were about to break. He had no choice but to try to climb up. The closer he was getting to the top of the hill, the louder his complaints became. He made it to the top with one last push up from the branches, collapsing on the wet earth. He had lost one of his shoes; his jacket and shirt were ripped all over. He was now drenched from the rain; it was washing away the blood but stung with each drop that was washed away. Only then could he decide what to do. It was a long wait; he could feel the pain from the cuts on his face, hands, feet, and chest. His body ached to the rhythm of the falling rain. He started to whisper curses at his father, at himself, at everything and everyone he could think of. He whispered to God, asking why everything had to be so hard, so complicated. He began pacing around like a mad man, hollering at the whole world as if it was seated in front of him, listening attentively. His voice became louder and louder and turned into yelling at God, questioning where he could possibly be; why was he putting him in these situations? Then, he noticed a middle-aged barefooted man holding a wooden stick, standing on a small hill looking right at him, laughing. He did not know where the man came from. He just appeared. He stopped for a minute and observed him, questioning what he was doing there at such a strange time. Who could this man be? From his appearance, he could have been anyone. Maybe he was a shepherd, but he did not know about any shepherds around that area. He assumed from his simple attire that he must be a Dervish. Dervishes, as already mentioned, have gained wisdom and power by controlling their inner feelings and destiny by connecting to all levels of spiritual energy that exist. Some Dervishes know many things about the great unknown, they are completely detached from the material world, spirituality reigns their existence. Some of them, they could be in different places at the same time; they could separate their soul from their physical body as if they were dead, and in fact, experience death, only to come back again. They could also control pain, regardless of the severity of a wound. Of course, each one has different levels of powers and the ability to do different things. They usually do not believe in claiming any place as home, the land is their house, and the sky is their roof. But Nader was not happy with this possible Dervish laughing at him. So, he walked towards him, ready to spit fire.

-What is so funny about this? He snapped at the man.

He replied with the steadiness of a slow-moving cloud,

-You are.

Then, he continued to speak, "Don't you think if God was willing to interfere with your problems, why would he bother to let you encase yourself in it to begin with?" Then, he walked away, going toward the hill, and Nader began following him with no hesitation. He did not know what overcame him, but he just followed with no reservations. He just followed the Dervish toward the hill. Nader disappeared into the rain after him.

*****

It was a cloudy day in Tehran, with heavy traffic and dense smog that added thickness to the clouds. A man was walking on the sidewalk looking like he had never seen a city street; it was almost as if people were unknown to him. His long black beard and long hair were uncharacteristic of the city lifestyle. His nose and two small black eyes barely emerged from his furry face. His clothing looked like rags hanging on his body. People were gazing at him as they passed by. It seemed he was the only one who was not in a rush. He walked through the streets of Tehran, feeling disturbed by the smog and traffic. He was a wanderer, lost in the forest of modern society, which did not sit well with him. Several people stared at the man so he would notice them and open a conversation. This would allow them to ask a question. But there was no answer from this strange man. Finally, he reached the area, which was a bit different than the south part of the city that he started his walk from. People driving or walking past him were very curious about whom the strange-looking man was. In a way, they were concerned and scared by his presence in their area. He had walked almost the entire day to reach there. Some perceived him as a bum and did not want to see him around. They were doubtful if he should be in the area at all. It was where the high-class government officials and foreign diplomats lived, and if you are unfamiliar, they would stop and check you out with complete confidence. But the man never looked back and just stared straight ahead like they were not even there. The way he walked, his energy, made it seem as though he did not belong there, nor anywhere, superior to all, and he was looked at differently, left alone. By the time he reached the most exclusive area of town, darkness had taken over, and it was like he was invisible, like a ghost. He was walking through the clean, beautiful, quiet streets, and every so often, an expensive model car would approach and pass him, then it was just him on the quiet street and the darkness and soft brize. Finally, he reached the alley he was looking for. He stopped for awhile and looked around while considering if he should enter or not. But finally, he disappeared into the alley. It was dark and quiet outside, sometime past midnight. A shadow walked through the room, finding her way by tracking the wall, trying to be quiet so she would not wake up others. The shadow tracked her hand down from the wall and onto a bed, finally touching hair, lots of hair. The hand stopped in surprise. Now the other hand moved to check the hair; both hands were running through the hair and touching someone's face. The two hands made their way to the side of the face, embracing it as she knelt down, sending the smell of the skin through her nostrils. Then, in the quiet room, there was now a voice of an older woman, weeping softly in the dark,

>   -God, is this a miracle?

The lights come on, and Parry walked up behind the older woman, Nader's mother, still kneeling down, holding onto someone's head with his back toward them, who was still a bit unknown at the moment. It is just hair, a messy man in a white outfit. Parry stared at his feet, feeling her nerves creep in.

>   -Oh God, who is this man? Get away, Mother, he must be a homeless person who got drunk and lost his way.

Parry was alarmed. By now, several others who were staying at the house appeared, a couple of them began to beat on the man, trying to provoke him to get out of the bed and out of the house. Nader's mother used her body to stop the movement in the room and whispered to them,

-Don't hurt him. He is my son.

She wanted to yell, but her voice would not come out. The beating stopped. She gently removed the hair from his face, pushing it in different directions to make the skin visible. It was Nader, everyone could see now. They realized a mother's instinct is never mistaken, and no matter how old their children are, they still are able to feel them. They can smell them, even in a dark room. As Nader turned over, his knees were folded into his body. Only his eyes were visible through the mass of hair. He stared at all of them with a blank expression. Then, tears welled up in Parry's eyes, and she reached out to embrace him, whispering with a quiver in her voice,

-Thank you, God. Hajji Khanoom, he is alive!

Within seconds he was wrapped in her arms and was soon bombarded by hugs from all. He was not a dead man any longer. He was back home, surrounded by family, and everyone was wondering what had really happened to him for the last six months. It was his mother who had walked to his bedroom every night all these months, some nights a couple of times into the dark, to check his bed and see if he was back. She used to check on him before, and she did not stop when he was gone. She never lost hope, and somehow, she knew he would be back in his bed one day. And for some reason, she had left the tall window to his room open, so he could get in anytime he came back. It was the same window he used to get in late at night, so he did not bother anyone. Nader did not know how long he had been gone. He did not know everyone thought he was killed in the accident or eaten up by some wild animal. Some thought he was arrested by the Savak. His brother thought he was killed by his radical friends who were anti-government. There was also a rumor he had left the country. But now the mystery was over, and they all had one question. Where the hell had he been all this time? More perplexing was that he showed up wearing a loose traditional outfit. But everyone was happy he was back, and at that moment, they did not care where he had been. They were just overjoyed to see him alive. Nader's first question spewed out quickly,

-Where is Forogh?

Within seconds Forogh was in his arms. Holding to her tight, she was still too young. It seemed he missed her more than anything. The night came to an end with such a happy ending for all, lots of unanswered questions, and peace in the house. But Nader knew this day would be the beginning of his problems again. But nothing mattered anymore. He would have risked anything to go through such an experience he had for the last six months. There was nothing of value that could replace the feeling, the understanding, the discovery of what he gained. The only problem he had was how to explain what had actually happened to him; maybe they would not understand the meaning of the experience, the wisdom he had gained. In his heart, he already wanted to go back; he missed the dervish and their way of life badly.

*****

Chapter 19

Up Close And Personal With The Dervish...

The rain was still falling hard. The Dervish's long steps were too much for Nader to follow. He was limping with one shoe and suffering from the pain of being barefoot; walking over rocks and bushes was not an easy task. He was pushing himself forward not to lose the Dervish. He ripped his jacket off and covered his injured bare foot since he had lost the other shoe during the accident. He was trying to catch up with the Dervish. He really did not know why he was following him or where he was following him to. The force that was pushing him forward was unknown to him. He just wanted to go. He wanted to get lost to ease his emotional pain, or perhaps find the true meaning of life, something with purpose, or at least something a bit better than what he possessed already. It was several long hours that he followed the Dervish on the curvy path way through the hills and mountain area. Walking through pouring rain, his mind was searching for purpose, but he was met with more confusion. Carefully, he was advancing, following the Dervish. He was bleeding underneath his clothes, and by now, he was freezing. Totally out of strength, his knees just gave out, and he collapsed like he was having a seizure. He needed a doctor very badly. Before he collapsed, he only remembered seeing a shadow of the Dervish as he lay in the heart of the mountain.

He could hear the sound of the sheep echoing in his ears, and it seemed that they were talking to each other and to him. He could feel the warmth of the flame on his face, and he could see the light of flames dancing through his closed eyes. Then, he felt a hand touch his forehead,

-He is back...

The man had an accent unknown to him, and he hardly could understand the language, but somehow, he knew what he said. Nader barely opened his eyes. After a few seconds, his vision cleared a bit, and he could see the Shepherd's hand still resting on his forehead. He found himself among a mass of sheep. They were lying around or struggling to make room among each other to sleep. The light of the weak fire, burning by him and lighting the wall, was like Heaven to see. He noticed, sitting on the other side of the fire, was the skinny Dervish that he followed with a kind smile on his face and another man, The Shepherd. He had a long white beard, long hair, and wore a hand-woven hat—two large dogs sleeping close by. Nader then felt the same hat on his head; he was covered with two heavy hand-woven overcoats to keep him warm. The two were staring at him; they exchanged glances with each other and again turned to look at him with smiles on their faces. They continued observing him for a few minutes, and meanwhile, he realized he was itching quite badly. He lifted up the overcoat to see they had treated him with some kind of medicine to take care of his cuts. His feet were wrapped tightly with small ropes. Nader sat up, still trying to get his bearings and figure out where he was. The Shepherd poured hot milk into a muddy cup that was being boiled on the fire and handed it to him. The cup was not clean-looking like he was used to. But it did not matter. He took it and began drinking, but he had to wait a bit because it was hot. Amazingly, it was the most delicious drink he had ever tasted in his life up to then. The two were still smiling and glancing at each other as if they were talking with their smiles, but he did not understand their communications.

-Thank you,

Nader whispered to them. He wanted to know where he was. He had no idea how long he had been unconscious. Then, the Shepherd grabbed the bowl he had drunk from, cleaned it with his hand and wiped it off with the corner of his shirt, then poured some hot milk inside, and then pulled out some dry old bread. He then broke the bread into pieces and threw it inside the bowl. He took a wooden spoon, wiped it off with the corner of his shirt, then his hand, and mixed the bread and the milk. He placed it in front of Nader and gestured for him to eat. Again, he was talking to Nader in silent language so he could understand what he meant. He looked at the food being offered to him and knew that any other time or place he would not have touched food such as this, he would have worried about getting sick. But he did not think about it then, and he began to eat. It was the best food he'd had in a long time. He was not done with the food when they offered him a cup of tea. At the time, he didn't drink tea, but he could not refuse their offer.

As moments passed, he was gaining more strength and feeling more aware. It wasn't much longer that he started to get into their routine. What he did not understand was why the two would hardly talk. They would just sit, staring at the sheep, or drinking tea, or smoking their pipes. And each time they said anything, it was only one or two words, then silence again. Even more surprising were the two dogs also were completely silent. He tried many times to ask them questions or for something, and they would just smile or hand him whatever he was asking for. Then, they would just continue to smile and glance at each other and him. In fact, he had more communication with the sheep than the two men.

Within a few days, he was feeling much better and ventured out of the cave. For a few long minutes, he could hardly open his eyes. The bright light from the outside world had him blinded. Everything was covered with snow, and he could not see a thing that was not white. In the distance, he could recognize a few trees also covered with snow. God, it was beautiful; he had never seen so much snow. He sat in front of the cave, looking out at a part of nature he had never experienced before. Or maybe he had never had a chance to notice it. But now he had no other choice, it was all around him, and he was surrounded by this beauty, along with the cave, the sheep, and the smiling Dervish and a Shepherd and few dogs who also were silent, and they were asleep for as long as he remembered. What else would he have been doing that could have topped this experience? At home, he might have been speaking on the phone or grabbing a book and pretending to read it. Or maybe he would be watching a movie or play and feeling superior to others. He could be chasing a girl for an animalistic desire. Although he had experienced what he believed to be real love, he had not yet attained the manifestation of a relationship. He was longing for the experience of making love in the holiest way with his soulmate. He believed this would be a holy union combined with physical and spiritual meaning, but so far, this had been elusive. If he were back at home, maybe he would take a stand and use his energy and intellect to manipulate and lie for financial gain or power. None of those customs or men made traditions existed or had any place on the white-covered mountain. It was just you and nature, the breeze, the sun, the silence, and the peace. You had no choice but to just get into yourself, and that was all. You were the books, you were the play, you were the movies, and you were the talker on both sides of the telephone line. You were the TV, and you were your only relatives and friends to talk to, to communicate with, to ask and answer questions. You were the entire universe. So, he became the entire universe, and the entire universe was his being. He was the earth, and he was the air.

He sat for hours and hours every day and watched the snow melt down. He sat hours and hours listening and watching the sheep play and live in their own world. Sometimes he would talk to them and try to speak their language, but they never turned to answer him. He sat and watched the Shepherd and the Dervish smile, drink, and smoke. He tried to spoke to the dogs, but they only stared at him as though they understood him, but there was no answer. By now, he began to learn their language of silence and the sign of their smile, and he began to communicate with them in the same manner. But he knew inside that his smile was not natural like theirs. He was faking it, but he felt it growing more authentic every day.

One morning when he woke up, the Dervish who brought him to the cave was gone. He had no idea where he was, he could not even ask, and they would not understand him anyway. He just stared at the Shepherd, looking for an answer, and finally, for the first time, he smiled and said,

-He will be back…

And then again was silence. As the time passed, Nader was getting used to the silence. It was not boring to be there, and the fleas would not bother him after the Shepherd covered his body with some kind of mud they had concocted. He never could forget the time he was standing naked in front of all the sheep, covered with black and brown mud, his hands covering his private parts from the sheep's view and others. Then, after it was dried, he had to rub the mud off and put on the clothing that a third shepherd brought for him. One man used to bring food every so often for the shepherds who were guarding the sheep. On one occasion, he came, and Nader handed him everything he had in his wallet. He did not count how much money he had and placed the wallet in some area in the cave, later he completely forgot he had a wallet. What was interesting was that they never asked who he was and what he was doing there, like he was one of them, like he was nobody. And with the outfit Nader had, he was one of them; he did not look different from them. By now, his beard was getting longer. His hair was already long. In fact, he had not shaved or cut his hair for about six months before he arrived at the cave, making it all that much longer. Now with his traditional hat, new long white outfit, and heavy overcoat, he was a Dervish and a Shepherd, just like them. He began to help treat the sheep, feed them, take milk from them and boil it. One night he even delivered a baby sheep and named it Peace. He did not know why he chose the name. It just came to his mind, so simple that one would scoff at it, yet it was exactly what everyone needed. If anyone had come up the mountain from the outside world, they would not have known that he was not a shepherd or a Dervish. The only differentiating quality about him would have been that he would talk more. But he had learned to live with silence by now, he hardly said anything, and it was becoming more peaceful and pleasant. Then, one morning, when he opened his eyes, the Dervish that walked him to the cave was back, he suddenly appeared again sitting by the fire, and there was his radiant smile. Nader did not know where he had gone, why he came back, and what he was doing. He decided to watch him, and the next time he left, he followed him. It was a few days later, and there Nader was, following the silent Dervish. He was sure that Nader would get tired and stop, but he hadn't yet. After several hours, he turned and looked at Nader, then smiled. He was walking faster, and Nader was trying his best to keep up with him. He was traveling through hills and rocks, and at several points, he stopped and collected bushes and stacked them together, placing heavy rocks on them so the wind would not blow them away. And there he was, helping him. Nader was wondering why he was stacking bushes. Several days into their journey, there was still just silence, not even one word. In the beginning, he was a bit bored, but by now, he welcomed the silence, and in fact, it was teaching him to contemplate, to discover himself within. The muted voices and music that flows within different levels of energy, he was discovering, experiencing.

He remembered laying on a bare rock staring at the stars; there were so many of them. As he watched the shooting stars, he began to speak with them. It was the next day when he woke up; something felt very odd. He felt a heavy weight on his chest, and when he opened his eyes, he noticed a long fat snake lying over his chest, staring at him. He almost had a heart attack and could not move or breathe. To the side of the snake, he could see the faded image of Dervish sitting close by, watching in calmness and smiling. He was so calm that it seemed he was not even there. It was then that Nader wanted to speak. He wanted to yell and say something, but he was speechless. Then he remembered it is through the man's fear that the snake would attack and harm them. So, he closed his eyes and decided to feel no fear, and it seemed he had no tongue to speak and no memory of how to use any words; he was dumb and deaf, like he was really dead. Just then, the sound of beautiful Ney echoed into his soul, and Ney is an old traditional flute. Then he felt the heavyweight was gone. He opened his eyes and saw the Dervish was playing for the snake right in front of him. The snake moved away and disappeared through the rock like never was there. He knew the snake was gone, but for some reason unknown to him, suddenly, a fear captured his thought and soul like he could not breathe or move. He just lay there feeling dead. In fact, he did not need to play dead; it was as if his spirit had left his body, just for a moment. But that was not the only experience he had with a snake. It was a few months later that he realized why the Dervish was collecting and stacking the bushes on his way across the hills and mountain. On one cold afternoon, he motioned for Nader to help him get a couple of the stacks of the bushes they left behind and place them underneath a big rock on the bed of a small mountain, which he was making into a small cave. Nader grabbed the stack and lifted it up, and as he was carrying it, he realized it was extremely heavy; he almost couldn't carry the stack. He thought he had picked up several rocks with the bushes, so he dropped the stack to check. Suddenly a snake rolled around his right wrist. It was moving toward his shoulder. It was a good size, and black. He stopped in his tracks and moved nothing but his eyes to look for the Dervish, but he could not see him. Clueless about what to do, he almost had a heart attack again. Then something caught his attention. He heard the sound of a musical instrument again. It was a sound of the Ney. But this time, he noticed no one. It seemed as though the wind was playing the tone. He closed his eyes, digesting the melody, remembering his first experience with the other snake. It was not the snake he was afraid of; it was himself. It was fear within him. He shouldn't be worried. The snake was not going to harm him; it would leave if it felt no fear, just calm and peace. Then, Nader thought he saw the older wise man sitting on a rock, smiling. Fear completely left Nader's being. He opened his eyes to watch the snake unwind, slithering off and away. He turned around to see the Dervish sitting calmly, smiling, of course, in front of a fire he had just made. Nader joined him. They both sat, staring at each other. He realized the importance of collecting the bushes for the invaluable fire on cold nights.

He lay to rest with his eyes half-closed; he was watching the Dervish through the weak flame. The flame gave the Dervish a much more holy and peaceful complexion. Nader was thinking, so many days and nights came and left, he did not know how many, but it seemed like a lot. He was following the Dervish all through the hills, accepting food from people on the way, surviving in the caves and hills, and having the time of his life. It was as though time was never a factor, like time never existed. He was just into the discovery of his soul, of his being, his connection to the earth, sun, and moon. Night and day, there was nothing else to do, you were forced to find something within you to be involved with, or you would have gone crazy. The mountain, the cave, and the total package had provided a safe haven for him to do just that. It was the best medicine he could have taken, and he did not believe there was any other way he would have healed from his internal and external wounds. He was spending peaceful nights on the hills, underneath the rocks, inside different shaped caves.

One of the places that the Dervish took him during his journey was an old monument situated on the top of a small mountain. To get there, one had to walk for a few days, and people used to ride donkeys, especially older men and women. But it was wintertime, and no one was there. It was just the two of them and the simple grave. He does not know who had died there, but there was something very spiritual about the place like it would cause time to stand still. It was there that Nader realized getting to the "light," to God and salvation, one must follow simplicity, to detach oneself from the material world allows a person to become attached to existence. He thought of all the enormous monuments built, immersed in gold and silver—such luxury, extravagance, things God does not need. Using religion to build wealth for man-made things is not what God wanted. Nader fell asleep picturing all the gold wiped from the planet. Oh, what a sight, what a sight. Then, an exceptionally mystical night came. He was laying down staring into the rain, and he had two vivid dreams. In the first dream, he was chasing a soccer ball. The second one was very different. There were two female angels, tall and beautiful. One was in a long green silk dress, and the other wore a long blue silk dress. They were flying him into the air, one on each side of him. He was mystified; they reached a building made from simple stone, which was sitting in the middle of nowhere. There were a few people walking around.

-This is the house of God.

The angel in green declared. Then the angel in blue continued,

-You asked to see it. Here you go.

He was baffled but very calm, enjoying the peaceful sensation of flying and the inner awakening that was coming about. Then, a soft breeze hit his face, and he opened his eyes, suddenly he knew he was not flying. He was lying by the fire in the cave, awakened from his dream. He was bewildered, dizzy, and did not know what had just happened. He only knew he did not ask to see the house of God and wondered if he had wished for something in his sleep. At the time, he used to go into deep meditations when he was staring at the fire, or blankets of white snow, or the pouring rain. By now, he was awake, but his eyes were closed; thinking about the angels, he felt something different within. He felt another presence. He opened his eyes, and from the corner of his eye, he realized the older wise man was sitting by the fire. This was the same older wise man that used to come to visit him in his childhood when he was sad. It had been a long time since he had seen him, and there he was, sitting across from him. His peaceful smile had always brought calmness and peace into his heart. He looked around for the Dervish, who was nowhere to be found. He does not know why he closed his eyes, but the feeling of peace and comfort that came to him was immeasurable. He could see the light of the flame from the fire, and slowly he opened his eyes again. But he no longer could see the older wise man anywhere. There was only the fire. He knew for sure the Dervish he followed was there that night before they had fallen asleep. There was now this burning question, but no one to ask to get an answer. The answer had to come from within him. He knew there had to be a reason for the older wise man to show up. Perhaps they were giving him a message, and he was not getting it, or if he was getting it, he did not understand. He only knew that every day he was more at peace and more relieved from his anger, detached from the material world.

When he would spend time reflecting on this experience of being on the mountain with the dervishes, he could not remember how he spent all those days and nights, except that he was watching the snow, feeling enraptured by nature. Maybe he had spent most of his time in deep meditation. He recalls staring into the flames for hours, and then he would see things. It was like searching for an unknown address, and every day he was getting closer to finding the address. During one meditation, he asked for an answer to appear to his conscience memory. But still, no answer appeared. And now, he was left alone on his journey. The Dervish was gone like he was never there. He had vanished, and Nader did not know where he was. He was left alone with his questions but guessed he had to find the answers on his own. He began walking to find a cave, but he had no luck. He did not know what direction to take. It was days later that finally, he found himself wandering beside a dirt road in the middle of nowhere. He began to walk along a tree-lined creek; a few hours later that an old beat-up truck approached from the distance. The dust covered him as the truck passed, but when the dust settled, he noticed the truck had stopped, and when he reached the truck, there was an older driver gesturing if he wanted a ride. He climbed on without any thought and was on the way, staring into the sky.

He was thinking nothing lasts forever, unhappy to be leaving, departing for home. Several hours later, the truck came to a halt in front of a roadside tea house. The old driver was staring at him to see if he wanted anything to eat. He opened his mouth to say the first words he had spoken in months,

-Milk...

He was given milk and then informed the driver he had no clue where he was and needed to get to Tehran. He left for a few minutes and came back with another man, gesturing for Nader to go with him. Soon he was sitting on a bus, in a row of seats all by himself. No one wanted to be seated next to a bare-footed dirty homeless wanderer. Everyone stared at him as he must have appeared quite strange. He was speaking fluent Farsi with no accent, but he was in a Dervish's outfit. The two did not match. He then remembered he had left his wallet in the cave and had forgotten to take it with him. Now he was on his way to Tehran and had to come up with a story as to why he had been gone so long. It would not be easy how he could explain what had happened to him. Could he not remember most of it himself? It would not be easy. How he could explain what had happened to him. He could not remember most of it himself.

*****

Chapter 20

You Can Run, But Where Can You Hide?

Back home in Tehran, the happy reunion lasted for just a few days. And again, his life turned to business as usual, struggling with whom he wanted to be and whom everyone else and society would require for him to be. All eyes were on him what he did. Now even the Savak has doubt about him and what he was up to and watched him closely. And for sure, Abbass had to do something. After all, in their eyes, Nader was abusing the privileges given to him. Their thinking was that he was naïve enough to let himself be used by anti-government activists, or he was directly involved, playing politics by acting innocent. Any way you looked at it, the situation was messy. Soon he knew what his options were. The choice given to him, he had to leave the country. Of course, his brothers had much to do with his departure. He could get out of being thrown in jail. But in his eyes, he was innocent, and he did not mean any harm to the government; he was just writing and doing what he felt right. Besides, how could he prove to them that he was living with a Dervish all these times? Would they never believe him? No one had ever done such things in a situation that Nader and his family were in. Was it unheard of? Even if they wanted to believe him, how could he find such Dervish to prove it to them? He even did not know where the Shephard and the cave were. By now, it was the end of summer, and all sheep were out, not at the cave. In fact, he could not fit in with the ideology of the anti-government activists either. The two major anti-government groups followed two paths. The path of communism, which he was against, and the other one was that of radical religious activists, which he was against. After all, his works were more about making fun of wrong traditions, trying to bring the topics to the table for discussion. So, the only choice he could see was to leave the country, and it was not easy for him to do so. First, he was very close to his mother; the two of them were like one soul in two bodies. Then, his concern was Forogh. Now he was both her mother and her father. He was her happiness and hope after the death of her mother. His older brother was now living with his new wife in a different city. His new wife was actually a nice lady; she became good friends with Nader. They used to talk all the time. Nader was trying to bring peace between her and the family. But it was not easy. He believed she also was abused by his brother's radical military behavior, and sometimes he felt guilty that it had to be him visiting her house, asking her parents to permit her to marry Abbass. Yes, his brother asked Nader to go, of course, his mother was with him, but he was doing all the talking, a favor for his brother, while at the same time, Boloor never left his mind. But Nader believed the past must be left behind, and life must go on.

The visa for Nader was arranged by the American consular that also was their neighbor. It was up to him to set the time of departure, and he realized that if he did not leave, he would harm his mother and Forogh more. He was sure he would end up in jail or would end up dead by religious radicals somehow. Besides, now he had more reason to take off; Fariba and Hussein were both in America. So, his choice was to go to America, and he chose Los Angeles because of them. The decision was made, and it was the night before he was leaving that he broke the news to his mother. He was concerned that she would be sad and worried. Supposedly she was not supposed to know about Nader's departure. But Nader could see that she seemed different, and she was more withdrawn into herself. She was asking him to spend more time with Forogh and wanted to take every opportunity to be with him.

Then the time for truth came. It was late into the night, and he tucked Forogh in her bed and kissed her goodnight. The time finally came for him to sit with his mother alone. He didn't know, but she had known all along he was leaving. She had him sit by her and began to stroke his hair as he was lying on her feet, just like when he was a little child at the farm. She told him the story of the unknown tall skinny man who came to the farm and spent some time in their small one-room mosque, the one their family had built for poor and travelers to pray and rest at night. She had tears in her eyes as she began to talk,

> -When you were about three years old, there was a tall, skinny, old man staying in the mosque for awhile with his wife and child. Your brother, Bijan, was going through some kind of final exam....

She did not need to tell him the rest; for some reason, he recalled the memory, just like it had happened yesterday. He remembered Bijan was fighting with their mother to get more food to take to the old skinny man and his family. He told their mother that by helping the family, God would help his brother with his exam. His mother said that she had already taken care of this family, but Bijan insisted on gathering more food and clothing to give them. When nighttime came, many of the villagers would gather around the Tall Skinny Man, and he would tell them about their future and even past, revealing hidden things about people. Nader remembered one of his female cousins was not convinced of this man's authenticity and tried to tell her mother that he was a big fake. But his mother believed that this man was valid. Later he heard their helper, Beby, point out to his mother that the cousin didn't like the man because he asked her to not be present at the mosque because he thought she was not a good soul. This really angered his cousin. The tall skinny man would not talk when certain people were present. If someone was not thought to be kind or have a good soul, the man would remain silent when that person was near him. His cousin had a bad reputation on the farm, and the tall skinny man was right about her. She had kicked her mother-in-law out into the street, causing the woman to beg for food in other villages.

One night he was at the mosque with the tall skinny man, Bijan, his mother, and several other villagers. The villagers had been brought by

Bijan to sit and hear their fortunes told, and then they would give a donation to help the tall skinny man and his family. The people were sitting around the man while Nader was playing with the older skinny man's son right behind and in between the tall skinny man and Bijan. The two little boys were in their own little world and were laughing and having fun playing. Nader guessed they laughed too loud because suddenly Bijan reached over and smacked Nader real hard on his butt. It hurt badly, and he was hurt but said nothing. Then, suddenly the tall skinny man, who had his back to Nader, without seeing what had happened, stopped talking. For a long moment, there was dead silence. The skinny man was staring at a wooden mat covering the floor, and he looked very intense. Then, his body began shaking, and he asked everyone to please leave. Nader was only three years old, but somehow, he could clearly remember everything when his mother was reminding him of the event. Nader remembered thinking he could hear a loud cry coming from him, although he was silent. His butt still hurt from Bijan smacking him, but he was not crying now. His eyes were fixed on the man. Bijan was staring at him with a stern look on his face, and he was sure he was blaming Nader for disrupting things. Bijan raised his hand to spank him again, but before he could, the tall skinny man yelled, "Don't touch him!" Bijan's hand was frozen in the air. Then, the tall skinny man asked Bijan to leave and for his mother to stay. Bijan took Nader outside and left his mother alone with the tall, skinny man and his wife. After several minutes, his mother came out. She seemed okay but a little concerned. Walking home, carrying Nader in her arms, Bijan could not contain his curiosity about what the tall skinny man had said to their mother, but she did not mention anything to Bijan or Nader about anything he had discussed with her. She just told Bijan he should never raise his hand to Nader again.

That night, Beby and his mother were examining Nader's back as if they were looking for something. They would continue shining a light on the back of his shoulders for days to come. He didn't know what they were looking for, but they were intent on finding something that seemed important to them. Then, his mother decided to prevent anyone else from looking at his back. Now, as he was about to leave the country, his mother disclosed the secret that the tall skinny man had told her. Nader was watching her, still confused. He was worried about how he would tell her he was leaving Iran. He was not leaving by choice. To his relief and amazement, his mother said that she knew.

> -The tall man said there is a mark on your back. It means that you are being marked, and whoever should hurt you, they will be hurt worse. Then, he said that one day you will leave for a faraway place, and it is your destiny to do something very important there.

Nader listened attentively as his mother continued,

> -The man said I will die while you are away, and I will not see you again. That is why I knew you were leaving.

He was spellbound as his mother continued this story. She revealed another experience she had had when he was very sick, and she continued with him, hanging on to every word.

> -One night, you were very sick, and it was raining very hard. There was just Beby and I taking care of you. I thought that you passed away. I was crying with Beby, and then out of nowhere, this older white-bearded man appeared. He looked like a Shepherd. He asked Beby to go get some hot tea. Then, he turned to me and said to not worry. You would not lose him to death now, but I would lose you to a faraway land. He said that you were going to go very far away, and you had to go. He placed a sugar cube in your mouth. You began to cry, and Beby became scared and fainted. She was stunned as I just watched the old man walk away. I guess I had fainted also, and it was a few hours later when I opened my eyes and found you playing as though nothing had ever been wrong with you. I had never seen the older man before, and I never saw him again. But that's how I knew you were leaving, and I was planning on going back to the farm after you left. I do not like it here in Tehran.

He was baffled by his mother's story but relieved at the same time that she was not upset that he was going away. The content of the story she revealed was not important to him. What was important was that the story or event helped her handle it all. He felt that he could say goodbye to this memory now. Then, she made it much easier for him as she continued to speak,

> -It is God's will for you to leave, and I have to live with it. But you must promise me one thing -- You never disrespect women, and whatever they want, just give it to them, then God will take care of you... and that is the only thing I want from you, son...

And without question, he had to accept the promise. Then, Nader went to sleep next to Forogh for a few hours, knowing when he saw her again, she would be grown.

As the morning of his departure arrived, many had spent the night at his mother's house where he was. His bags were packed, and relatives wanted to take photos as it was tradition. He could see that his mother and sister Parry were hiding their tears from him; He knew they had cried all night. But he only had one thought, and it was about three-year-old Forogh. He could see the change on her face. He had been so busy for the last ten days getting ready to depart that he hadn't seen her as much, although he had tried his best to spend as much time as he could with her. He couldn't grasp if she knew he was leaving, but later, he realized he was dead wrong, and she knew all along. He could see her being quiet and slightly plaintive for the last ten days prior, and he didn't know how he would be able to go through with leaving her. He was looking all over for her, but he could not find her. He went to his room and sat behind his desk to call his sister to see if they had taken her to their house. Before his phone call was answered, he felt someone touch his legs from underneath his desk. He leaned down to see Forogh hiding, looking at him as if she had a mountain of sadness in her eyes. He was holding onto the receiver, and his sister was yelling,

-Hello…hello?

But he could not hear her. He hung up the phone and moved underneath the desk to sit next to Forogh. He was full of heavy guilt about leaving her. He did not know what to do, and soon tears were running down his cheek. By now, his mother was looking for him and wanted to tell him to spend some time with Forogh, not knowing he was already with her. Others joined the search, and minutes later, his room was filled with many relatives looking at the two of them in tears. It was his mother who walked in and yelled at everyone to leave and let them have their peace. But soon, he was on the way to the airport with her sitting in his lap, holding on to his designer shirt that he designed himself. A few hours later, he was flying away from Forogh, from everyone, from Iran, his beloved land. It took him a few years to recover from the sadness of leaving that little girl. Tears still gather when he recalls those memories.

*****

Chapter 21

His Second Home Land, Is It In Exile Or Born Of A New Life For Him?

There was dead silence on the airplane. It was almost as if he wasn't aware of the other passengers on board. He was lying back in his seat with a myriad of thoughts swirling around in his head. He was headed to an unknown, uncertain new beginning. He had heard such a wide range of stories about this land known as America, and the reports were greatly mixed. At the time, it was a dream of practically every young boy or girl in Iran to go to America, a dream that many could only imagine but never experience. He was not sure if he should be happy or not, given the bad and good things he had heard about this foreign land. He was happy, though, that finally he would escape all his problems and was happy to join Hussein once again. Maybe, he would find Fariba. But Nader loved his home so, the smell of the dirt, the fragrance of the flowers, the taste of the fruit. He knew he would close his eyes on many occasions and see what he no longer had. He felt a hand touch his shoulder, and he came out of his deep thought. He turned to see a girl about seven years old holding a magazine.

-My mother asked if you can sign it for her.

She said. He glanced at the page she was holding. He gazed at a photo of himself. There were a couple more inside as well. He turned and looked to see who her mother was,

> -She was there, the night that they wanted to arrest you... in Kerman... she said she was among the people who held hands to keep the police away from you...

The voice of the cute girl was whispering into his ear as he stared at the pretty woman in her late twenties, sitting, and two rows away from him smiling a hello. He signed the magazine, handed it back, and the little girl walked away after two more words,

> -Thank you.

It was then that a sad thought captured his soul. He could have been a great artist in his home land, he could have helped educate his people, and this opportunity was taken away from him. This thought was eating through him slowly, like a worm to an apple. What can he possibly do in America to satisfy his artistic urges and passion? How could he find a way to express his creative and innovative ideas in a new culture that he knew nothing about except what he had seen in movies? And they were mostly "B" movies on top of it. Movies with very little authentic meaning that spoke about a real subject. America was known to Iranians mostly by these commercial "B" movies which were known for coming from Hollywood. Whether or not they all were Hollywood blockbusters is up for debate.

It was common to hear people discuss their experiences about visiting America. Often you would hear stories about Black people in America. They didn't know the term African-American in Iran; politically correct terms were unknown, no matter the ethnicity. And this does not mean that people meant it in a derogatory way as well. One has to imagine a place where, generally, everyone has the same features. This is accompanied by the same culture and traditions. There was not a large population of people from different ethnic groups, nor were there a large number of tourists.

Many may have gone their whole lives without meeting someone of African descent. At the time, there were crazy stories, urban myths of Tehran, about how black people would rob you, shoot and kill you, over anything. If they asked you for something, you just give it to them. Nader learned quickly that propaganda came in many different packages, and most stories were just sad, twisted truths, far from reality. He was amazed at how stereotypes traveled so far and so intensely. Also, there were stories about sex, that everything was open in America. He remembered one person was saying that if a girl invites you to her house and you go in and do not sleep with her, her parents will think there is something wrong with you. They were told you could get rich fast in America. You could just buy or rent a dry-cleaning machine, install it right on the sidewalk, and you just go every other day and collect the coins. The rest of your time is having fun with ladies. This was the image of America they had been given: sex, violence, money, and unlimited fun.

The plane landed in New York, and Nader had to rush to catch a plane to Los Angeles. As he ran, the movie poster for Rocky displayed under lights caught his attention. He kept going, looking at Rocky when he remembered before he gets on the plane to Los Angeles, he had to contact Hussein to pick him up from the airport, which he had not done yet. He didn't speak English. Unfortunately, he only knew a couple of words like yes, no, and how are you. He also knew the sentence, "It is good to be good." He asked someone to write that quote for the play he did, the adaptation of the John Steinbeck book, Of Mice and Men. He was going to be late for his flight, and he didn't even know where to go or how to ask for help, standing in the middle of the giant JFK airport, holding two bags and carrying one on each shoulder, wondering which direction to head. One of the bags was so heavy that he was leaning to his side. It was full of pistachios, about thirty pounds of it, his mother forced him to take it, and she made sure he took it inside the terminal. Just then, Nader heard the words, "Bye, bye." It was the cute little girl from the plane holding her mother's hand. She touched him on the hand again to say goodbye. Then, the mother spoke a couple of words, he began to walk with them, and he told her about his problem, she was a great help. Her name was Ziba. She took the initiative to call Hussein and let him know Nader was on the way to Los Angeles. She then showed him where to go; she even walked him to the gate and left. She had been living in New York for few years and knew her way around. Nader was grateful for the help. It was nighttime when the plane landed in Los Angeles, and Nader followed the crowd, carrying all his bags. The pistachio bag was so heavy that by now, he had no control of his right shoulder; in fact, the weight had ripped off the sleeve of his white designer shirt. He did not know what to do, embarrass, but realized no one was looking, no one cared. That was the first difference he noticed between America and his homeland. Everyone in America is rushing, minding their own business. They do not care what you do or what you wear. Soon he passed through customs leaving the window with his many suitcases and bags. As he stood in the middle of the crowded Los Angeles airport, he was hopelessly looking for Hussein but could not find him. He was getting worried, especially when he saw many African-Americans. What if Hussein never showed up? What would he do with all his suitcases? With thoughts swirling, he began to walk through the airport, hoping to see someone familiar. Then the pistachio bag fell off the cart; while he was placing it back on, he noticed Hussein rushing through the crowd looking for him. Nader began calling him, pushing the cart with full force. But Hussein was getting away, so he had to speed up to catch up with him. Just when he was getting close, a young woman rushed across in front of him, also carrying her suitcases. He had to come to an immediate stop as he yelled for Hussein; this caused the bag of pistachios to fall again. This time it landed right in front of the cart, on the floor, and broke wide open. The fresh, moist pistachios scattered all over the floor, flooding the dirty tile. He was motionless and embarrassed, like he did not want to be there. The crowd stopped, and it was two African-Americans who approached him first. Despite his worried thoughts, they approached to help, not to kill. Luckily Hussein had heard him and turned straight around, headed towards him. By now, many others began to collect the pistachios for him, but he still could not react.

-Welcome to America!

Hussein's voice with a sarcastic tone and a smile on his face was right in front of him. Nader was happy to see him, so he reached to hug and kiss Hussein as they do in Iran, and he pulled back from him. For a moment, Nader was so insulted and confused, wondering if Hussein didn't like him any longer. As he was helping to collect the pistachios, he turned to Nader,

-Here men do not hug or kiss. Everyone takes it wrong, as if you are gay, no exceptions; just a handshake.

He was relieved and surprised as he continued to collect pistachios. Hussein noticed his ripped sleeve hanging. He reached over and ripped it off completely and handed it to him.

-No one here cares if you have it or not or if you are even naked.

From the moment he landed, he began to understand how different things were; everyone moving at the speed of light, chaos, blinders on, trying not to get left behind. Sleeves, who cares! It was so much different than home. He learned not to believe any rumors until it was proven by experience. Comparing America to home, it was as if Iran was going in slow motion. He noticed Hussein was now different. From the beginning of his arrival, Nader could see a big change in him; he could feel he was not the same Hussein he knew six years ago. He began wondering if America would change people, every person that touched its soil. He did not have to wait long to see the new parts of Hussein. It was not much time later when they were sitting in his green fiat, going down the freeway. Nader could see Hussein was watching to see if he would be impressed with the freeway systems and how fast traffic was going, and the number of cars. Then, he surprised Nader with a song he began to sing. He had never seen Hussein sing or dance; it was the first time. He was amazed at how he sang with passion and soul. Nader could feel he really meant what he was singing, and what was more surprising to Nader were the lyrics. It was one of the songs written for the anti-shah activists who were chased and killed or captured by government forces in the forest in the north of Iran. It would never have crossed his mind that Hussein would even consider joining the anti-shah forces, and more shocking to Nader was the communist group, which was the most radical one. He had heard about it from other friends but did not give it serious thought. However, he knew Hussein's family background, which was pretty intense, and Islam and communism did not fit in the same envelope. At the same time, Nader was confused by the freeway system, and he was more confused about Hussein. In that moment, he was exhausted from his twenty-four-hour trip that he did not know what to do or what to say. But Hussein did not stop. From the first hour, he hit him with his ideology, his mission to change the Iranian government, to get rid of the evil shah who was an American puppet. These were his words that followed his song. The song was the warm-up for Nader, and the speech came right after. And Hussein meant business.

Soon they arrived in Westwood by UCLA. He was living in a two-bedroom apartment with his brother and a friend. They walked in, and there was Hussein's father and stepmother sitting waiting for them. It was the first time Nader had seen them after Hussein's departure from Iran, and he did not know they were in America visiting Hussein. He was told by Hussein they were waiting for him, and it was the next day he realized why. The first night he found out what he needed to now know about Hussein; he was heavily involved with the communist group and had completely changed into a radical individual. If you were not aligned with his ideology, you were out. He did not hesitate to tell Nader that he had wasted his time all his life by being a writer and filmmaker and that his brother is evil because he was a member of the Savak. He went on to say that Nader should join his group and use his talents to accomplish something substantial, which would be the only way to help their people. Luckily, Nader passed out while Hussein was still talking; the other friend Abbdi, who also was staying with them, was now asleep as well. Hussein's apartment was being used by his parents, so they were staying at another apartment they had rented for a short time. By now, Hussein, who realized he had no effect on Nader, was getting more passionate or maybe more frustrated. What he did not know was that Nader had changed a lot since the two were together as well. He was much calmer and more reserved, and Hussein could not understand anything about the world of spirituality. The two were completely on opposite fronts. In fact, Nader was not sure with what he had experienced so far that he would be able to survive in America. But there was one hope left to keep him positive, and that was locating Fariba.

The next day, Hussein's father approached Nader to talk after Hussein had gone to school. He began to talk about the past and reflect on the good and bad aspects of life. This was the first time Hussein's father actually spoke to Nader. It felt like the first time he considered him an actual good person. Before Nader would have a chance to say hello and goodbye, he began to talk. Soon Nader could see the strong feeling of concern in his voice; he was trying to explain to him why Nader should have a talk with Hussein. He also wanted to know why Nader was in America in the first place. Hussein had talked about it the night before, but briefly, the reason for his father being in America was to convince him to get out of the communist group and sign a letter of apology to the Shah. He wanted Hussein to get married to the lady he was in love with and now dating. Hussein had not told him about her yet, and Nader really wanted to know about his new love. His father was the best source to get the entire story since he was asking for help. Nader thought Hussein had a girlfriend, an American one who was still in Iran with her family, looking for her father. But he was hearing from Hussein's father in complete detail that Hussein was in love with Shirin Neshat, the daughter of Commander Ali Neshat, the head of Shah's personal army called "The Guard the Javidan." But when she went back to Iran for her summer vacation and revealed to her father that she was going to marry Hussein, her father would not let her leave the country, and she was stuck in Iran. So, a condition was offered to Hussein, and if he accepted it, he would be allowed to marry this girl. The condition stated that Hussein was to write an apology letter to the shah and leave and bash the communist party. They also offered him a ministry position within five years, and they meant this as a serious offer. For this, he would be able to marry his love. So, his father was sent to America to bring Hussein back, and it just happened to be at the same time that Nader had arrived.

Despite the fact that Nader did not know he nor Hussein's father could change a thing, he promised his father that he would try to talk sense into Hussein. He was sincere with this promise because he was completely against communist ideology reining in Iran. But his efforts were unsuccessful and caused a rift between him and Hussein. He did not want his friendship ruined by their different beliefs, so he backed off. A week later, Nader left Hussein and moved to another city. Later he found out Hussein's father left without any success. Hussein had come to Nader and asked him if he wanted to buy some stuff that belonged to his girlfriend Shirin; she would not be coming back. It was then that Nader found out the Fiat Hussein was driving belonged to his love, and whatever income Hussein had was used on furthering his cause. Nader bought a black and white Sony TV and some other small stuff and paid Hussein whatever he asked, but he didn't buy the car. Regrettably, Hussein's love never came back; Later, he heard from Hussein, she was forced to marry one of the up-and-coming high-ranking officers underneath her father's compound. This was like pouring salt in a wound for Hussein, it had created a personal animosity in Hussein's heart toward the Shah, and Nader knew that the Shah probably did not even know about Hussein or his story. But no matter what would have happened in Iran at the time, even if it were done by the clergies, the Shah was the one to be blamed, he was the leader, and leaders get blamed for it all.

*****

Chapter 22

Still Searching For A Childhood Crush A Decade Later...

Soon Nader could hardly spend time with Hussein. Their conversations always revolved around ideology; they never had a conversation that was not heavy. In addition, Hussein constantly criticized Nader for searching for Fariba. He called him a silly fool who needed to get over it and join the cause. Nader was spending quite a bit of time at UCLA hoping to find Fariba, to have at least one glance. But Nader also had his reasons for not joining any government group out of the country or inside the country. He had made a promise not to. Besides, he did not wish to jeopardize being able to go back to Iran and see his family, to see his niece Forogh and his mother. Most importantly, he did not believe in the communist ideology. Nader was a loner with no real home. Now, it was time to learn English. It would be to his advantage to learn for many reasons, so he rented a room from two kind older ladies to soak up those daily conversations. The older woman was in her seventies; they both called her Mom. The second was her daughter Janet, who was in her late forties. They both were so kind and fun. He remembered Mom used to sit in the corner of the living room on her wheelchair and point to the photos on the wall describing each for him. One was very important to her; it was a photo of her great grandfather, who had happened to be a former president of the United States. He could never remember which one, but anytime she would get to that photo, he could see a smile of pride in her eyes. There were two big dogs as well, a Doberman and a German shepherd. Some of his friends would not come to visit him because of the dogs. Janet would tell him the story about Mom in the Second World War; she was in Europe working for the American army. She told him so many stories that Nader almost felt like he had been around all those years as well. He began to visit with all their friends and join in all their gatherings. Nader would help Mom and take her around, and they enjoyed each other's company. It was about that time that Nader decided to stand on his feet and support himself and not accept any money from home. Getting money from home always came with some kind of attachment, and of course, be followed by many demands, suggestions, and expectations. Basically, he was still being controlled from Iran by his brother. He had to break away from and do him, free of any influences. The first thing was to get serious, to accept the fact that he may never go home, this realistically, was permanent. He realized his soul would be dead soon. He needed to stop wasting time and do something useful. Nader had never really worked a day in his life; getting a job would be interesting, to say the least. He always had money, and he only knew how to spend money, but not how to make money. In fact, that was the biggest challenge of his life; learning how to make money while working an average job, like the other ninety percent of the world's population. He also thought if he ended up staying in America and wants to break into film, he must get familiar with their customs and culture here. He had to keep the news of him getting a job from his mother, and it would depress her. He had to cut himself off from the people who knew his family, and that meant leaving Los Angeles. He picked San Francisco. Settling in San Francisco was not easy; it was complicated getting a place to live and looking for a job.

By now, Nader could speak a few words of English and was learning more every day. Sitting in his studio apartment, thinking what kind of a job to take was fun. When he looked back on this, it was amusing; a grown man, acting like a sixteen-year-old, trying to figure out what to do with his life. Once he heard Hussein comment that America means getting dirty in order to learn how life works, from the poor to the rich, all had either washed dishes or pumped gas. There was not any shame to work at any job. This was way different than Iran. It wasn't like back home where if you are from a rich family or a family of high influence, it would be shameful to work as a laborer in a gas station or restaurant. It would be an insult to the family's reputation; you would bring shame to your family. Nader already loved America because of this standard alone. Everything was so much more relaxed and real in this regard. So, he decided to take the dirtiest job he could think of. He could learn how America had become America. At the time, he felt America was like a giant computer that he stumbled into. He could not figure out how the system worked, so organized and easy when compared to Iran and even Europe. He contemplated what kind of disaster would ensure if this huge complicated computer broke down. America was the best guide and example of success. So, he had to learn how this system worked and to understand that he felt he had to do every kind of work he could get into. A list of a plethora of jobs was sitting in front of him; the first on the list was dishwashing.

He began to hit the streets, knocking on doors of any restaurant. His second try landed him a job as a dishwasher, and the next day he was as dirty as he ever had ever been in his life. It was surprising to him that he did not feel bad. In fact, he felt happy and proud, and the first thing he did was to document his work by taking a photo stamped with the date. But the job only lasted four days, and he was fired due to a fight he had with the manager. The results were no pay from the work he had done because he had to pay for some broken dishes. The fight started because Nader had not realized he got a job at a gay bar. Late one night, he was approached by the manager, and he shockingly put his hands on him. When Nader hit him, he broke a stack of dishes. Being gay at the time in Iran was unheard of, so the first time he encountered gay men was quite a surprising experience.

The second job he got was at a gas station working the night shift pumping gas. He was doing well, and for this photo, he had an outfit and posed proudly when the picture was taken. All the photos were hidden and guarded so they would not reach Iran or his mother. It was a late spring night, and he was helping a customer. He noticed a white beat-up van stop by the building, and a short but buff African American man got out and approached him. He was creepy looking and Nader thought he was on drugs or something.

　-Hey man, where is your head?

The man asked. Nader didn't know if he should answer him or not. He was asking himself why he wanted to know where his head was when he could see his head sitting on his neck. So, he ignored him and walked away to help an older African American lady who was sitting in the car waiting to get her gas. The man followed him as Nader went to charge the fee to her credit card,

　-Hey asshole, I am talking to you. I asked you where your head is?

Nader felt anger in his voice, so he had to respond,

　-This is my head on my neck. Don't you see it?

Nader thought he should act tough, or the man might go farther and start a fight.

　-You mother fucker, I will be back, and I'll show you where your mother fucking head is.

He looked around in anger, walked to his car, and took off as the smoke from his tires covered the station. Nader walked to the African American lady to hand back her credit card and the bill for her to sign. Then she asked,

　-You must be new here?

　-Yes, I am.

　-What he meant by a head was the bathroom.

-So why did he not ask in regular English language so people could understand? How would I know the head is the bathroom?

-You do not need to be worried. Soon you will know more than enough.

Then, she drove off, and Nader walked to the office, thinking why he did not take the time to find out what he meant. Minutes had not even passed when he noticed the same white van stopped right in front of the office, and the same man jumped out. He kicked the office door open and entered holding a gun, pointing it at Nader, his friends right behind him with one still sitting in the driver's seat.

-Yeah, mother fucker, now I'll show you where your fucking head is. Get in the fucking head.

And before Nader could react, he pushed him forward into the bathroom, commanding him to put his head in the toilet. Nader was in a state of shock and did not know what to do. He had never been assaulted in this manner or treated that low before. The man continued yelling as he pushed Nader down, unzipping his pants. Nader was leaning over the toilet. A foul stench mixed with bleach filled his nostrils. He did not know if he wanted to rape him or not. He could feel the gun on his head and was thinking, *What if he pulls the trigger? Do you want to get killed or insulted*? The man, still cussing, shadowed over Nader's body. Nader could now feel hot water hitting his head. He just closed his eyes and tried with all his force and energy to hold back his anger and frustration, to not do something stupid, as his head was getting warmer. He could barely hear the police siren from outside getting closer and becoming louder. Or either, he hardly could hear the man's friend, who appeared in the bathroom door and yelled at him to come on and leave the motherfucker alone. But the man continued to pee on Nader's head. By then, he had had it, and Nader felt so insulted that dying was not important anymore. He did not feel like a man at that moment but an animal. An animal that wanted to attack, ripping the head off his enemy. But his time with the Dervish and meditations came to help and just closed his eyes and killed the anger within in. Just then, several police cars came to a stop at the station, and several officers suddenly broke into the bathroom, their guns pointed at them. Nader did not know what to do or what to say. He just moved to the sink and held his head underneath the hot water. A few minutes later, when he lifted up his head, through the water dripping through his hair and covering his eyes, he saw the middle-aged African American woman who he just helped. She was standing by him and handed him several paper towels to dry up and she was apologizing to him for what had happened. Later he found out her name was Mikki. When she was driving away, she noticed the van waiting on the corner, when they entered as they did she called the police. That was his last night working at the gas station, but Mikki and Nader ended up being best friends for years to come. Fate had brought him a great friend. She had a small corner restaurant, and it became his regular stop. Anytime he was frustrated about anything, he would sit in his regular chair, and there was Mikki to talk him out of frustration. Nader used to blame himself for not fighting to defend his dignity and his manhood even if it cost him his life. And more importantly, she was also involved with few filmmakers, and that was a great opportunity for Nader to get into the film business. It seemed as though the moment he placed his feet in America, all his spiritual power was out the window, and he did not know why. He knew it could have helped him in that situation to be patient, grounded. But for some reason, that part of him felt congested, hazy.

His other jobs were at McDonald's, Burger King, and selling vacuums door to door. With all of these jobs, he still could hardly speak English. The more time that passed, the more he was getting used to America but was still not convinced he should settle here. Soon he was feeling the pressure of financial shortage, still refusing help from home. He had told them that he was doing well. In fact, he had lied quite a bit just to make his mother happy. He talked to his mother and Forogh on the phone almost every other day. This wasn't even enough for his mother, and she wanted him to talk to her every day. But phone calls alone were breaking his back financially. Nader was always very busy working; he was also attending school to continue his studies as well. He had to take classes, otherwise, his visa would expire, and he could not remain in the States any longer. He decided to enter a graduate program. School was the only thing keeping him on American soil. His life was not what he thought it would be and certainly not what he wanted. In the crevices of his mind, he felt as though this whole situation would be temporary; the fact that he may never return home and continue doing films was not a valid conclusion. He wanted to do films, and there he was, in Hollywood, with a million-plus people crashing around with the same dream. Besides, his English was not good enough, and he had no connections. He tried several times, and everything he wanted to do, you had to have a manager or agent. If it wasn't hard enough locking down a good agent, you had to be a member of the union too, which required previous work in T.V. Or the cinema. The doors were all closed.

    Now he was falling into depression, something big in his life missing if he would not get a chance to do his art. It was like a sickness you have, and there is no medicine or doctor to cure you, and you will gradually die within in and out. It seemed he was in his biggest turmoil in his life. He closed his eyes and was lost in thought and hopelessness and fell into sleep. It was then that he had a dream that helped him to get his hope back. In the dream, he found himself at a young age when he was first year in dramatic art college in their large garden in front of their family house at the farm that he was borned and spent untill he was 6 years old. He was with several of his nephews and nieces all in their young age. They were picking fruits and grape from the garden. Nader was at the end of the garden overlooking a wild running river where most of various fruit trees were. He was standing underneath a special red berry tree. The tree was planted in his name,when, he was just 5 years old, and his dog went to war with the wolves, and sacrificed his life to save Nader's. Then his mother decided to plan this tree and they buried his dog's corpse underneath it and named the tree for Nader, so he could keep his dog's memories alive and help him handle his dog's death that he loved so much. Now it turned out to be a big tree, and it had lots of red juicy sweet cherries. As he was grabbing some cherries from it and was sharing it with others his foot hit a glassy old bottle buried underneath the same cherry tree and where his dog was buried. Small part of the bottle was showing. Nader bent down and pulled it out from under the earth. Relatively, it was a large glassy old unusual shaped bottle, full of brownish old liquid . Also, inside of it was an unusual brown worm that looked neither like a worm nor anything else Nader had seen before. He was dancing in the liquid trying to get out. One of his nieces, Efate, asked him to throw it away because she thought the worm inside was too scary. But Nader thought otherwise and was not scared of it. He was trying to open the bottle, and finally opened the lid, and as the lid was opened in a sudden move, the worm jumped out of the bottle and in an instant turned into a white unicorn and began jumping and running through the garden and near Nader, back and forth, celebrating his freedom. All the children ran away in fear, but Nader was there, watching him, laughing and wanting to touch him. It had jumped around and started kind of dance around and for him. Finally, the white Unicorn slowed down and calmly and playfully approached Nader and stood in front of him for him to touch, Nader had not yet touched him, that Nader was surprised as the unicorn began talking to him,

> -I'm Unicorn ... Every thousand years one of us comes alive and belongs to special person. I belong to you, I was burned to help you with the things you are going to do ...

Nader thought for a while and put a smile on his face as he touched and enjoyed him. He brought Nader a special comfort, peace and feeling he was not familiar with. He looked up toward the other children, and raised his voice,

> -Do not be afraid, he is harmless ...

But they all were long gone out of fear. Nader woke up as he was having fun and talking to a unicorn.

Just as he was having the time of his life with the unicorn, a sound knocked on his apartment door awakening him. He opened his eyes, still engaged with thought of his dream. It was the second knock on the door that he came to his senses and raised up, and opened the door. As the door was opened he stood motionless for a moment. His body did not know how to react; it was the last person he would expect. Abraham spoke up first,

> -Are you going to invite me in? Friends always stay friends no matter what. And a friend does not need invitation either.

Nader, still surprised, watched Abraham look around and then turned to him,

> -Why do you artists always have to be different? Always have to make your life miserable? I never understand it. Look at you, from such life you had and still could have, you chose to live like this, just like the homeless.

Nader had no verbal answer, but his mind was screaming the answer to his questions.

> -But you really do not have to live like this any longer. We were and still are friends, and I am here to help you. You can start working with me. In real estate, soon, you will be big, and you do not need to be worried about money. You are so conceited and full of pride. I know you suffer, but do not ask for help from home. That is what I do not understand.

The more Abraham spoke, the more Nader was surprised. He did not know Abraham was in America, and he knew his family was not financially strong, particularly not strong enough to start a real estate empire. Besides, how did he find him? And why was it that every time things were not going well, he appeared out of the blue? Deep down inside, Nader was a bit happy to see Abraham. He would never utter this out loud, though. Before the revolution, there were not a multitude of Iranians in America, so if you crossed paths with one, you were sure to begin a friendship. They all would organize their group of Iranian friends to gather and play music and party on occasion. Nader was disconnected from all, and having an old friend, even if it was a complicated friendship, felt good. Abraham told him that during a recent trip to Iran, he found out Nader was in America, got his contact info, and decided to look him up. He told Nader that after the incident with Bahman Reesh, he decided to leave Savak and left for America to get away and start a new life. Nader believed everything Abraham said; he had no reason to really doubt him at the time.

Nader and Abraham began to meet on a daily basis; Abraham was so generous and kind to him and would not let him pay for anything. This was a typical Iranian tradition or show of courtesy and respect. The two always fought over who would pay the bill, and it seemed Abraham always had the upper hand. Everywhere they went, people knew Abraham. It became clear that he already owned many pieces of property. He was getting Nader started in real estate. Both were positive and motivated to grow. Their friendship became how it was when it first began. They ran around like schoolboys, with Abraham always harassing Nader as to why he would not get a girlfriend. Abraham was convinced that Nader needed a woman. His wife had informed him that she had a cute American friend that wanted to meet an Iranian man. Nader agreed, and dinner was set up. Later Abraham called and suggested they meet at his house, and his wife would cook for them all and would introduce Nader to her girlfriend. All was set for Friday night.

It was a cold winter night, pouring rain. Nader had a silver Honda civic. He drove up and down the hills of San Francisco and finally found their house. It was an average-sized, cute, older house sitting on a hill. Just as he stopped in front of the house, he began to have an eerie feeling in the pit of his stomach. Why was he there? He was a filmmaker, not a real estate man. The thought of getting serious with someone American made him miss home. But he hadn't even met her yet. Just then, an older model Jeep stopped and parked right in front of him. A pretty young American woman exited and walked up to Abraham's house and rang the doorbell. The door opened, Abraham appeared in the doorway, she entered, and he glanced around outside and then closed the door slowly. Within minutes Nader was ringing the doorbell, wishing he had never touched it. The door opened, and he was frozen in his tracks. He was speechless, and so was the woman who opened the door. For a second, both of them thought they were mistaken, or their eyes were seeing something else. It was an unbelievably long minute that they just stood there staring at each other. Both had lost words,

>-Oh, you are here, finally, good. Nader, this is my wife Fariba. Why are you guys standing in the door? Come in.

Abraham had appeared and broken the silence, and he was acting so cool that it seemed he did not know anything about Fariba and Nader, or if he knew, he missed his calling and should have been an actor. How could Abraham not know about them? It was him who helped Nader get back at Bahman Reesh, who was distributing Fariba's photos. Abraham must know; this must be why he wanted them to meet in their house. Abraham broke Nader away from his thought once again,

>-Are you going to stay there in the rain all night? She has a beautiful lady waiting for you inside…

Nader could not remember who said the first word. He was thinking perhaps it was him. He guessed he said something like,

>-I am happy to meet you,

Fariba answered the same. And that was the first word that was an exchange and spoken between Nader and Fariba since they got to know one another. Abraham reached and grabbed his hand, escorting him into the living room. Smiling, Abraham walked Nader over to meet Julia, who was very beautiful and waiting. He thanked God that Julia was a shy girl and pretended that he was too. He could not have asked for a better gift at the time. Now, he was embarrassed to meet Julia, on the surface. He was embarrassed and wondered what was really going on with everything. Maybe he had set everything up to embarrass Nader. He had lost his balance being in the same house with his Violin Girl and Abraham. He could not get her beauty out of his mind. She had on a simple blue dress with her long soft hair lying on her shoulders. He could not be interested in any girl in front of her. Abraham yelled for Fariba,

-Azizam, where are you? Do you need help... Guys, you two keep each other busy while I go help my wife.

He was playing so cool like nothing was wrong as he left the living room, Nader was still standing, and it hadn't occurred to him that, perhaps, he should sit. His only thought was what he would do when Fariba entered the living room, and he even did not know he was rubbing his hand together like his hand was dancing together? He knew she had to come out at some point and face him. She handled the situation much better than him. She kept her composure.

-How long have you been here?

Julia started the conversation with her soft, shy voice. He could see her face turning red, as was his. She continued,

-I am sorry if you are uncomfortable. This was Fariba's idea.

Nader could hear her, but he could not respond, and he did not know what to say, but he had to say something,

-I am sorry I am a bit shy. I have not done this before. It is my first time. I am not a talkative guy. I'm reserved... and do not speak much English...

He was just mumbling words that meant nothing to him. Maybe if he talked a bit, it would help him relax, so he could be ready when Fariba entered the living room. Then, Abraham entered, carrying a tray with several teas on it.

-Sorry, I did not know my wife had a bit of a headache. She will be out shortly.

Now Nader knew she was as surprised as he was, confused and nervous as he was. He failed to realize how hot the tea was in his hand and gulped the tea too quickly, burning his throat. It was very painful, and he could not breathe. He had to sip cold water right after. God, he really wanted to walk out. He was thinking how he could possibly sit in the same room, eating, chatting, watching Abraham call his violin girl "azizam." Oh, azizam, my dear love.

His mind focused back on reality when Fariba walked in smiling brighter than the sun and prettier than any flower Nader had ever laid eyes upon. She was holding some fresh pastries and placed them on the table as Nader motioned a thank you with a slight nod of his head.

-You are really welcome, Mr. Nader. Abraham talks about you all the time, but he never said who you were.

She said, then she turned to Julia,

-Nader is a great playwright… I saw one of his plays last time when I was in Iran…

For a moment, Nader was shocked to hear Fariba had come to his performance, and he did not know. He responded quickly before his ability to speak was lost for the night,

-I am humble, and please, I am not a big eater. In fact, I am fasting to lose some weight, so do not worry about me…

He did not even know why he said he was fasting and needed to lose weight. So stupid. He was in the greatest shape one could be and had absolutely no fat anywhere on his entire body.

As the night was passed, he became more comfortable, and she was the reason he began to feel more relaxed. Fariba made things easier for him by being so nice and outgoing and act normal. It was a very strange feeling like she really wanted him to feel relaxed. They were all relaxed now, enjoying each other's company. But Nader began to have mixed feelings about the situation. By watching them, he wondered if there was real love between Abraham and Fariba. She turned to Nader and spoke again,

> -I think you should take Julia to an Iranian restaurant. She likes Iranian food.

Fariba spoke quickly, almost with a sarcastic twist. He watched Abraham to see his reaction. Maybe she was trying to coax Nader to move on. Real love never dies, but what was he supposed to do. She was married. How had she gotten married, and to a man who at the time was his worst enemy? He wondered if she knew who Abraham really was. And now, his violin girl was asking him to go out with her friend; he would never ask her to go out with his friend, even if he was married. He did not like it and did not respond to her comment. Just stared blankly at her. Abraham noticed and thought he might not be that into Julia. He suggested they all go out together sometime.

Later the same night, they were all sitting at the dinner table. Fariba was sitting right in front of Nader. He could have touched her warm feet from underneath the table. Abraham had arranged for Nader and Julia to sit together. Nader noticed Fariba placed her drink right in front of him, so Abraham was forced to sit across from Julia. Anytime Nader looked up, his eyes would sink right into hers; they would burn all the way through his entire skull. But she was relaxed, and it was beginning to bother him very much. He did not know if she was playing games or perhaps she was making a statement; she was trying to give him a message. To tell him, "I love you, I don't, go away," and "rescue me." Looks are always deceiving. Abraham began to notice her behavior; Nader could tell he was trying to control himself. But there was something in her glance, something that started a fire in Nader's heart that he could never brush off. There was such a deep, sad, and meaningful feeling in the way she would glance at him that he had no other reason than to feel she is still loved him. She still wanted him; that was the only way he could continue sitting there. Abraham began to talk about her cooking and how great of a wife she was to him. How happy and proud he was to be her husband, how much in love he was with her. Then, he landed a couple of kisses on her cheek. This provoked so much anger within Nader that he wanted to smash Abraham's face and claim his love. He wanted to tell him that she did not love him and never truly would. He wanted to scream she was miserable being his wife. He wanted to tell him so many things, but he didn't. He just sat politely and quietly and watched his love wrapped in Abraham's arms, warming his bed, bringing light to this house.

Dinner was over, and dessert with more tea was brought out. She asked to play a game of cards, and soon they were sitting at a smaller table for four. Abraham organized the teams, him and Fariba, against Julia and Nader. Every move he made to Nader looked deliberate. Abraham was bragging about how great his wife was playing. Again, Nader wanted to punch him, especially when he reached from across the table to give her kisses. Nader did not know how he could have told him that he was deliberately losing to make Fariba happy. But he knew Fariba had understood, she mentioned several times that he was an expert player, but he was having a streak of bad luck that night. Finally, the night came to an end, and they were about to leave. They were standing by the door. Traditionally the guests and the hosts would plant a friendly kiss on each other's cheeks to say goodbye. This was custom for hellos as well, kissing one another cheek, and both cheeks were pecked in the same manner as French custom. Abraham started with him, then with Julia, then it came to him and Fariba, and he did not know what to do. He really didn't know if he should reach and kiss her or not. While he was debating, she reached and landed a kiss on his right cheek and one on his left. He couldn't remember if he gave her a kiss back or not; he only knew she had made his night the most pleasant one he had ever experienced. Driving in the pouring rain, he was drunk, but not drunk on alcohol. He was intoxicated from her kiss, from her hug, her smile, her entire being. He did not know what time he got home. He only knew he began to whisper as many love songs as he could remember, and not just once or twice. It was about six in the morning that he fell into a deep sleep. He was still thinking of what he must do next.

*****

Chapter 23

Weeds That Always Reappear Right After Picking...

Life sometimes treats you well, yet this treatment can drive you insane. Fariba appeared in Nader's life again, yet still unreachable. Abraham as well was a puzzle that was never completed for him. He was always left wondering what his motives were. He could not escape him, a friend who turned into painful weeds in his life, weeds that would always reappear right after picking. What was more surprising was to find out that Abraham was Jewish. All along, they all thought he was a Zoroastrian. Abraham could have only become familiar with Fariba through the Bahman Reesh incident. He must have seen her, fallen in love, and concocted his own plan. But Nader wasn't quite sure about this yet. The situation was in shambles. Just as he was starting to relate to Abraham, accepting him as a real friend again, old feelings began to rise. He reminded himself to watch his back. About to start something new in his life, taking on real estate full time, he was now between water and desert, stuck. He felt as if he would never be able to see Fariba all the time in his arms. He was unsure if he could trust himself to not do something crazy if Abraham had set this all up and was still working for the Savak. Yet, he felt guilty that he may be misjudging a loving family. The paperwork for his new deal with Abraham was ready to sign. How could he break such news to him?

A few days after the evening at their home, Abraham was calling Nader constantly. He didn't answer his phone or return his calls. Then, one night there was a knock on the door; Nader looked out to see Abraham. He had already visited Nader's apartment a couple of times during the day, but he had not opened the door. Just like a frightened cat, he hid inside. But how long could he hide? How long could he avoid him? Nader knew he had to come clean, demand the truth; even if he didn't, Abraham would now suspect him of something because of his behavior. He had handled everything horribly and was now backed into a corner. He was missing Fariba terribly and wanted to see her. The sound of her first words was still echoing throughout his soul. The taste of her first kiss was mixed into his spirit, and he could not be free. Now, it was part of him, a part of his legacy. Abraham was still outside, standing in the pouring rain. Nader opened the door, they both stared at each not knowing what exactly was going on. Abraham sat on the stair, facing the rain. Nader was watching a man who once was his best friend, his enemy, then friend again. He waited for Abraham to speak,

-I am here as a friend. I know I have done some good and bad toward you. But ... maybe I really did not know what I was doing, or I should say I was forced to do them because I took a job. Savak sent me here to work for them. Everything was fine with my marriage, and we were in love, with laughter and happiness, until I heard you showed up in LA looking for Fariba... what can I do now? It was my father, and her's who set everything up, introduced me to her, we met here in Los Angeles, and I did what was asked of me. They invested for us. You see, after what happened to you, I was feeling guilty, they sent me here to do some training, and I stayed working for them here. But I did not mean any harm toward you, and you see what destiny does to a person. After all this time, I need your help. I feel less of a man and powerless with you... you could destroy my life... you could take the best thing that ever happened to me, my happiness. My wife, who I am madly in love with...

Abraham wiped heavy tears with a corner of his shaken hand, and that was what Nader could not handle. But he did not know if he was playing one of his games or he was really suffering? As Nader watched Abraham beg to let him live his life, it hit him. Nader was responsible for it all. He should have acted sooner, stepped up, and demanded what he wanted. But he really wanted to know if Abraham knew he and Fariba had something, something one could call real loves? Or if he, Abraham, was madly in love with her? And she had no real feeling toward him? When Abraham saw his silence, he did not stop; he continued,

> -I swore if I knew anything serious about the love between you and Fariba, I would not have touched her nor done such a thing. She gave me the feeling that she had no real love for you. I left Los Angeles when I found out you were there looking for your lost love, who happened to be my wife. Then you are in San Francisco, chasing her. I knew sooner or later you would find her, so I had to do something. I thought... I should see you and tell you what was going on, but I couldn't... then I thought if you come and see how happy my life is and how in love we are, you would leave... I know how your heart works. You are a man of honor... you are different. You are a good man... Nader? ... I do not want to run anymore. I brought you to our home to see for yourself that we are happy, we are in love... that I wish the best for you and want to provide you with the funds to start your own business. You are my friend.

Nader was sitting next to Abraham, staring at the rain, heartbroken. He watched his old best friend weep, begging him to let him keep his life, to accept where fate had placed them all. Abraham stopped talking. It was dead silent, just the sound of pouring rain. The two friends sat in a land far from home, watching the rain, feeling powerless.

Driving around in the night's sky through the streets of San Francisco, with no idea where he was headed. Nader left the house at 1 AM. He was tired of sitting. He ended up in front of Abraham's house. He had promised him that he would walk away, leave them be. He had no intentions of going there, but he sat in front of the small quaint house as thoughts flooded. He was in mourning for something he never really had and could still try to get. He sat for hours, then started the car and headed down the hill. The red warning light began to flash; he was out of gas. At the next exit, he pulled off and stopped at the first gas station. A man approached, and he asked him to fill the tank up. He stocked the car with crappy food to last a few days and hit the highway. The approaching freeway sign read *Los Angeles, 200 miles*. He hadn't planned on such a drive yet kept going as the hours passed. It was about 6 AM tired, hardly able to keep his eyes open. He pulled to the side of a road, contemplating what to do.

Two hours later, he was awakened by a truck honking. He realized he had fallen into a deep sleep next to a stoplight on the side of the road. The truck was honking for an older lady to open the road for him. His eyes had landed on the old lady. She was nervous and in a state of panic. Just before he was about to help her, she drove away. Seeing her, he suddenly remembered his mother; he also, recalled Mom and Janet. It had been about eight months since he had a chance to visit them. There was no more thinking to do; he was on the road to his American mother and sister. Soon he was knocking at the door, but there was no answer. He could not hear the dogs running to the door like before; something had to be wrong. A neighbor walked out of her house and informed him that Mom had died a few months ago and Janet had moved back east to stay with her family. The house was sold, and new tenants were moving in.

This hit Nader like a ton of bricks; he missed his mother in Iran terribly. What if she died without seeing him again? He needs to be there with his mother and Forogh. Standing on the doorstep of a home that was no longer sheltering his American mother, he began to prepare himself for how he would handle the death of his mother back home. Driving with no direction, he stopped at Hussein's. He sat in his car observing his apartment, wondering if he should go in. He really wanted to see him and give him the news of Fariba, but he knew he would have gotten a speech and was not ready for Hussein's criticism for being a romantic dreamer. He didn't want to hear that he should join him and fight for his country, die for his country. Nader became keenly aware of the fact that Abraham could be working for the Savak there. They did have agents in America. He thought the least he could do was let Hussein know about Abraham's past so he would not get too close to him.

Nader's drive back up the California coast was consumed with thoughts of his mother's death that had not occurred. He thought of Forogh, Fariba, and Abraham as well. He did not have a talk with Hussien about Abraham. He knew he had to stand firmly with Abraham. He had to claim his love back or walk away peacefully, unable to see her all the time in the arms of his friend. By the time he got back home, he had made his decision. He put up everything in his apartment for sale. Within days all was gone but few small items, and he was sitting in the middle of an empty apartment having a few drinks in silence. It was late in the afternoon; he leaned his head back against the wall and closed his eye, taking in the sound of pouring rain again. He would be returning to Los Angeles the next day with an uncertain future. He had avoided Abraham as well. His neighbor informed Nader that he had come by many times looking for him.

A few hours later, his eyes fluttered open, hazy. He was immediately startled by what he saw. He thought he may be dreaming. He rubbed his eyes, assuming he was drunk and had to correct his visions somehow. But his eyes were not mistaken; sitting directly across from him, leaned delicately against the wall, was Fariba. She had on a lovely, airy, pepper-colored dress, her long black hair cascaded over the olive skin of her arms. Her body was almost too lovely to view, with a graceful openness that he had never seen, and she was staring at him. They looked at each other for a long time; again, he had lost his speaking ability. They both knew they had to get out of the apartment. Abraham may show up trying to catch Nader. They said no words; she rose, walked over to him, and took his hand, helping him up. As she was holding his hand, he was hot as fire, and suddenly, he believed there was a God. As they left the apartment, he felt he was flying like a bird. He was ecstatic that he had accidentally left his door unlocked. Asleep, she came in and watched him rest in such a peaceful state, something she knew would never happen again.

Hard rain still poured, Fariba drove through the streets of San Francisco with Nader in the passenger seat. She used back alleys and small roads to ensure no one would see them. She came to a stop at a rocky beach, they both got out and began to walk, she grabbed his hand. It was pouring but still a beautiful day. The temperature was perfect, the humidity just right. She led him down a small hill to a secluded area, still holding his hand. They sat, staring at the ocean. Barely any words were spoken. They did not need to. Both were afraid words would ruin the intrinsic peace between them. As if words would remove the feeling of holiness that flowed through their fingers. Their hearts need no sound, just the ability to sit close to each other, to feed off each other's energy.

He was watching two seagulls fly overhead and land underneath the rocks to find shelter from the rain. They move closer together to shelter one another from the rain and the cold. Just then, Fariba leaned over and placed herself into his arms. Just like the bird, it was a feeling that he had never had before. He knew heaven felt like that. He was flying way above the sky, surrounded by the breeze. His hands reached out held her with all the energy he possessed. He was holding on to her like he would never let her go again. He would fight for her if he had to. He would go to Abraham and say what needed to be said. He was lost in time, daydreaming with his violin girl in his arms. She turned and looked into his eyes for a long moment, her fingers brushing over his lips and face. He was motionless, staring into her eyes, playing with her hair, touching her neck. Now darkness had covered the earth. They could hear the sound of the water hitting the rocky shore. Water splashed into the air with each wave that crashed as soft sprinkles splattered the surface. Then, a moment Nader thought would never happen came into reality. She reached closer, placing her lips upon his. He forgot everything, forgot Abraham, he forgot he was leaving in just a few hours. His mind pushed all his guilt down into his gut, something it knew he would have to deal with later. He forgot Fariba was not his wife. They were kissing, breathing each other in. He was just, there; his soul, his spirit, his entire being was with her. Then she spoke,

-I want you to make love to me,

Her sweet request took his breath away. Hours later, they were still holding each other, watching the shooting stars, and listening to the sound of the water. The rain was still falling but to a calm, soft beat.

-That was the first time I have actually felt like I was making love... like I was one with my soul and heart....

She whispered into his ear. Both had lost track of time. It was now close to midnight. The moment they left each other, a feeling of acute pain took over his body, but she had to go, and he watched her drive away. Nader knew after this unusual disappearance Abraham would definitely suspect Fariba of something. She had informed Nader that she had spoken to Abraham, telling him the truth. She revealed Nader and Fariba's whole story. She told him this was why she did not want to have any children with him; he left the house crying like a wounded child. He left quickly, without saying a word. This was why Abraham had been around Nader's so much. He was afraid his wife was leaving him. But she came to Nader only for a few hours, to have a moment in time with a love that was too wounded by others to hold on to. She would stay with her husband, bringing true happiness to Nader and leaving him in sadness. Once again, Nader was standing in the rain, alone. He had to leave; it was time for him to disappear.

*****

Chapter 24

Are You From Saudi Arabia?

A few days passed, he was now living in an empty apartment, with only a blanket, a pillow, and his clothing, hoping for Fariba to return. He was supposed to vacate a week ago, but he sat debating with his conscience, unable to arrive at a final decision. He thought he had made one but not yet. He knew Fariba told him she was staying with Abraham, but he knew she was doing it because she felt sorry for Abraham, worried over the implications it would have on their families. In the back of his mind, he thought she would come up with something for them. He always thought she would change her mind and would leave Abraham. A week went by, he was worried; he had not heard from her. There had been no phone calls, no visit; even Abraham had not shown up. Nader drove over to their house; he did not stop, did not leave the car. The lights were out, the house silent and dark. The next night he drove by again, hoping to catch a glance of her; again, no lights, no movement. He slowed down directly in front. Put the car in park and stepped out. He wondered if they were out of town and stepped slowly. He realized there were no curtains on any of the windows, then approached the front window, peeked in. The house was empty. A deep and familiar sadness captured his heart.

The best person to contact to get information was Julia. After a few apologies for not returning her recent phone calls, she suggested meeting him for a drink to talk. They met at a small coffee shop. She told Nader that Fariba had had an affair with an old flame, and Abraham found out.

He didn't waste any time. He immediately moved them within days. Even Julia didn't know where they went. Her father and mother also showed up. Julia had no idea it was Nader, and that night sparked a new relationship between the two of them. He remained in San Francisco for a few more weeks, hoping things may change. He saw Julia every night. She had read many books and was knowledgeable of every subject, so carrying on conversations with her was not a problem. He was enjoying their time together and found his English improving. He was completely broke because he had not worked for awhile and had to get back to it immediately. It was time to leave San Francisco and head back south to Los Angeles. They sat at the same small coffee shop, and he told her he was leaving. Her face became concerned and saddened. She became quiet and left within a minute. He sat alone, thinking he should call her. He got up, walked to the payphone, and dialed her number. Her voice was still quiet, sad. He asked her to come with him. There was a long silence. He thought she had hung up then heard her voice,

-Why do you want me to go with you?

-Who knows...? We like each other, maybe it will work out, and we will end up married.

He did not know why he even said such a thing. But he did not stop there, she was quiet, and he wanted to get her to talk, so he continued,

-Would you marry me?

He couldn't believe the words that came out of his mouth, and then he heard her whisper one word, softly,

-Marry you?

*****

It was four weeks later, and he was a married man, living with Julia, and unsure how exactly it all happened. His friends were in as much shock as he was. Most didn't believe he was actually married. And if he was, it had to be for a green card. But there was nothing he could do to prove otherwise. What he could prove was his wife was not only intelligent but extremely kind and nice. He was a lucky man. He could have carried hours of conversation on with her and still continue talking. But he felt a small part of him, lingering in the back somewhere, knew he may have done it to get over Fariba. He had guilt from sleeping with a married woman. He couldn't even imagine someone sleeping with Julia. He always had the choice to say no, but he just couldn't. They were both victims; their love would have been great or ran its course without others interfering. In his mind, she was always his, letting that idea which was rooted in him had been painful, and blurred many lines. He also felt guilty for not being honest with Julia. He cared for her, and they had a good life, but he wondered if they would even be together if what happened with Fariba had not occurred. Sometimes, he thought marrying her would help him walk away from Fariba and help him forget her and give him a reason to put the thought of going back home behind and would pursue his life in America breaking into Hollywood. At the same time, he created a lot of feelings, respect, comfort, and trust toward Julia. But he did not know if it was love or something else; he just knew when he was around her, he was happy and safe. Whatever the reasons were, it was in the past, and nothing can be done with it, he only could make it right now, and after, so, he committed himself to treat her like a queen. He had a wife to take care of, and his cultural upbringing taught a man to treat a woman well and provide for her; you make a marriage work. Now it was time to hit the streets and find a job. He knew he did not want to wash dishes, and steering clear of Burger King and all that was similar was crossed out. His school had just ended, now a master's degree was added to his pocket. Even with this, he had problems. He was still not qualified for most positions. Five days into his search, he still had no luck. Wandering down Sepulveda Blvd. Nader stepped aimlessly at a loss as to what to do. His eyes landed on an Iranian man about his age, working at a small car lot. He stopped and watched him, marveled at how he could sell cars, and barely spoke English. He waited for some time until he was done with the customer he was helping, then noticed Nader and approached,

-Are you Iranian?

-Yes, hello, how could I get a job selling cars?

Nader asked

-Just go and tell them you worked at a car lot in Iran. They will give you a job. But go across the street. We do not have any openings here.

He turned and saw a Honda dealership. Two days later, he was an official Honda employee. After a week at the dealership, there wasn't much progress. Every time he approached a customer, three older Americans, Spanish and Filipino salesman would snatch the customer away. Nader was not used to this type of treatment. He had to learn so much, he approached his manager to inquire when payday was and if anyone could teach him how to sell.

-Are you from Saudi Arabia?

Was his response. Nader was thrown off.

-No, I am from Iran.

-Iran? Get the fuck out of here. You're fired. You did not sell anything to get paid. I thought you were from Saudi Arabia. I needed your help there. You can leave now.

The manager left the office, stopped, glanced at the rest of the sales team on the porch, lit a cigarette, and drank coffee while waiting for a customer. Nader walked away from the dealership discouraged. But the next morning, he was more determined than ever to get a job at a car lot. He had to take Julia with him because of his English. Nader would take the applications back to the car, and Julia would fill them out with him. He remembered visiting a Dodge dealership, the manager who was Spanish took a liking to Nader. He offered him a job, but the only condition was that he had to shave his beard. Nader had not shaved in fifteen years; this was not easy for him to accept. That night he took to the razor and was actually amused by how younger he looked. Two days later, the manager fired Nader. He said he really needed someone who spoke Spanish and didn't have time to train Nader. Although Nader was as upset as when he was fired at the Honda store, he left with pay for the hours he worked and a sincere apology. The next day, he was at a Buick dealer across from the Dodge dealership. He stood in front of a younger manager, about eighteen years old, named David. He looked up at Nader just as an older, slim and short, distinguished Jewish man walked in holding a folder,

-You couldn't have possibly filled out this application; you cannot even carry on a conversation, so how could you expect me to give you a job?

Then, David was staring into his eyes, he could feel he liked him, and he wanted to give him the job. Nader responded firmly,

-Because I have a family to feed, and I am hungry...

The older distinguished man dropped the paper on the desk for David and turned to Nader.

-Son, no one dies of hunger in America and especially not you.

Then the older man left. David turned to Nader with a smirk,

-You got yourself a job.

Nader did not know at the time, but the older man was the owner. The next day he was working, and it was not easy. He was running around for fourteen days, not selling a thing. Frustration was all he felt. Then, one of the salesmen who did not really like Nader approached him with a smile and informed him he would be fired at the end of the shift. He did not know how to handle this news. Even though he was exhausted, he was enjoying himself, and he could not afford to lose the job. He had to sell something, and he looked around for help but was only met with silence and no support. He was watching the lot, and he could not see any prospects. Then, David approached him several times, asking if he had anything in the works. Nader's answer was always yes. David would just leave with a smile on his face. David genuinely did not want to fire him, he could tell.

Finally, a middle-aged African American woman walked onto the lot, and no one wanted to help her. Nader immediately approached and began to show her a car, but he could not land her on any, so he turned it over to another salesman from his team. He stood in front, looking for another customer, praying for the magic to happen inside. The system was set up for two salesmen to speak to the customer; if they could not write up an offer and close it, they would turn the customer over to their team leader called a closer. Often a closer from another team would get involved. It was about nine in the evening, he realized no one could do anything with her, and she was about to walk out. David was standing outside looking at him,

-Nader go stop her, I know you could sell her car, I take any offer...

Nader's feet began to move, and he quickly ran up to the woman who was now on the sidewalk, he informed her that they had a quota to make so she could leave with a good deal considering it was so late already, he asked her to just look at one more car before she left. Within minutes she was back inside looking at more cars. A smile appeared on David's face while the other salesmen just huffed and puffed. The reason was that if one salesman had a customer, the rest had to stay no matter how long it would take to close the deal. They used to go to a bar called "Stony" and didn't want to stay after nine missing out on drinking time. They also assumed she was a lost cause; the two most experienced closers had talked with her and couldn't close a deal and now were standing around for nothing.

Less than a half-hour later, she was sitting in the office to sign an offer. She wanted to purchase the demo model. It was a red Buick Skylark, but was offered the same price for a brand new one with no mileage. He had the write-up in his hand, staring into the mirror in the bathroom, talking to himself,

> -Nader, you are going to sell this car, you are good, you are hungry, and you are going to sell this car... no matter how... no one can stop you... you are not going to lose this job...

He walked out looking for David. He was nowhere to be found. He walked through the dealership as one salesman approached him who wanted to grab the write-up, Nader did not give it to him, but it did not stop him from cursing. He spewed some comment about how he was wasting his time, then he heard David's voice paging his name to go to the sales office, and he did. As he entered the sales office, David snatched the write-up from Nader, looked at it, and then he turned to the other salesmen and hollered for them to leave his office. He then sat in his chair, smiling, and grabbed a pen. He wrote up a voucher and handed it to Nader. It was small yellow paper. Before he looked at it, he whispered, "Am I fired?" David was silent and shook his head to the side. The voucher was a $200 bonus for writing up the paperwork all by himself. Nader even did not know how the system worked; this was the first money he had really earned. Magic happened that night. The nice woman bought the car, and Nader needed no help from a closer. The dealership made thirty-five hundred dollars that night, and David had an ear-full for the rest of the employees. He felt no one was doing their job. It didn't matter that the woman returned the car the next day; he had become one of the favorites. That same month, December, he became the top salesman. Within six months, he was a closer, and a year later, Used Car Managing. Even with this success, Nader still knew nothing about cars, very little English, and needed more income to provide a good living for his family.

*****

Chapter 25

Revolution, The New Direction Of Iran/Persia...

Sitting in his office, thinking about the past, marveling at the twists and turns of life. How could a simple farm boy ever have imagined where he would end up? From the peacefulness of green trees, fascinating scenery, mountains covered with wildflowers and gorgeous rivers, to Tehran, the city that is forever fighting to get a past back that no longer exists. And now, in the giant computer wonderland of America where all are fed fast food and the American dream. His struggle and fight to be a filmmaker, writer, and explorer of truth through his art were at the forefront of his thoughts. Soft sentiments floated around for the people he had come to care for. He was sitting behind an aluminum desk, running a dealership of mediocre cars with a bunch of immature adult salespeople.

His eyes lingered past all those outside, taking in how their lives had all crashed together at this dealership. Outside the window was Roger, who later he found out was a child abuser in Ohio who fled to California. Sandy, who had been a drug dealer in New York, was now working to stay on a clean path. Bo, who had been let go from the army and accused of being a mad man, was next. Joe, who was in hiding because he shot his girlfriend in Puerto Rico, Javier, was an ex-gangster from Chicago who "relocated" because he was shot in a drug deal. And finally, Mike, who complained every second he possibly could about the unjust treatment of Black from

Whites. And ten more, they all, worked for him. The Persian man from the most beautiful village, by way of Tehran, fleeing the constraints of his family and with mixed painful and enjoyable past with uncertain future. He was pensive about how his destiny led him here, to his wife, to this place. It was unbelievable to think that he had been married to Julia for two years now. She had become his best friend, the love of his life.

He was thinking about his mother, about Forogh, and his brothers. He thought maybe his brother was right. If he would have listened and studied hard, he would be a doctor now. He would be in a respected hospital treating patients, not dealing with a bunch of lost souls who never fully matured to their true potential. But if he had done all that, what would have happened to his dreams, to the ideas that made him feel alive? Made him be him? His deep contemplation was interrupted by the phone ringing; he went into automatic reaction as he reached to answer the phone,

-Sales office,

-What are you selling? Your people to the evil government of America? Or your soul to the devil of imperialists? Aren't you ashamed of yourself? Your people are being robbed by the evil Shah, the puppet of imperialists, and being helped by your brother, and you are sitting here teaching a bunch of crooked salespeople how to rip off poor working-class people? Damn it, Nader, you used to be a man of ideas, truth, and strength. I thought of you as a man who could lead and educate people through his art, but now all I see is a man who has sold his identity, has sold his principles and soul to money and blonde women!

Hussein would not stop. He yelled into the receiver with passion, anger, and the unmitigated strength of a radical. Nader stunned, did not know what to say or how to respond in this moment. It just happened that the owner, Mr. Harrison, walked into his office at that very moment wanting to speak with him. He just hung up the phone on Hussein and turned swiftly to his boss,

-Women! You work hard; they complain you are not home. Then, if you spend some time with them, they complain that we are short on money. Yes, Sir...?

Nader caught his breath, waiting for a response.

-Maybe you should take a couple of days off and be with your family. Your wife is right. I see you are practically living here. I will have David take care of what I was going to ask you to do.

Mr. Harrison was right. Nader needed a few days' rest. He had been working two years non-stop, ten-hour a day. The only vacation he had was a year after his wedding. He took Julia to Big Bear for a couple of days. He had bought a van conversion, but they just used it once to go to Big Bear. She wanted to visit Santa Barbara, but he thought it would be a good time for him to visit Hussein on the way from Orange County, where they now lived. On the way to Hussein's house, he was thinking that he had never hung up on Hussein before; he had never insulted him or ignored him as he did a few days ago. He did not know how Hussein was going to react, but he was going to see him and had Julia drop him off. She was going to take a tour at a museum then pick him up a few hours later so he could be alone with his friend. After he was sure Hussein was home, Julia took off, and he was knocking on his door. When Hussein opened the door, he was surprised to see Nader. He was still living in the same apartment near UCLA. Hussein had a smile on his face, but he was serious and at a loss for words. He started in with teasing him,

-If you have anything to say, say it to my face so I can understand it.

It was then that Nader saw a smile on his face. He handed Nader a drink and took one for himself. Hussein had many things spiraling around in his mind; he did not wait to tell Nader about what he knew or what he thought was going to happen to Iran,

-The Shah will be kicked out of Iran within six months. Ayatollah Khomeini will be leading the revolution. I know your brother is a good man and means good, but to save his life, he has only one choice; to join the people's revolution. You must talk to him, you must take a trip and convince him to join, and convince him to also talk to his friends to join so there would not be so much bloodshed....

Nader was surprised and concerned by his words. He was astonished by how it would be possible to throw the Shah out of power. The Shah was one of the most powerful leaders in the world, or at least it appeared that he was. He was leading the fifth strongest army in the world at the time; the Iranian army could have taken over Iraq within few days. But Nader knew that as a leader, people need to be with you, and if they are not, sooner or later, you would be gone one way or another. At the time, the Shah was not popular and had lost touch with his people. He had lost the people's trust even though his intentions were to make Iran stronger and loved his land. The problem was and is for many that to have a great vision is easy. To make it work and have millions follow is the hard part when you are running many others interest to help your country and your people.

Nader knew at the time the Shah took a different approach towards the clergy than his father had. After his father was sent into exile during the Second World War, the Shah took the crown when he was only twelve years old. From this point, his mother influenced and advised him. He decided to be closer to the clergy and treat them with respect, and he used to reward them with oil money. But he did not understand the clergy was the manufactured voice of foreign policy. They also played the field for the English, who could not be trusted. Hussein's conversations had finally gotten to him.

Two hours had passed, and he was still with Hussein. As time passed, he was becoming more concerned. Hussein seemed nervous, and he did not know why. Nader noticed Hussein was glancing at the phone every so often, and he knew he was waiting for an important phone call. Once Hussein made a phone call and asked someone on the other end of the receiver if they had heard anything, the answer was no. Then, he went to use the bathroom and shut the door. Ten minutes passed, and he was still in the bathroom, then his phone rang. Hussein ran out with his pants still around his knees, grabbed the phone, and ran back in, forgetting Nader was there. Then, Nader could hear Hussein yelling from the bathroom.

-Zendehbad Iran-e-azad. Marg bar shah.

This translates to

Viva, free Iran! Death to the shah!

Nader didn't know what was going on, but he did not have to wait any longer. Hussein walked out of the bathroom elated, but this time his pants were up.

-They passed, they passed, and people are with us.

Nader was still confused and at the same time curious, what had passed? Hussein entered his room and waved for him to follow. He pulled out two Israeli-made machine guns. He thought they were model Z3s and pointed to him.

-Four of these just passed through customs at Mehrabad airport. They had people promise us they would ignore it, two of our friends decided to try and see if their word was true. It went through American customs and Iranian as well. They did not even look at the bags. You must join before it is too late. People are joining everywhere. You must join. We need help with money. You must help your people. It was then that Nader could hear Julia honking outside, calling for him. Hussein went to the window and looked out.

-Maybe you have been sold to the imperialists and its blonde devils like I thought.

Nader left Hussein ignoring his comment. He knew he was trying to get to him by hitting a deep-down crevice. Nader was truly sad, Hussein had turned into a radical fanatic. An activist who didn't understand that his way would just lead to more bloodshed and a new puppet leader. There were no guarantee things would be better, just hope. He had been his best friend since childhood; he knew he had a great heart and was in it for others. Nader firmly believed that if you joined any group or religion that you should respect its philosophy to the fullest. And this meant that if Nader joined Hussein, he would be a murderer of his people, even if he did not pull the trigger. He did not want to join. He did not want to bring death to anyone.

The two days in Santa Barbara were the longest couple of days for Nader. He tried his hardest to make it enjoyable for Julia, but he could not sleep; he couldn't stop thinking about Iran or his brother. On the second night, he finally decided to take a trip to Iran immediately. He had not returned since his departure, and he hadn't even told anyone he had been married for two years.

Only a couple of his friends in Iran knew. He decided to bring Julia and let a few people back home know, so no one had a heart attack that he had a wife in tow, especially his mother and Forogh. He had no idea how his brother or mother would react. A week later, he was sitting on the plane to Tehran with Julia. The pilot was announced they were about to land at Mehrabad Airport. Two years away from his homeland, his mind was flooded with memories from the past twenty-seven years. He was taken over, his whole body numb. He could not wait. All he wanted to do was get in the car and drive straight to his mother and Forogh. He had told two of his nephews to pick them up from the airport; he didn't want his mother to come. He knew that if his friends and relatives were aware that he was coming, they would all come to meet them at the airport and make a big deal about his arrival, and he did not want that.

By now, he thought Julia must be a bit tired of hearing about Forogh and his mother and how much he missed them. They were going through customs as he glanced up behind the glass window. He thought he saw

Abbass's wife but didn't see her anywhere and looked again. He didn't see any relatives, so they walked out of customs. As they exit customs, he was blindsided. Almost everyone he knew in the country was there. As soon as they saw the two of them, happy chaos began. A mass of flowers fit for twelve hands was ushered over to Julia. She was moved to tears but had no idea what was going on. His nephew had told his sister Parry who could not hold it in and told everyone. They all decided to come and honor his new wife. She needed a warm welcome to Iran.

While Julia was lost inside the sea of his enthusiastic relatives, he didn't know where she was and just asked to see Forogh. He knew his mother would not be there. She never used to go anywhere unless it was a matter of life or death. Besides, she would never leave the house because she would want to be sure everything was ready for her new daughter-in-law and her favorite son. Receiving a new guest, especially one from America, for her, was like receiving a gift from God. All would be grand. And there was Forogh, touching his legs for a long moment that he didn't notice. He looked down when she pulled on his shirt. Then, he sat, and she was in his arms, and he was holding her tight. He was so happy that he did not want to let her go.

A little later, he was sitting in one of almost a hundred cars that came to welcome him and his wife. He still did not know where Julia was, and they got home before her. The second the car stopped in the private alley by their house, there were many more waiting to welcome him back. Among them was his mother, Hajji Khanoom, waiting in the doorway. There were many tears. She hugged and kissed him, her hands clenching his arms like she would never let go again. Julia arrived, and all attention was reflected back to her. She was now feeling Hajji Khanoom's tears and strength in her firm embrace. She walked Julia in, holding her hand firmly. It was many hours later that Nader finally saw his wife again as she was led back by the multitude of relatives and friends. She had been taken to visit his relatives outside and to his sister's and brother's house, which were next door to his mother's. Julia was so surprised and impressed by the welcome she had received that she was still crying into the night. Something she was not accustomed to in America. She insisted on calling the states and explain what had just happened to her mother. It was an outpour of love she had never experienced back home, ever. She was explaining to her mother about her experience. Nader was surprised that no one, and he meant no one, said anything to him about being married to an American. They immediately loved her. Nader was bombarded with questions as to why he had not informed them he was married!

During the next few days, his mother's house remained full of people. Julia had received gold and many other presents from his family members. Every day she was so impressed that he used to see tears of happiness on her face. But Nader knew from the first moment he arrived in Iran, he had another mission. He was back to see what is going on in Tehran. He was here to see the political situation with his own eyes. He was here to speak to his brother and see if what Hussein was saying was true so he could convince his brother to leave the country. But Nader already knew he could not outright speak about guns entering through the airport. That was his best friend's secret, he had revealed it to him because he trusted him, and he was not going to break that trust. He was in a position in which he needed information out of his brother but to also warn him without being straightforward about the information he had. After several indirect conversations, Nader posed the question to his older brother. He asked if the Shah's situation was stable and if he had any idea that a coup of some kind was in the works. But the more he pushed the issue, the more he hit a brick wall. Abbass kept insisting that no power could touch the Shah, and he was in charge. Not even after Nader finally revealed to him about the gun passing through Iranian custom. But his brother laughed and thought it was just a rumor.

*****

Chapter 26

A Lot Of Sadness And Doubt...

It was now two weeks later, his mother and sister were in tears. He was about to return to America. By now, they all had accepted that Nader had a second home called America. There is a saying in Iran, you ask a man where his home is, and he replies, "I am not married yet." Then it was time for Nader and Julia to leave Iran. So many tears fell that all faces were wet. Hajji Khanoom and Parry tried their best to stop the tears, but they couldn't hold back. And there was Forogh; her solemn silence was more effective than crying, Nader was heartbroken walking away from her.

As they flew out of sight from the land he loved, his unanswered questions flooded back. There was lots of sadness and doubt in his mind about the future of the country, and he knew Hussein knew more than he told. He also had given Nader more information about Khomeini's return from France and other occurrences. The things he revealed to Nader were all correct. Only the dates they would occur were different. He was convinced Hussein was right and he must do something to save his brother and his family. He must do something to help the future of his country, his homeland. He knew if Khomeini was going to be the leader, the clergy would take over power, and this would be a disaster for Iran. Every effort the Shah and his father, Reza Khan Pahlavi, had done to create a strong and independent Iran would be in jeopardy. He knew the long-term plan of the west was to weaken the Iranian army in the region, to keep Iran weaker than them by supporting the ousting of someone they called an ally who was trying to build more than just infrastructure. The Shah had been trying to create a balance between America, Europe, and Russian so they would be safer against attempts to get rid of him.

Nader could not just sit back and do nothing. Without hesitation, he contacted Hussein and began to get information. He offered to help them where he would feel was right and appropriate for the country but would not participate or aid in any and everything. It was about six months since his visit to Iran, and the situation there was beginning to escalate. Every day there was a different event being reported in the media around the world, the tone of all messages reported was against the Shah. Suddenly, the Shah had become the enemy of the west and exiled Khomeini was the hero to them. BBC Radio London was leading the campaign of destruction in Iran by smashing the Shah and his policies and praising the opposition, especially Khomeini. Khomeini had moved from Iraq to France. He had every possible access to media to get his message out everywhere he wished.

For many, including Nader, it was clear that the west, led by America, France, and England, wanted the Shah out. They played the field to gain benefits for themselves. They did all that they could. In fact, if the west had stopped giving media attention to Khomeini and disallowed his message to be distributed all throughout Iran and the states, there probably would not have been a revolution in Iran. It was during this time that Nader knew he had to return to Iran without letting anyone know. He joined Hussein and his group and worked with another group as well. He had supported many organizations financially to get them stronger for the oncoming challenges and struggle for power after the Shah's fall. What people didn't understand was that having a successful revolution was the easy part to Nader. Making sure the right people grabbed and sustained power and order after was the hard part. He was against the clergy taking over Iran. He knew it would be the destruction of over three thousand years of history and culture. Thus, he was officially active in working against the Clergy, gaining power after The Shah. not because he wanted to, but because he knew the stage was set for the Shah to leave regardless, and they had to be sure the clergy would not take over the country. But the climate was so strange, and everything was unfolding so rapidly that you did not have time to think. No one had time to think. Suddenly, and for no reason, everyone hated the Shah and was in love with Khomeini, but no one knew really why. All were swirling around in chaos, in the excitement of ideas; ideas that in reality may never actually occur.

Nader had returned to Iran, but no one in his family knew, not even his wife. In fact, he had traveled back and forth four times in secrecy. He was making short trips pretending to be on business trips to check out potential land to invest in. Every time he went, he re-evaluated the situation and made sure the right people were in contact with each other. Nader quickly realized nothing could really help; the stage was already set. The cast was already hired. The script was written, plans for the whole country to fall on a specific date were set. It was just like clockwork. The Shah and the Iranian people were betrayed by the Shah's best friend from childhood, general Fardoss. Of course, he had a few other cohorts, but he tied the noose around his best friend's neck. The Shah was also betrayed by his best ally, America. Suddenly he had no friends, no one knew him, and he had no place to go. The man who once was welcome everywhere was like a disease. By now, Khomeini had returned to Iran. Nader never forgot that during his last trip to Iran, he sat with his mother, watching her pray. He realized she was staring intensely at Khomeini's photo. He asked her what was wrong.

-Nader, I am afraid of his eyes. I do not trust him.

He should have listened to his mother; his peers should have listened to people like his mother. But at the time, there was a magical spell upon all; everyone believed in Khomeini. He had captivated the country to the fullest extent. Everyone was misled by a man they thought was an angel, including Nader.

Surprisingly, even Nader believed him when he spoke of not being interested in power and would reside in the city of Qum (pronounced Ghoom) as a religious leader. He believed him when he said the clergy would not rule, that Iran would be led by a civilian government. Every speech he would bellow about giving the people their share of the oil money the Shah stole, that they would be able to not even work if they wished. He promised gas and electricity would be free for all. Sadly, the money never came, but oil was still being sold. This empty political promise was realized when the clergy's bank accounts throughout the world became fat. The killings of vibrant intellectual minds in Iran began. The killing of the young began. Masses fled their homeland; some hoped to return one day with skills that they had acquired to contribute to the betterment of Iran. But returning home was a dream of many that melted away.

Those that were mesmerized by Khomeini quickly began to awaken. As the executions of innocent people rose, the hazy eyes cleared. These killings also included many key players of the Shah's government who could have revealed the whole truth. The clergy was scared their secrets would be revealed and ordered them to be executed immediately. One incident, for example, could not get out. The clergy was responsible for the burning of the Rex Movie Theater in the city of Abadan. The doors were sealed, and over three hundred were burned alive. They were just disposable pieces in a game of trying to make the Shah look bad; the blame was all on him. Massacres after the revolution set the stage for many to rise against Khomeini. He did not honor any of his promises as well. The internal power struggle among the greedy and power-hungry involved within the revolution had begun. Killings, assassinations, executions, and bombings became a daily occurrence. What was worst of all was that the wealth and brains of the country began to storm out of the country, having no choice but to leave. The advancement and progress of the country became stalled. Today, Iranians are the richest and most prevalent immigrants throughout the world due to the fact that the wealthiest and most educated were able to flee.

It was not difficult to realize that many people participating in the revolution were in danger, including Nader. It was now Nader's sixth visit to Iran; this time, his wife and family knew. Hussein met Nader in the back of a small back alley shop. He was given the message to leave. He informed him that his brother was going to be arrested as well. This was the first time he would ask Hussein for help. He asked him to help save his brother. But he looked into Nader's eyes with an unforgiving expression,

> -His life is not as important as the many people who have died and shed their blood for the revolution. He had his chance to join, and he did not.

Hussein left a few minutes later; Nader sat glued to the chair, unable to move. He did not expect such a reaction from Hussein. Nader remembered when Hussein rose to leave, he turned to Nader and said,

> -I am only left with this one pair of pants. If you have any Levis, give me one pair before you leave. I can say that Levi jeans are the best thing America has contributed to the world.

Then Hussein walked out of the restaurant, and Nader watched him get into a taxi. He smiled at Nader as the taxi disappeared.

After a few days, Nader had visited everyone he could think of to see if he could get any help to save his brother, but no one wanted to or was able to help. He was disgusted with the radicalism that had overtaken everyone. All they could see was blood and revenge with a blind eye. Whether you were a neighbor or friend did not matter. Disheartened and confused, Nader went home to talk to his brother. As he entered, his eyes became. Still, shock took over. He noticed his wife, and his mother-in-law, sitting with his mother chatting. First, he could not believe what his eyes were seeing, how could this be possible? But it was real; it was his mother's doing. She wanted to surprise him. Nader's head began to spin in both directions. Here he was stuck in Iran fighting for his life, fighting for his brother's life, and now had to worry about his wife and mother-in-law. And to make matters worse, they were two American women; they would definitely stick out. He did not know how to break the news to them. He looked above to God for a teeny, tiny bit of help.

The only release Nader had from worrying about himself and his brother was the fact he was now worried about them. He informed them they could only stay a few days and then began concocting an exit strategy keeping the eminent danger out of their minds. He knew he could not leave the country through the Tehran airport. He knew they may already have his name on a list, and the moment he arrived, he would be arrested. Especially now, he had two American women with him right after taking over the American embassy, and many Americans went in hiding and waiting for an opportunity to escape from Iran. The decision was made to drive out through the Iranian/ Turkish border, making their way through for a "sightseeing tour of Iran and Turkey." One of his friends promised to join him with his mother and young daughter so they would not appear so suspicious. The plan was set; within a few days, they would be on the road, hopefully headed toward keeping their lives.

During these few days, Nader had spoken with his brother several times, pleading for him to leave with them, but he was stubborn and constantly repeated he had done nothing wrong, he would not leave. Abbass was confident he would be safe. His reasoning was that there were several people helping Khomeini with this new system who he had worked with before collecting information for the Savak. He had treated them well, respect, he felt was present. What he really meant was that many of the clergies were field agents for the Savak; they were paid by the Savak through his brother. The irony was that those people were the ones who really wanted him dead, so they could bury their connections to Savak forever. He could not get to them and was standing his ground cursing at the Shah for leaving the country. He thought the Shah had betrayed them; he should have stayed and died in the land he loved, just like Abbass. Thus, Abbass was staying firmly on the ground he stood, even if death was waiting around the corner.

Nader's last stop was to visit Ayatollah Talaghani, who was supposed to replace Khomeini after him. He was sitting with him the night before his escape from Iran. He revealed to him that many close relatives of his brother's first wife had complained about him; they had filed a petition stating he had killed his first wife. This news struck a painful chord within Nader. The same people who put his brother in long-term pain, the ones who really were responsible for Boloor's death, her quiet suffering, were laying the responsibility all on Abbass. As Nader watched tears run down Ayatollah Talaghani's face, he whispered to God for this justice that he never saw. Ayatollah Talaghani spoke slow and solid,

> -Some of my old friends... now want me killed because I would not support their crimes. They are harming innocent people under the name of Islam; how could I support such wrongdoing? I am ashamed of our people, I have committed a sin by supporting the people in charge, and now I know they do not mean good for the people. I cannot go out this door and look into their eyes. I wish God would take me so I would no longer see these injustices being committed under the name of The God....

Those were the last words Nader ever heard from him. The next morning, he noticed people were rushing to the newsstand; some yelled that Ayatollah Talaghani had died. There was a state prayer on every media channel. The government was using his death for their own benefit as if they weren't the ones responsible.

The next day, they were ready to move out, and Nader was doing it very quietly. He arrived at home a half-hour prior to their departure, and his friend Nasser with his family arrived at their house. Nader spotted the green cargo van which Nasser had bought from the asset department; this van had been taken from the American embassy at some point. Those days if you were traveling through Turkey in a car from the Iranian border to Ankara, the second-largest city in Turkey, you did not want to stop for gas or anything at all. First, there was no gas to buy, and second, it was not safe, especially if you had pretty American women with you. Blondes were rare in that part of the world, especially during that time period. There was also fighting in parts of Iran towards the border. They had to have enough gas for the majority of the trip, really for the whole thing. The plan was always to keep driving.

They could not waste time, and they had to hurry out. His wife and mother-in-law did not know anything about the fact that they were actually escaping from the country, and everyone's life was in extreme danger. He could not reveal this to either of them because he knew his mother-in-law might accidentally blow their cover; in addition, she would drive everyone nuts and crazy. They both needed to be calm and relaxed as possible. Nasser informed them they were to be given a driving tour of areas of Iran then headed to Turkey for a few days of sightseeing. They both were happy about this hospitality. They did not know about the fighting and chaos in the north and the danger in Turkey from the Iranian border to Ankara. They were making their way out when Nader saw his sister, Parry was yelling for him to stop. He looked out and saw two of the workers carrying a large package towards the car; Parry was asking him to open the back. He asked what the package was, saying they did not have room.

> -This rug is for your mother-in-law. She said she likes it, I am giving it to her.

Nader realized his mother-in-law had praised the beauty of a large twenty-meter Persian rug at his sister's house many times. His sister had it wrapped up for her to take as a gift. But he had no room to take the rug and fought with his sister, explaining she would just have to lose this fight for now. They drove away, leaving Parry, his mother, and Forogh in tears. His wife and mother-in-law looked perplexed over the commotion. He explained to his mother-in-law a new lesson about Iranian culture. If you talk nice about somebody's belonging, no matter what it may be, they will offer it to you as a gift. This is a sign of respect, love, and kindness. He had to explain this again to his mother-in-law after she made some nice comment about Nasser's shirt, and he took off and handed it to her, and she was insulted. It was then that Nader had to give both of them a speech about the differences in cultures and asked Nasser to put his shirt back on.

Sitting in the car cruising through mountain roads, thinking about the future, Nader was crying inside but kept a smile on his face so everyone would be at ease. He was just like a clown making everyone laugh with tears welling up inside. Just like a candle that burns to lighten the dark, he filled himself with energy. He was thinking about Forogh, about his mom, and when would be the next time he could see them, or if he ever would again. He was worried about the people who he helped come to power, many of them were his close friends, and he wondered if they would stay away from his family and from his mother. He knew they would go after his brother. He had made one last phone call from a public phone to give it one last shot,

> -You have sold your country. I would rather die than leave. This is the only home I know how to breathe in, how to laugh in. The ground soaks up my tears and feeds me life. This land is me. America betrayed us. Why would I go to America... you should go and stay out of here, make a future for yourself there. There is not one here for you. Pay attention to your family, your wife.

He hung up on him, and Nader began praying for their safe passage. Quickly Nader's mind came back into the moment. They were approaching a war zone where the local tribes had revolted against the government. They were controlling the mountains and most of the roads through them. Now, the biggest problem they had was his mother-in-law. She wanted to stop every hour, and anytime she would see something interesting. Her reason was that in her mind, they were taking this trip to show her and his wife Julia, Iran, and Europe. They had to do whatever they could to get to the border as quickly as possible. So, they finally told her that the rebels were attacking and they had to leave the area, but that was the worst comment they could have made. She did not stop talking for almost three hours. It came to a point where Nasser had to stop the car and sit on the side of the road, she made him never want to drive again.

She stopped talking long enough to get them to where the rebels had set up a checkpoint. One of their leaders, a young man in his twenties, approached them, holding a machine gun. He looked around and made a comment that the van belonged to the American embassy and perhaps they were trying to get the Americans out. But the fact that they had the green army van helped very much with him. The young man said they would help them because if anything were to happen to Americans, they would look bad in the world's opinion of them and their cause. They were relieved, but his next comment raises both Nader and Nasser's eyebrows,

> -You will be stopped at the border for sure. Driving an American green army van and having two Americans will be enough reason for them to not let you pass through.

They had never thought that using a green American army van and posing as students was a bad idea. The same young leader spoke up again,

> -If you guys have a problem getting through, come back here, and I will find a way to get you out through the mountain paths. But the easy way is going through the border. I used to live in Miami, Florida; maybe one day we will see each other in the states.

Until then, it had not occurred to Nader that he was speaking English all along. He gave them a note to use in case they were stopped by other rebels, and then they headed through the war zone again towards the border.

They could hear the sound of gunfire from a distance and could see rebels running through the mountain path, getting in position to fight the government forces. By now, his mother-in-law was completely quiet and very scared; she did not say a word. His wife was sitting by her, holding her hand. He was now worried she would have a heart attack. Nader had something else very important to worry about as well. It was quite possible one of the bullets could hit the gas tanks on top of the van. No one knew who they were. A decision was made to hang a long white piece of material from the antenna. The nice rebel leader had given it to them. They quickly made their way through the war zone and entered the city of Ardabil. A few hours after that, they were approaching the border; he remembered it was about four in the afternoon, and they wanted to cross before dark before the border closed for the night. They were stopped behind other cars waiting to get through the checkpoint. He did not know what to think or expect; he just prayed, asking for help. Nasser was as worried as he was but was constantly making jokes with the few English words he knew and asking for his help to translate. They were about five cars away from the checkpoint when Nader noticed one of the guards walk away from the checkpoint with his eyes fixed on their van. Nader became worried immediately as he began to walk straight towards them. Within minutes they had moved them out of the line and to the side to begin questioning.

Nader knew at the time border control could not communicate with Tehran very easily, but to be sure, they had brought a friend of his nephew's to accompany them until they got to Ankara. He was a mechanic who came with them to help them in case of mechanical problems with the van. He was going to fly back to Tehran. He took Nader to the side and told him it was time for him to leave. His reason was he would stop at three or four places on the way and cut the wiring so they could not contact Tehran by phone or telegram for some time, to give them more time to think about what to do. Nader could not have heard better news. Nader hugged him and watched him walk to the other side of the road and get on a bus. He knew they had time until the morning to do something, so Nasser tried to convince the officers at the border that they needed to go back to the city and stay there for the night. He used the women for this excuse. But they would not let them move an inch.

It was a few hours into the night, and he was pacing back and forth, feeling trepidation. The rest were kind of sleeping, and Nasser was making sure they would not get too worried. It was close to midnight, and Nader was sitting outside behind and few yards from the van on the curb, holding onto his knees, feeling worried and praying to God for help, thinking what to do next. What would happen to them, to his wife, to his mother-in-law, to the lady in the tank? Yes, a lady in a tank on top of the car. They were smuggling her out. Her life was in jeopardy. No one knew she was there inside one of the gas tanks, except Nasser. Nader would knock on the tank lightly and wait for a soft knockback which meant she was OK. She was the daughter of one of his friends, the lady Hussein has sent to Iran to find her father. It was then that Nader noticed there was an older man, pacing around in front of the customs building, about seven-eight hundred yards from him, playing with his beads, and it seemed he was observing Nader. Nader had a feeling he was one of the bosses. Nader thought he was trying to scare him, so he stopped looking at him and looked away; he placed his face on his hand that was holding to his knee; everything went dark, heartfelt and humble with a lot of emptiness within in began to talk to God,

-My God, please save my wife and my mother in law... Please, I was a good man to all, all through my life... now I need your help... can you hear me?

-Young man, is this your family?

Nader was taken away from his talk with God with a voice he heard; he looked up and realized the old man was suddenly standing by the van. He was shocked and confused, questioning how the old man could get from where he was next to him? It was not even a minute that he took his eyes off him and began to speak to God. It should take him several good minutes to walk to him, but he had to answer him. Nader got some kind of good feeling and trust toward the old man, he raised and began to talk,

-Yes, my wife, my mother-in-law, and my friend's daughter and his mother. I brought my wife here to visit my mother, she was sick, and they are stopping us. My wife and her mother are scared to death. I was here helping with the revolution...

The old man cut Nader off.

-What is your name? Nader?

-Yes, Nader.

-What school did you go to? Jam, in Gholhak.

-Yes. Jam, in Gholhak... Hajji it seems you know everything about me. Please Hajji if you want to hold me here, I am okay with that, but please let my wife and my mother-in-law go... they had nothing to do with what is happening here... it is my fault; in fact, my mother is the one who invited them here, Please Hajji, I helped the revolution....

Hajji, of course, was a nickname for religious people who went to Maque to pray at God's house and become a trend after the revolution. The old man cut Nader off, and he asked Nader to get in the van and follow him. Nader watched the old man head toward the border checkpoint. He was confused and did not know what was going on, but he followed his orders and got in the van, quietly woke Nasser up, and asked Nasser to follow the old man. Nasser did not want to follow and said,

>   -Nader, he is the main man here; he wants us to leave, and before we reach the other side, they will shoot us dead....

But Nader had a different feeling and almost forced Nasser to follow, and he finally gave up and followed him to the very front of the checkpoint at the border, which by now was closed. They could not understand or believe what the older man was yelling to the guards,

>   -Why are you stopping my cousin? Open up, let him through! He has to attend his test at the university early tomorrow... open the border....

The guards were confused at first but obeyed, "Hajji even if we let them out, they may not let them in on the Turkey side... let them cross in the morning....

But the older man did not stop yelling, and finally, the guard lifted up the checkpoint, and then, the older man came to Nader's side, reached, grabbed his hand, and gave Nader a goodbye kiss on his cheeks gestured for him to leave. Nasser drove through while they all exchanged silent glances thinking about what had just happened. They were through the border, as Nasser was worried and waiting for the bullets to be fired after them. Nader had something else in his mind; he could not leave; he had to know who the old man was. He told Nasser to stop, which he did with hesitation. Nader jumped out and ran back to the Iranian border. The older man still was standing by the barrier to be sure they were gone safely. He reached him and, for a few seconds, stared quietly.

-Who are you, please? God?

-Astakhforelah!? You are the God, Not me....

Which translates into forgiving me, God. Then, he whispered into Nader's ear,

-You have given shelter to a man whom his uncle kicked out of his house. His name was Ali, from the city of Sarri in the north. I saw you at his house in Sarri, the summer you came to visit. I am his grandfather... Just remember, good deeds are always rewarded in some form, now go son, go before it is too late. You will be okay.

He was still looking into the man's eyes and tried his hardest but could not remember if he ever saw him in the city of Sarri, and Ali never told him anything about having a grandfather. Nader turned and began walking back to the car, looking at the van ahead of him, lighting the dark night. He was a few steps away when he remembered the older wise man that would appear to him. He had such a resemblance. He spun around and darted his eyes across the land behind him. The man was nowhere to be seen. Nader knew he could not have walked back to the office within such a short time. The office was a good distance away from the border entry. So, he turned back and walked briskly to the car, got in, and they took off down the lighted road. Everyone inquired as to who the man was. But Nader only had one answer.

-God.

He did not want to elaborate on the story of Ali and his high school times, and he was just happy they had successfully crossed the border. Several years later, he contacted Ali and told him about his experience at the border. But Ali said his grandfather had died several years before, and he had no idea who the man was.

It took them about an hour to convince the Turkish border control to let them in. Now they had to get to a safe place and get the lady in the tank out of her misery. Nasser was now driving fast on a curvy one-way mountain road in Turkey. The infamous mother-in-law now could not breathe and began to complain about Nasser's driving insistently. But Nasser was not in the mood to even listen or hear her, and he just kept cruising. After a few hours, they reached the first city. They finally located a small hotel, but they did not know if it was a safe place or not. The plan was to drop the women off at the hotel, and Nasser and Nader would drive to a safe place to get the lady out of the tank. They had missed the people that were supposed to meet them and take her away. They had left because Nader was stopped at the Iranian border for so long.

Nader noticed the street was jammed with people, and he felt there must be something wrong. Soon the street was covered with soldiers and police controlling the crowd and dispersing them. They then found out that Turkey was also in turmoil. Of course.

The soldiers approached and asked Nasser to move the van, and he had no choice but to take off without Nader. He knew it was not safe to leave the women alone with the conditions he was witnessing anyway. Nader took the women inside and into the two rooms they had rented. But his mind was with Nasser and the two gas tanks which still held over forty gallons of gas and the lady inside one of them. Then, Nader realized the hotel lobby and the upstairs hallways were packed with people that the soldiers had pushed off the street. Nader was concern they might decide to break into the rooms. Nader knew their rooms were a target of the intruders. Some of them knew there were American women in the rooms, so he moved Nasser's daughter and mother in one room with them and stood guard. He was yelling, asking for his gun, hollering if anyone entered, he would shoot them. But he was yelling in Farsi and English, not Turkish, hoping someone would understand. He did not sleep the entire night, but no one broke in, and they were safe.

It was about ten in the morning when Nasser showed up. He was also tired and sleepy. But Nader was happy to see Nasser and the van were both safe. The soldiers had ordered Nasser to move out of the town because of the gas tanks on the roof of the van. They did not find it safe and were worried that someone might decide to use it as a target and blow it up. Nasser drove out of the city and spent the night in the car, and returned in the morning when everything was calm. The rest of the way back to America was also full of interesting events. They made their way back, finally, to the safety of America.

*****

Chapter 27

Please Go To The Living Room. I Will Be There...

How can a person survive, move on when all their loved ones are getting killed and dying on you? How do you go on when all your dreams shatter in front of your eyes as quickly as ice cracks? You do, you continue to live, normally, when you have witnessed the massacre of innocent people throughout your homeland? How do you enjoy your day when every morning you open your eyes, you know you have supported people who became unjust, and you are forever partly responsible for unjust killings? What do you do when you have spoken of their kindness, their honesty, their principles, and know they wash the blood off their hands?

After returning from Iran, Nader did not want to live. He saw visions flashing images of innocent men, women, and children dying cruelly. He always felt religion was there to bring peace and love. To create a world that existed based on the energy your heart created. Nader had to rediscover himself. He thought back to his time with the Dervish. He knew he had to ground himself. Save himself from self-pity. Soon he began to have his dreams back quite often, and he was seeing the images much more clearly than before. He started to see the two beautiful angels, one in blue and one in green; they always flew on each side of him, taking him away. He always knew he was dreaming, even where he was sleeping while in the dream. In the beginning, he did not think much about this because it had just started, and he thought it was just a reoccurring dream that was insignificant. But it was after the death of his father and one of his brothers that he became keenly aware that these dreams were more than just dreams.

He was in bed, asleep with his wife. His father appeared out of nowhere. He stood in the doorway and stared at Nader. He leaned up against the frame, and Nader spoke,

-Please go to the living room. I am sleeping with my wife. Please go there. I will be out to speak with you.

-Do not be worried. She cannot see me. I know you are scared of Khomeini and cannot come home. So, I just came to say goodbye, I am leaving for a long trip, and I came to ask you to forgive me. I know I was not a good father to you, but you are the only son who never insulted me... goodbye Nader....

-Please go to the living room, I will be there.

But his father just smiled, turned, and disappeared. Nader attempted to get off the bed to go after him. He was completely awakened, realizing he was being held back by Julia. She was awakened when she heard him talking in his sleep.

-My father is dead.

Julia sat motionless as he rose to make a phone call to see what was going on. He was told his father had gotten into an accident around the farm, and everyone, including his mother, had gone to see what was happening. Later, his mother told him he was hit by a car while he was crossing the street. While his father was at the hospital, he had turned to his brother-in-law and his mother and whispered to them,

-I will die, but my only wish is to see Nader before my death. But he is worried about Khomeini, and I know I cannot see him. He was the only son who did not insult me; I was not a good father to him. I hope he will forgive me for that.

His brother-in-law felt bad for the dying old man, so he went out into the streets and looked for a young man who looked similar to Nader. He worked a deal with a young man to come to the hospital and pretend to be Nader so the dying old man could be happy for a few moments before his death and die in peace. His brother-in-law entered the hospital room with a big smile on his face.

-See, I told you Nader will come to see you. He is back from America just to see you.

The young man had reached to his father to hug him with an empathetic smile on his face. But the dying old man knew who his real son was. He held his hand up for him not to approach. Then, he turned away and closed his eyes, never opening them again. The incident had happened exactly at the same time when Nader had the dream in America. He had forgiven his father a long time ago, he had paid for his wrongdoings in many ways, and Nader wanted his spirit to be at peace. It was about seventeen years later when Nader finally returned to Iran and sat with his mother. When she told him the story again, he realized how much she was in love with his father. He realized she was still missing him. Despite all the abuse that his father had inflicted upon her, the power of love had brought peace into his mother's heart, and she had forgiven her husband. He realized love could do wonders.

His mother and his family had not yet recovered from his father's death when another tragedy hit his mother within weeks.

It was about six months after Nader's return to the States from Iran. He hardly slept still and was tired all the time. It was one of those days of heavy rainfall on the California coast. He lay down to take a nap; He was in between sleep and the world. It was about three or four in the afternoon in the states and about four to five in the morning in Tehran. He noticed his brother Bijan driving in a white or yellow-colored car. He was watching him zigzag through traffic like he was trying to run away from something. He felt something bad was about to happen to him, and he must warn him to stop. But Nader knew he was sleeping in America. As he tried to think of a way to warn him, Bijan's car had disappeared between two eighteen-wheelers. He tried very hard to see him, but the only image Nader could see was his whitened face staring straight ahead at the string wheel. But he would not say a word. Nader pushed himself to awaken and rushed to the phone.

Julia was in the kitchen and became worried when she saw him break for the phone in a panic. Those days she was watching him very closely. She knew he was not doing well. He called his brother's flower shop that was on the corner of the dead alley his family used to live. One of the workers, a nice older man, finally answered the phone. It was very early morning. Nader asked for his brother Bijan and his whereabouts. The old man said,

-He just left for the city of Saveh.

Then, he continued,

-All the family is going there to visit one of your nieces.

Nader told him he must be stopped immediately.

-Can you go after him?

-Mr. Bijan is long gone, I only can see his backlights in the distance, and I would never catch him. Besides, I cannot drive or leave the shop.

Nader hung up the phone and called his other brother, Kamal. His mother was living with him during this time. He could not tell his mother about his dream if he could just get her on the phone. He told his brother he must rush to go after Bijan and stop him. Nader told him about the dream; he was not amused and replied;

-Please stop eating at night and stop dreaming....

But he was worried enough to take off after Bijan after he told him he would talk to their mother.

Nader was worried all day and night, he could not get through to anyone for a long time, and that gave him the feeling that something bad had happened. He did not want to call his mother because he knew even if his feeling was right, no one would have told her yet, and his constant phone calls to her would make her worried and upset. So, he had no other choice but to wait. Finally, the next day, he got in touch with Parry. Her response was that nothing was wrong; everything was fine. But Nader could tell she was lying. Then, his brother Bijan began to appear in his dreams.

-Why are you sleeping... call Hajji Khanoom... tell her she should stop crying for me... I am fine... every time she cries, my soul is in pain... it would suffer my soul, please tell her to stop crying... get up and call Hajji Khanoom....

Of course, they called their mother Hajji Khanoom, he told Nader he was dead, and their mother would not stop crying. Every time she started, she never stopped. And every time, her tears seemed like they wouldn't end,

-please tell her to stop crying...

Nader would be visited by Bijan, beckoning him to call their mother and stop her tears every time their mother would cry. Nader was constantly on the phone with his mother even though all were still denying to him that Bijan had been killed. So, all Nader could do now was call his mother, ask her why she was crying, and try to calm her, even though he knew where her sadness was coming from. He told her what Bijan told him.

-Bijan has come to me. He is asking me to ask you to please stop crying. He cannot be free if you cry.

But she was a much better actor than he was. On the phone with him, she would pretend there was nothing wrong, and Bijan is traveling north. They just had a light accident and, still, were traveling somewhere in the north.

But Nader knew she was play-acting. But he did not know for sure how he died; maybe the car accident, and execution, assassination. This game went on for forty days. They then had his last prayer ceremony in his mother's house to say goodbye as tradition called for on the fortieth day of the dead person to say goodbye and stop the mourning. It was daytime in Tehran and nighttime in America. That morning his mother began to cry early in the morning, so Bijan began to appear to Nader, and he asked him to call their mother once again. His constant phone calls began as the night passed on in America and day was passing in Iran. They had set up a man with a microphone by the phone, and anytime the phone would ring, he would yell into the microphone and ask everyone to be quiet, and the clergy who was speaking had to stop. And every time it was Nader calling, his mother or sister would answer the phone, and he was told there was nothing wrong. But the minute Nader would place his head on the pillow and try to relax; it was Bijan again and again, with him,

-How can you sleep when your mother is crying herself to unconsciousness? Get up and call her. Please tell her she is bothering my soul. I am happy here.

And he was on the phone again. By now, he was calling home every half hour, and the answer was the same. Then, finally, he heard his cousin Daash Mahmood yelling in the background,

-Why are you guys playing games when he already knows? Don't you guys hear him?

It was Bijan's wife who took the phone and cried to Nader,

-What do you want to know? Yes, your brother is dead, along with my two-year-old child Ghoncheh, is that what you want to know... he is dead....

Nader could hear the scrambling of his mother and sisters. All were echoing through the receiver. It was like they were challenging each other as to whose cries were louder. This is somewhat of a tradition in Iran; through the cries, you show your grief, and your grief is measured by the sound of your whaling. Those that are silent at a funeral may be perceived to not care that the person has passed.

Bijan's death had not hit Nader until that very moment and after he hung up the phone. He knew he was dead because he had been talking to Bijan almost every night, but he still was living in a warped denial. But after that moment, it hit him hard. He had such a difficult time trying to get over his grief when his brother was appearing to him all the time. Nader needed to settle this, and after some time, he felt this was unfair to him, like a sick game. So, he began to talk more instead of just listening. He asked Bijan about the world of death, the unknown afterlife. He had tried to speak with Nader, answer his questions, but he was always taken back to his mother crying uncontrollably. She continued her endless crying for a year after his death. Nader was in turmoil. He felt he had to be by his mother's side in Iran to really settle this, to give them both peace. The two people he needed to help were dead and on the other side of the planet. But he knew going back to Iran was a big risk. He may be arrested or killed, and this may be too much for his mother to handle.

What made matters worse was that his eldest brother Abbass was constantly getting arrested. And each time, people from several cities interfered and marched into the streets until he was released. The government could not publicly get rid of him. Then came a rumor that people did not like Bijan, and some had staged an accident for his death. His young daughter being a helpless victim. This all piled on top of the fact the entire family was again having financial problems. His aging mother had a lot to bear on her shoulders.

Nader's body was filled with guilt, longing to help, to be present spewed from his pores. He was depressed. During this time, he was not doing great financially as well. For the life of him, he could not hold down any type of job. The sadness, confusion, and depression were making it very hard for him to function. But it was Bijan who used to keep him going. He still came to him in his dreams. Nader knew why. Because he did not give the share of the property their family bought, and when Nader was young, they put it all in Bijan's name, and he was supposed to give Nader's back when he became 18 years old. But he did not, and their mother always used to curse Bijan, and now she felt guilty, she felt her cursing was the cause of his death, and Bijian was keep coming to Nader's dream and asking Nader for forgiveness for what he had done to him, somehow he let Nader know his children will pay for his greed and mistake. No matter how many times Nader said he forgave him, Bijan would not stop, and he kept coming, and he was always asking for forgiveness. But at the same time, Bijan showed him again the real purpose of life, helped separate him from the material world he was drowning in. Bijan shared many things with Nader, but one dream, in particular, was especially significant. And Nader knew it was meant to give him a message.

There was a beautiful river at the farm their family used to own, and in the noon hour when they were young children, they used to go to a rocky part, dive into the river and swim. Bijan took him there many times when he was very young, but this time in the dream was different. Nader was sitting on the rock, and Bijan was diving into the water, and instantly, within the blink of an eye, he would appear right behind him and dive in again. Bijan was tall, young, and handsome. He was also naked. Nader was worried that the farming women would see him and get insulted, so he began to plead to Bijan,

-You must cover yourself. If the women see you, they will get insulted, and they will go to Hajji Khanoom, and she will get upset.

-You do not need to be worried. You are the only one who can see me; they cannot see me.

Then, he dove into the water, and his routine continued. It was then that Nader turned to him and began questioning him about the other world, the world of the unknown, the world of death that Bijan now knew.

> -You see, Bijan, you practically do not let me sleep. Would you at least tell me what is going on there, where you are?

He pointed to Nader and the farm, and with a look of sadness and concern, he turned to Nader,

> -Hell, to this world, I was mistaken; everything is here in this realm. Hell, to that world. I was wrong... everything is here... you should forgive me ...

Bijan was not done talking when suddenly seven men who were the same size, tall and handsome just like him, all naked, appeared directly behind Bijan, grabbed him, and would not let him finish. They all dove into the water and disappeared. Nader could sense that they wanted him to know, to feel, the seven men. The number was significant.

Nader woke up, wondering what kind of dream he had just had. There were so many unanswered questions. After this dream, Bijan did not come back to him in any dreams. And the only time he had a vision of him, he was fat, unhappy, and depressed. Two years later, he came back, just once. It was on the day of his daughter's birthday, the day had been interrupted by their eldest brother, and Bijan wanted Nader to give him a message about his being displeased.

*****

Chapter 28

Smiling While Torment And Sadness Festered Inside; Moving House To House And Every Other Day...

Nader's struggled with the dreams and tragedy after tragedy that occurred. By now, he could see or dream most of what was going to happen back home or here in the States that had to do with his family. And it was beginning to drive him crazy. He was really losing it, and then came the last blow. The president of Iran was now Abolhassan Banisader, who was one of the closest advisors to Khomeini. He was like a son to him. They all knew he was ordered by Khomeini to go around the country and give speeches. This would ensure that he would be the first president of Iran. And as if by divine appointment, Nader's high school friend, Hussein, was the one who was Banisader's right-hand man; he was the one who was writing for Banisader's daily paper. When Hussein's articles were in the paper, the paper would sell out within hours. So Banisader was the president, and Hussein was a very close and trusted advisor to him. In fact, he was told no decision was made by Banisader without Hussein's advice, so Hussein knew very much from the beginning of the revolution to the end. But Banisader began to fight the clergy over power, and the clergy did not want him around anymore. There were complaints from both sides to Khomeini, and the result was Khomeini taking the clergy's side. Suddenly Banisadder was not his son anymore; he was the Enemy.

Nader was sleeping one night, and he had a vision of Banissader dressing up, covering his face, leaving the country. He was having a conversation with Hussein, who was very angry, shouting he was selling his homeland. He must not leave. He must stay and fight the clergy because this is the time the country really needed him. But Banissader left, entered the dark area at the airport, and Hussein was wandering around mad, running alley to alley. He was entering different houses. He would rush out and run into another house. Quickly he entered a large building with a tall wall surrounding it, and Nader heard a gunshot.

Nader woke up, and he knew something must have happened to Hussein or would soon enough. He called Hassan, their other friend at the time, who left America and went back to Iran; he answered the phone. They did not talk for about two years because they had gone into an argument about Khomeini, and Hassan did not like Nader's opposition to Khomeini. Before that, they were best of friends. Besides, they were classmates in high school, but their real friendship started when they met in America. That is why Nader was hesitated to call first, but he could not find Hussein, and he had no choice but to call Hassan. To his surprised, Hassan was so kind and so happy to hear from Nader that made Nader relax. Then Nader to him about the dream. After Nader's phone call, Hassan left Banisader's office right away, but Hussein thought he was crazy. It was just a few months later those things changed, Banisader had escaped from Iran, and the rumor was that he had a veil on as a disguise to get onto the airplane to be flown out. With Banisader's departure to France, his office was closed, and his staff, including Hussein, was in danger of being arrested and killed. Hussein was the first target, and they were looking for him. So, he had to go underground, but he did not want to leave Iran. He was moving house to house, and every other day he was at a different friend or relative's house, so he could not be located. His father was arrested and was hung upside down. He was slashed on the bottom of his feet to force him to reveal Hussein's whereabouts. But he remained quiet about his son's location.

And finally, the news of Hussein's death came to Nader on a rainy day in the late afternoon. These rainy days kept bringing Nader news he did not want. A friend stopped by and handed him a letter that was sent to him by Hassan. He opened it and was taken aback to find Hussein's will. It was written in his jail cell on the last night of his life. He had written his will after they told him he would be executed early the next morning. Hussein had been in hiding for few months when he was arrested and tortured. He was then given an ultimatum; to write an article denouncing whatever he had written before, to admit his guilt and praise Khomeini and ask him for forgiveness, or die. He stated he would rather die than write what was not true. He was shot to death the next day. His father had to pay for the twenty-one bullets which were used to kill him in order to get his body back. This was his reward for helping a revolution, for trying got support his homeland, his people.

Hussein's execution and what he wrote in his will, was the last blow for Nader. He was already walking on the edge of reality, of leaving sanity. He was on the edge of destruction. He was on the verge of giving everything up and joining the opposition, even dying for revenge, to make things right laid before him on the table. So far, the only thing that was holding him back was Julia. This incredible and kind person that he was married to was all that was keeping him from completely going off the deep end, and he didn't want to ruin her life. How could he leave her and break the commitment he had made to her? But the situation was beyond repair in many ways. No matter what, someone would suffer.

A few days later, he received a letter from a friend who had changed his life direction. He was informed that he had been included on a list of those to be assassinated by the government. They were scared that he might possess information given to him by Hussein or his brother. They thought Hussein may have given Nader certain documents to keep safe that proved dishonest actions taken by revolutionaries who were now in power. They pretended to be followers of Islam, but in reality, Islam was the last thing they were thinking about. They used Islam like a pair of worn house slippers, trekking it through the mud, morphing practices and beliefs to benefit themselves. He was told that perhaps his family could be in danger as well. He knew who he was dealing with, people who showed no mercy even upon their own children when they spoke the truth. Now, there was Julia. He could stay, putting her life in possible danger, or leave to protect her. Every time he answered the door, it could be someone blasting a few quick shots to wipe the past under the rug. Even a car bomb slipped in during those few minutes when he wasn't watching. Even in America, they were not safe. He had to leave.

Julia never knew what was really going on. As always, everything dark was a secret to your wife, and Julia was no exception. When he broke the news to her, she was in absolute shock. Her heart became heavy, stunned. She knew they had a few problems, but nothing major. Every couple had a few problems. But she knew he had been struggling with something, a sadness and pain she knew nothing of. His departure was tough to fully unravel, yet she had stood by her man the best she knew how. Much later, Nader found out he had never really been on that infamous list. The information he was given was just a strategy implemented by the new Iranian intelligence agency. They wanted to see if he would talk if he knew anything. But it was too late to return to Julia. The damage had been done, and Nader knew he would never fully recover. He had such a deep respect for her, he knew it was unfair for him to return and play with her heart. He knew he had to fight to get his land back from the radical heartless innovator.

*****

The news of Nader leaving his wife had shocked their friends and relatives more than it did Julia. They could never have imagined something like that would happen. No one believed that he was gone for only a few months, but he was gone for good. Nader was deeply depressed. He felt horrible and hoped Julia was doing well. He always prayed to God to keep her safe and gift her better life. Then he moved back to San Francisco. He needed to be farther away to protect her from the danger and chaos of his life. He had to move every couple of months to be sure he would not be located, just like a gypsy does. The hardest part of his life now was keeping a job. He had to change it every few months, which didn't allow him to have an element of trust when interviewing for his next job. By now, he was just like a drifter who had no purpose in life, a man lost in time, a man who had no home and no real life. He, again, was just like a clown, not knowing where he would be the next day. Smiling while torment and sadness festered inside. Every day presented more depressing news from his homeland and more tragedy to deal with. His mother still had to hear his voice every day, and the cost of calling home constantly left him broke.

But his mother and Forogh were the sole reason he had to stay alive and in good spirits. By now, Forogh had grown up and was attending high school. She constantly made Nader promise he would take her to America once she graduated. His mother and Forogh now lived together. They became their own small family unit within their larger whole. Forogh was always butting heads with her father the same way Nader had, and his mother was like a lost soul. Nader was always trying to make peace through the phone lines. It was all becoming so hard for him; he began to crack, desperately wanting normalcy. He was beginning to contemplate returning home, even with the possibility of death or arrest looming in the air. He needed something different in his life besides pain and suffering. He needed something new. He decided to begin writing again and try to break into the film industry in America. Nader had also met some new friends. A group of Iranian women whom one could call party girls entered his life. For him, it was like a breath of fresh air, a time to relax and wind down a bit, to have a bit of fun out and about.

Many years had passed, and Nader's two missions in life were to help his mother stay alive however he could and help Forogh finish school. Then, one of the ladies from the group he used to party with suddenly fell in love with one of his old college classmates, Ali. Nader had run into him and took him to a party the girls had invited him to. They started dating, and within a few days, they fell in love. Within a week after that, they were engaged to be married, and of course, Nader was invited. But this wedding party ended up being a reunion with a past love.

There were about a hundred guests at the home of the bride's sister. An Iranian wedding has two phases, Aghd and Aroosee. Aghd gathering consists of close relatives and friends of the bride and groom gathered together. The bride and the groom are dressed up and sit in front of a beautifully designed set called "Sofreh Aghd," which means the set of the wedding. In the set, there has to be seven items, all starting with the letter "S," a candle, a mirror, a colored fish, homegrown greens, and the Koran if they are Muslim.

There would be elaborate flower designs everywhere. In fact, there is heavy competition for the best flower designs for the wedding set, as well as on the car the bride and groom drive in. When the set is ready, the bride and groom sit in front of a mirror, and four ladies hold a white or blue organza over their heads while all take turns grinding two pieces of large sugar cubes over their heads upon the organza. Then, the clergy comes and reads vows to them. Generally, he will ask the bride three times if she would take the groom as her husband, and it is the third time that she will finally say "yes." Then the same question will be asked from the groom once, and he will answer yes. This is followed by cheers of joy and a party. This is when presenting big presents to the bride from both of their families occurs, but the bride and groom exchange their rings and place honey or cake in each other's mouths first.

But the poor grooms only get a few small presents from the parents, sisters, or brothers of the bride. Then comes the Aroosee, the party, which is usually the same night. The party starts early without the bride and groom. Tradition calls for the groom and the bride's drive to the main party in a beautifully designed car with flowers. Of course, there are tons of relatives and friends who are following the couple's car. There is also a custom that calls for those following to answer the tune that the driver of the car that carries the Bride and the Groom plays using the horn. So, everyone through the streets is notified that a wedding is taking place, people stop to watch and join in the festivities from the streets. Finally, the arrival of the couple is announced with the playing of a special song called "Mobark Bod." The bride and groom walk through the party chit-chatting while exchanging kisses and handshakes. Quickly the party continues, and the couple hits the dance floor, all celebrate into the night.

Nader was still surprised they were actually getting married. He wondered how two people could fall in love in just one week. He was lost in thought, contemplating love, when his eyes landed on her. After that, his mind forgot there was even a wedding in progress. He was watching the dance floor; he was watching his love, Fariba, his violin girl.

Standing in a corner, hiding from the crowd, he was watching her floating through the shifting dance floor, moving just like a butterfly, and she was looking at Nader. He could feel she was missing her soulmate, her partner, on the dance floor. She wanted him on the floor, in her embrace. But her soulmate was playing shy and wondering if she was for real. He thought he may be hallucinating and looked around for Abraham but saw him nowhere. He knew that whatever was happening, he still loved her. Nader knew he wanted her to be in his arms for his entire life, he knew he wanted her to be happy, and he could feel that finally, she was. He could read it in her smile and in her body the way she was moving around the floor... and with the way, she was looking at him. He could see the change in her from the last time they met. She was reaching deep down into his soul with her eyes; Nader felt the familiar burning in his being that only she could cause.

It did not matter how shy he could have played. She was free of all inhibitions. She was alive even if he was not. She would dance away on the floor like flying into the air, and he could see her reaching out to him again and again, beckoning. When she was dancing freely, it was as if there was a burst of light, and she wanted him to join her feeling of freedom. Then, he was holding onto her, moving into her flowing spaciousness, feeling her warmth. Looking into each other's eyes, they traveled into each other's spirit. There was just him and her and the moment, and time was standing still as they dissolved into one soul, for one moment. Just she and him. Silence blocked out the extraneous sounds, and there was peace. He could tell she seemed freed. Freed from everything that plagued their past, but he couldn't tell why.

It was after the third song that she reached into the air, being marvelously sultry for him to watch, divine as a ballerina, and there were no rings on any of her fingers. It was clear that she wanted him to know she was finally free. She had broken free from the one-sided contract of her marriage forever. She was internally freed, and she was happy and delighted to have him in her embrace. He was separated from his wife but not divorced, and he wondered what would happen next between them. Is there hope finally that he would be happy with her for years to come? But he had a feeling that she was just enjoying the moment at the time, and she did not want to even think about the next one.

The night was coming to an end, and they had completely forgotten about the fact that the evening had belonged to another couple who had invited them to celebrate their vows. It seemed they were the ones who had the party to become one. But before the bride and groom were bidding farewell to their guests, they were long gone. They were passionately embracing each other in the elevator going up, and when the door opened, they did not want to leave the elevator. They were holding onto each other so tightly as if something was going to happen, and they would lose the sweet moment. They were headed to his place. Soon they were at his apartment on the thirteenth floor of a high rise facing the ocean. His place was simple and elegant with wood floors and oak and leather furniture.

It was a bit past midnight, and they were still holding onto each other so tightly that there was not a force possible that could separate them. All through the night, they may have said one or two words, not more. It was always the silence that spoke the best between their hearts. They did not need to use fabricated words to communicate or to manipulate the feeling of their union. It was just the feeling, the energy, the peace which had bonded them, and they did not know how. He could never have imagined the bittersweet feeling from her lips or the captivating magic of her kiss. Never in his wildest dreams had he experienced such a high, and he was drunk not on booze, but the connection with this being that was his soulmate, felt like eternal love. They both were in the heat of passion, so hot that they could have burst into flames. Peace, freedom, fear all flowed throughout the night.

The next day he was consumed by the bittersweet feeling from the past night. She was free from her husband, yet he still could not have her embrace. Something else was different; he felt another change had occurred. The truth that she did not want to be with him either defied his logic as well. Her words echoed,

-I feel… it would be better to be away from each other; then our love will never die. What if we got married and found out that we were not a match, and then I would die. It is beautiful the way it is, it is holy, it is peaceful, so why should we ruin it? Let it be what it is, not tainted by everyday life. Let it last forever, my love. Besides, I need to think about my son. He is very close to his father; I am not sure how he would react, especially if Abraham decided to tell him about all of our history… or use him against us… love you forever….

He was sitting at his kitchen table reading her note, but he could not think or move his mouth. He noticed a photo of a young boy leaning against a kitchen counter. He stared at the photo, then reached and held it closer. He turned the photo around, written on the back was My Son, Nader. He sat motionless, stunned, wondering what the extent of this meant. He was frustrated she had left while he was asleep. He ran her words through his mind again. He understood what she meant yet longed to have his love with him each day. They had such a beautiful thing, something that many never experienced in life, not even for a day. He knew he had to go on with his life. She was gone again, but for how long, he did not know. All he could do is waiting for that next sweet moment, for another moment in time that would come by surprise and leave him in wonder again.

*****

Chapter 29

The Revelation Of His Life...

Sitting in his apartment, watching the rain hitting the window, again, he was not feeling anything. He stared out into oblivion, hypnotized by the rain and the majestic view through the windows. He then noticed a small bird moving around the corner of the balcony, searching for a place to be safe from the pouring rain, and for a long moment, he did not notice the poor bird crying for help. He reached and opened the window; she flew in after a bit and landed on the ceiling fan. He took a break to watch the lost little bird, as he needed a breather. He was in the process of rewriting his script, and the bird and the rain were a wave of fresh energy. Now he had a little friend, this bird, who seemed to be speaking to him with silence. She seemed to be yelling for help to find her way out, for a way to leave and join her friends, or perhaps her mate. But to him, she was just singing a nice tune, as if she was talking to Nader, but he was deaf and dumb to her language. He was lost in thought, thinking he was just like the little bird. He was free to go out, but his room, his apartment, and his world was just like a small cage. It did not matter where he was. He was in prison within himself. It did not matter how close the ocean was, how easy it was to run upon the open road; he was like a captive bird. As he watched the little bird, he began to fall more deeply into recollections of his past with full intensity. Each memory seemed to be accompanied by an entire set of unanswered questions, but he was beginning to doubt the purpose of each event less and less. He had stopped asking why certain things had occurred in his life, and now he knew better than to ask, "God, why me?" Even as he looked back on things he didn't like, he was learning to accept a grander possibility for his life's situations.

One particular situation, and the results, he would never forget. How would he be able to forget that upstairs corner room of the Motel 8, on 8th street, in the Wilshire district of Los Angeles?

Earlier the same night, he was staring at two suitcases full of money, each hiding about two million dollars within its solid leather binding. It was at a motel room in Pasadena. A chubby Spanish man of about fifty was sitting on a chair, looking at him, and the suitcases that two of his armed bodyguards had just pulled out from underneath the bed,

-This is four million, and we will provide you with three million more later. I need just the seven million by the same time next year, and you will deposit it in our bank account. I hope Richard has told you who we are.

Nader was confused but not as confused as he would have been if he accepted the money. He had to find a polite way to refuse the money so he would not offend him. He looked around the room then at the two bodyguards standing by watching. He offered an excuse,

-Richard has to handle the accounting, not me. I am just the creative man, writer, and director, he has to accept the responsibility, and I am not good with money... beside my trunk is full and there will be no room for this...

A few minutes later he was driving into the light rain back to his motel room, thinking about what had just happened. He knew he only had about a hundred dollars left to his name, and in a few days, he would be kicked out of the motel where he was living. He had worked on his script for a year and had given up everything to develop the script, which illustrated the situation in Iran. He thought that was the least he could do for his people, who he felt he had betrayed by supporting the revolution. His partner

Richard, a known attorney, promised he would bring in the financing now after he had spent all his savings. Richard had not shown up, and he would soon find out why. Maybe because he knew the money was drug money, laundering, and didn't want to be involved directly. He entered the Motel 8, on 8th street, in the Wilshire district of Los Angeles, where he was temporarily staying. He stopped right at the entrance, turn toward the office, and could see the motel manager, Maria, a beautiful lady from El Salvador, sitting behind the window waiting for him. She knew the story and who he was meeting. She had lots of problems with her redneck, drug-addict boyfriend, and he had promised her when he got the film going, he would give her a job, so she could disappear from her boyfriend's sight. He stopped and looked at her for a second and then took off. She could tell he didn't have the money, and he didn't have enough energy to get into a discussion at the moment. He went upstairs, not even feeling the rain, and watched her lights go off. He fell onto the bed and was lying down, just staring at the ceiling until finally, he fell asleep.

It was about three in the morning when he was awakened by the lightning from the storm banging against his window. He got up and went to use the bathroom, stopping in front of the mirror, staring at himself for a long while. Then returned to the bed, adjusted the pillow; his right elbow was holding him against the bed, his right foot was found underneath his left food that was laying straight. After adjusting the pillow, heartfelt, sadden, empty within in, he looked up again to stare at the water-stained ceiling. He could not figure out what to do next. He hadn't said a word since he left the men in the motel room, refusing four million dollars, and now it was time for God to answer, hopefully,

> -God, I do not understand, why do you help people who always hurt people and ignore the ones who want to help others? Why? Eventually, the good turn bad because they do not feel you; they do not sense your help. Can you hear me? Please answer me?

He wished he had never opened his mouth. He was just about to turn his head and settle back to sleep when within a second, the ceiling opened up, and he was sucked up into a black, green, and white tunnel of light. He was going, up, into this tunnel at the speed of light. He could not move and began to yell, if not out loud in his mind, his right elbow still bent, his right foot still was folded underneath his left, his right eyes were in pain and half-close, just his left eyes were wide open, "I am sorry, please, God, please forgive me. I am sorry. Please forgive me!" He did not know for how long he became a part of that tunnel, but he was dropped back onto his bed, the light disappeared, and the ceiling closed up. He was completely disoriented, totally numbed. His right eye was still half-closed as his right leg, which was folded under him, was still locked in place. He was on the bed, motionless. A bit later, there was a knock on the door, and he stayed as he did not know what to do; he was spaceless and did not know where he was.

-Nader, it's Maria. I have the police here. Are you okay?

He could hear her voice from behind the door, but he could not respond or think about responding. He continued staring, "Nader, the police are coming in." The key turned in the door, the door was opened, and several policemen entered pointing their guns, with Maria following. The police checked the room and the bathroom as Maria was staring at Nader. He still could not respond. He could hear them but had no ability to move his lips, his vocal cords were numb. Maria continued,

-The man next door heard you yelling for help, so he called the police… are you okay?

One of the officers checked his closed eye, and as he opened it, he asked him,

-Did you smoke anything?

He could not answer. Maria knew Nader didn't smoke, so she answered them,

-He doesn't touch drugs... but he dreams... he sees things in his dreams.

The officer turned to Nader and asked him,

-Were you dreaming?

He shook his head up and down toward the officer. Yes. They all waited a few more minutes before leaving him, shutting the door firmly. He was scared to death, and suddenly he came to life. He jumped up, scared, within a few minutes, grabbed whatever he could, and left. Ten minutes later, he was sitting in his car, still kind of in shock, driving away from the Motel 8. It was the next day that he realized he had left many items of clothing and a couple pairs of shoes in the motel room, but he never went back to claim them or contacted Maria. In fact, he has not driven around that area since. He was so scared that he could not sleep in any room for a month. He began sleeping in his car. The fact that he was awake and had experienced such a frightening answer from God, or the creator, had him thinking twice before asking any questions again. It caused him to wonder about what is taken into account when you wish or ask for something. His partnership with Richard was dissolved because he did not want to get involved with drug money. He found out Richard was an attorney to several big drug dealers. And the last thing Nader wanted on his plate. But by now, he knew he could not doubt the events that were happening to him. He had to live with circumstances and be patient. After his experience in the motel room, he accepted the fact he could not change anything and could only control the path of his life to a certain extent. Destiny was in charge, and he was co-captain. The two angels, one in blue and one in green, began to visit him often between the hours of three and six in the morning. They took him to many places.

*****

After what had happened at the Motel 8, Nader began seeing more visions and dreams. On one of those nights, Nader was sleep at Sherman Oakes apartment located in Van Nays Blvd. Then suddenly, the two angels appeared. One was dressed in long light blue silk, the other in very light green. They just stared at him, and they said no words. Then Nader found himself with the two angels again. Frustrated, he began to talk,

-I do not understand what do you guys want from me... why don't you guys go find someone else... I'm no good... I'm a salesman....

As always, the Angel on green showed frustration in his appearance, but the angel in the blue, who was much younger and always was following the green one, had a smile on his face. Her smile never faded. Always was there. The Angel in green gestured to Nader to look at the artwork that was on the table. Nader knew they brought the artwork, and it did not belong to him. It was in the shape of a rectangle. It is a beautiful work of art, like a painting, but in written language. He could not understand the writing. It was a combination of Farsi, Arabic, English, and several other alphabets. It was perfectly straight in organized lines. Only in the right bottom corner of the rectangle was there a mark out of the rectangle that looks like the English letter "y" to break the balanced and the harmony of the structure. All other writing was inside the rectangle. Nader examined it more closely. It looks like a Persian miniature painting, but he could not understand any of the words in the beginning.

Finally, the Angel in the green breaks her silence,

-This is the name of God.

Now Nader was confused. He looks up to the Angel in Green and in testing mood,

-You mean the name of God is y....

The Angel in green spoke up again like the one in blue was smiling and was watching the two,

-Don't see it with your eyes… close them and see it with your heart.…

Nader debated if he should follow her directions or not. But he did and closed his eyes and look at the artwork. And suddenly, after a few seconds, he was looking at an incredible artwork. But this time, all words were known to him. It seemed the artwork was moved around, and this time the letter "y" he saw on the bottom right was located on the top left of the rectangle, and still, it was the only letter out of the rectangle. But this time, Nader did not see the letter "y," but he was looking at an "L" for love. And now, in the maze, he could recognize and understood all the words. He saw the word of love in every language in the world. The languages Nader even did not know existed. Now excited, he began to read the word and the language it belonged to. But his celebrations did not last much as the Angel in a green broke his focus,

-there is more to see for you… come with us.…

And suddenly Nader found himself been escorted by the two angels. They were fly away with Nader to be in between them, through rosy clouds and shimmering multi-colored spheres of light, which flow into rainbow light tunnels. They pulled through the tunnels of multiple lights and arrived in a pristine, ethereal old mystical Egyptian-looking abandoned town. He looked around, confused. The two angels in blue and green silk stood each on a different side. He suddenly found himself in an ancient old city. It looks like the entire place was an oldish brown color; he looked around more confused as the Angel in green speaks up again,

-This is a form of God.

Nader looked at what she referred to as the shape of God. He saw the bust of a statue sitting on an older, broken post from his chest up. He only could see the left side of the face, which is iridescent in color, brownish. He moved to see the other side of the face. But each time, he moved he could still only see the same side of the face.

Frustrated, he moved faster and faster to see if he could see the other side of the face, but he had no luck. Frustrated, he turned to the Angel in green,

> -I always thought God was shapeless... now you tell me God has shape and only has one side of a face?

> -This is for you to find out why....

The Angel in green respond to Nader as the Angel in blue, as usual, was laughing quietly and had a good time watching the interaction between Nader and the Angel in green. Nader, now was lost and frustrated again, he turned to the angels,

> -What kind of game is this? Don't you know that if I tell my mother or sister that you have shown me the name of God and the shape of God, they would laugh at me, and they would think I have gone insane?

> -Let's go and see what they would do and feel.

The green Angel motioned, and they were in the air traveling again, with him in the middle as usual. Soon, they were at his old house in Tehran, in his old room, during the time he was attending the College of Dramatic Arts. They were standing by his bed, by the tall window facing the balcony, and as he was looking at them, Nader knew he was in America sleeping on his bed yet simultaneously standing in his room in Iran, so many years ago. Then his mother and Parry appeared in the doorway, entering another room, surprised to see him back. The Angels were motioning to him to speak to his mother and sister, and finally, his mouth opened,

-Hajji Khanoom, Parry, those two Angels just showed me the name and the shape of God.

He was not finished speaking when his mother stopped him with her worried voice,

-Astakhforelah, Astakhforelah, do not say such things. You will be punished. It is a sin. God will punish you. I think America has driven my son to insanity. You must not go back, Nader....

His mother just kept talking away as he could see a smile of confusion and surprise on his sister's face. His mother turned, and he turned to the Angels.

-I told you they think I have gone insane. Didn't I?

-Shake the sheet.

The Angel in the green outfit pointed to the silk bedspread and motioned for Nader to do as she said. He hesitated and turned to his mother and sister. His mother spoke up again quickly.

-Who are you talking to, Nader?

-I am talking to these two Angels in green and blue. They want me to shake the bedspread.

-You have gone insane. We have to take him to a doctor, Parry. America has driven him into insanity! Parry go, call Doctor Fatahi... we must take him to the doctor, American drove my son into insanity... what are you waiting for? Call Dr. Fatahi

His mother was still talking without taking a full breath as Parry stood with a questioning smile on her face. The angel in green asked him to shake the sheet; he turns to his mother and sister again,

-Hajji Khanoom, Parry, these two angels want me to shake the bedspread... I do not know what would happen... but do not be scared....

Huffed softly, then Nader leaned in, grabbing the bedspread, and shook it. Suddenly, out of nowhere, flames appeared in the middle of the bedspread, burning strongly. It stayed confined to the middle of that silk bedspread, dancing so beautifully, creating something like blooming the Lotus flower. His mother and sister both became scared. His mother ran away, followed by Parry laughing. As the Angels began to smile, he woke himself up from the dream. Nader walked to the kitchen, thinking about what he had just experienced, and was contemplating whether or not God really did have a shape or a universal name. He grabbed some water from the fridge, perplexed. He was still drinking it when the phone rang. It was his sister, laughing through the receiver. She was explaining to Nader that their mother had run out of the living room and was standing out at the patio and was scared to come in. Nader could hear his mother in the background, yelling to him,

-If you want to kill me, just do it. Why do you want to set me on fire and torture me to dead... why are you giving me a heart attack...?

Then his sister Parry began to explain that their mother, as usual, was sitting at his praying rug in the living room praying. Then she had seen Nader appeared and sat in front of him, talking about God... then he grabs corners of the prying rug and shook it. Then suddenly, a flame started in front of her in the middle of her pray rug dancing. That scared her, and she ran out to the balcony and yelled for Parry, who was living next door to her. Nader could not explain to her why she had had such a vision, but he told it all to Parry, knowing she could handle it.

*****

Chapter 30

The Bird Had Found A New Home Now...

The bird had found a new home now. Nader used to keep the window half-open. She would fly in, amuse herself, and then leave when ready. He enjoyed her presence. She was his company. He spoke to her often, and she always had the same answer, silence. He was at a very weird stage in his life. He needed someone to talk to. Someone who would not judge or gear him toward what they felt was best. It was as if he was being put to the test as if someone was trying to give him a message that he was not ready for or could not digest. He really did not want any type of special message. He felt that he had enough problems, problems he would be working on for the rest of his life. He wanted his life back to normal, or as normal as it could get. Challenges were not on the top of his list; in fact, they sunk to the bottom, being held down by thick boulders. He wanted to feel peaceful. Many times, he thought there must be a devil within him, there must be something wrong with him, that he must have personally created all these illusions. He had to be the source of all his problems. He knew that he was part of the problem, but he didn't think he was responsible for creating it. He had tried many times to stop dreaming about what would happen in his future, but the dreams would not cease to come. He decided to try to change the direction of the dreams. If he had a dream and he knew a change was coming, he would try his best to not let it happen.

But no matter how hard he tried, he could never manage to stop things from taking place; his plans crumbled. He knew something would happen soon to change the direction of his life. His work would be transformed, and meeting a woman was in the air. Losing a woman was also a possibility.

It had been about six or seven years since Nader and Julia had separated. He remembered that they still had not filed for divorce. Within days she filed, and soon their divorce was official. It seemed without knowing the minutes, there was divorce, and he began to search for love again. It seemed as though this was the story of his life. He found himself very lonely, and he thought if he could have a steady relationship in his life, things would be better. He was not sure if Fariba would ever return again. He had a feeling that even if she would, and it would not be permanent. She would appear and disappeared, just like one of his dream. He informed his women friends that he wanted to find love. They alls cuffed at him because he constantly had new women around; they said he had a new flavor every month. Some of his friends joked he was like a magnet for women. But he always treated them with respect and affection. But he hardly looked for one. They would appear in his life and disappear. There was a friend of a friend named Mahrokh. This woman liked him, yet he always ignored her and never called. His friend came to him again, saying Mahrokh was still talking about him. He needed to call her and set up a date. He seized the opportunity and set up a meeting for the next day. They met at a nice beach house restaurant. The weather was crisp and warm, the beach perfect for a walk. She was beautiful, even kind and caring. They dated for a month or two, and then his friend started suggesting he should ask her to marry him. She believed that his life would change for the better if they were to get married. He would become more settled and would be able to think about moving forward. He would be in a good place financially and also in his personal life, two things that brought him closer to normal. But for some reason, he did not. Then, another big surprise came. It was a rainy night; Mahrokh picked him up and drove him to the same beach house restaurant they had met the first time. He had a feeling something was different this particular night. It was in the air. The waitress brought a simple candle sitting firmly on a clear glass plate. She placed it within the center of their table and lit it quickly. The significance of the candle could only mean a few things; Nader did not have to wait long. She grabbed his hands firmly, yet with the softness of a woman, "I wanted to ask you to marry me, I know you care about me, I have a great job, and I will support you so you can focus all your energy on your writing. You must write. You are not a car salesman or any type of salesman, you must write, and I can help you fulfill that." He was stunned; she was touching a deep place in his heart. She was sincere and also beautiful when she spoke. Why should he not marry her? But for some reason, he could not say yes or no. He just stood up, walked over to kneel by her, and hugged her like he had loved her forever.

He sat next to her the rest of the night; she was in his half embrace as they ate. She took him home, and, in their minds, it was as if the deal was done. But he had not verbally answered. The word yes had not pierced the ear giving his vocal proclamation of acceptance. After she left, he sat up all night. By morning his decision was made. He would marry her and decided to take her out with all their friends and propose to her in front of everyone to show he admired her courage. He picked up the phone and made arrangements for the gathering. And then a dream came again. Nader knew that he was sleeping in his bed when the dreams came. He was at his apartment getting ready to leave. The green and blue angels appeared. They were trying to take him away, where he did not know. Frustrated, he refused to go. He turned to them, "What do you want from me? Why me? I am getting married. I am going to ask her to marry me. Can you guys just find someone else for all this?" The two angels were now frustrated as well, ignoring his pleas insisting he come. Finally, he turned to them, and with a serious and firm tone, spoke,

> -I will not go anywhere. I am tired of the game you guys play with me. I want to get married.

The angel in green frustrated yet calm, politely responded,

-You cannot get married. Why don't you understand?

Now Nader really was frustrated,

-What do you mean I can't get married? I want to get married. And I will.

The angel in the blue outfit spoke with a softer tone,

-I am sorry, but you cannot.

He was at a loss for words, his body sank into his toes, and helplessness took over. The voice of the green angel cut his attention,

-Because your wife has been chosen for you.

Nader turned toward the Angel in green to see her point to the woman who was standing next to her; she was about 5' 7" with a good figure and a round face. She looked somewhat Oriental, yet hints of Persian were found in her traits. She was just standing there with a look of innocence and sad feeling within in, and she was staring at him. Nader could see the kindness in her being. He did not know what to do or say. Then, he was awakened by the phone ringing. It was about 4:30 in the morning. He answered the phone to hear his friend's voice yakking at him through the receiver,

-What in the hell did you do last night? She just hangs up the phone when I call. She is crying and doesn't want to see you anymore. What happened? He just listened in shock, taking a deep breath, trying to gather his thoughts as they stirred about still half asleep, "Nader! What did you do? She called last night and was very happy, and then now it is all tears. Are you there?

He finally broke his silence and said,

I did nothing. I do not know what is going on. As usual... you know?

Frustrated, she yells again,

-Did you have a dream again? Please stop dreaming! Would you already?

After that, he never saw her. He knew he could not have her. He also did not know if he should wait or look for the one, the one that was chosen for him, not by him.

This loss of love was just another occurrence that showed him he did not run his own life. He was tired, frustrated, still craving stability. Peace was his mission. He began to recollect all his past dreams. He made notes of everything and sought outside help, people who could translate dreams. Among them were a couple in Chatsworth, California, Tom and Janet. He was told they were good at seeing things. There he was, sitting in front of them. He met with them several times, sometimes with them individually and sometimes with all three of them. Both had many good insights, but everything good would come later. Most interesting to Nader was that Tom wrote his name with one letter different. He had not told them about his real name before. During his first visit alone with Tom, unrest occurred. Since he was usually cheerful and smiling, it surprised him when he suddenly began to shake and was almost in tears, "You are here for a purpose. I am sure you are seeing images. You must write them down and reveal them somehow." Nader reached and turned the tape off; they always taped the conversations, and both would keep a copy. He did not want such things like that to be on the tape. Then, Tom settled again and continued and told him that he will suffer through his life until old age and then compared him with the head of the large corporation, General Motors, at the time. He predicted Nader would be a big shot at an older age.

Later Nader sat with Janet, who had such a peaceful and warm essence. He took her into his confidence. He told her about a few of his dreams quickly to see if she could make any sense out of them. One was more interesting than the rest to her. It was the dream Nader had at the hospital when he was waiting for the doctor to operate on his broken arm. Janet's interpretation was that it could mean that he had, in fact, dreamed his entire life, and he was recalling everything that had happened to him in Iran as a whole. Then, coming here to America, the culmination of his new experiences was being shown to him all at once. He came to an understanding that she may be right. She had translated the first part of the dream, where he was looking for the soccer ball in a messy river; this representing his messy life in Iran. The second part, when he went over the wall and jumped into a beautiful garden which everything was utterly organized and perfect; had to be America. The ball he was going after was his goal, his destiny, and the suffering he went through. And finally, to catch the ball is what he was going through now, and the end will be beautiful. The results he craved, what he was chasing, would come in old age. Everything she said was beautiful, but to think that he had to wait until "that one day at the old age…" to get the results was just unacceptable to him. He really wanted the turmoil to end and to have a peaceful, regular life. To see his dreams flourish as he worked hard. It was now after the 1993 Northridge earthquake, and then the September 11th tragedy occurred. He realized, reading his notes one day, that he had seen it take place before. There was another instance when he was truly involved in a personal struggle. He had a vision of Buddha.

 He was standing on the Santa Monica pier. The wind blew up the raspy smell of seaweed and sand inter-tangled within each other. Then, he saw Buddha sitting right in the middle of the ocean. The entire ocean, surrounding him, glowing. It was lit by the most astounding sunset Nader had ever seen. The spectacular array of hues consisted of a shiny red and brilliant yellow blend. Buddha just stared at him, and he was pacing. He had a sensation that Buddha was asking something of him,

 -Yes, what do you want from me? I am just a salesman. What can I do for you?

Then, suddenly, he was standing on a different pier in San Diego. The same scenario occurred. He was pacing in frustration, pleading with Buddha to just give him peace. The scene happened again, now at a different pier. But the same ocean, same Buddha, same sunset. He did not know where this third pier was located. By now, he was calm. He stared at Buddha and decided to go to him. He stepped off the pier onto the air, attempting to walk toward Buddha. He was awakened. Again, during the dream, he knew he was sleeping, and he knew he was dreaming. From then on, he gave up the notion that he should try to challenge destiny and just enjoy the ride.

Strangely after he saw Buddha in the dream, he felt much calmer and at peace. And after a long struggle with these two angels and rejecting what they wanted to teach him, for the reason that was not clear to Nader, he decided that it was better to stop fighting them. He thought, what if there good message in this, and he came to the understanding that this is out of his destiny and he can not fight with his destiny, especially since it did not matter how much he tried to prevent the occurrence of what he saw in his dreams, but he failed, and it was out of his control, and things would happen as he has seen in the dream or vision them. The only difference was he did not know when they would come to reality. It was just like someone wrote a script of a pre-written film; they played and were shown. Sometimes they would happen in a short time. Some would take years. But what was more painful for him was that all these messages that reached him were completely contrary to what was sold to the people under the name of religion, especially in Iran by the clergy under the name of Islam, they were forcibly imposed on them, which had nothing to do with the principle of Isalm and they did not have the essence of the religion of Islam and were only for personal gain and power. Again, to understand and digest these messages, Nader began to recall a Dervish who had lived with him for several months in the foothills of Iran. And this helped him to avoid feeling sorry for himself and complaining about his fate. After reaching this conclusion, two beautiful angels, one in blue and the other in green, came to see more rarely.

*****

Daily, tragic news from Iran exacerbated his depression. His heart could not be still. The entire world had forgotten about Iran. And the people in power made deals with other people in power. But his mother still plagued his mind. He had been away for over seventeen years. He missed the land, the air, the smell of the dirt, every corner of his homeland. He thought of Forogh. She was almost ready to graduate from medical school. He knew his mother was very sick. How bad it was, he was not sure. But she was already in her eighties; the years were catching up. They all, of course, would never tell him exactly what was going on. They probably would not even inform him of her death for a long time. That was the way it went for most. If you were not in Iran, you should not be bothered. There was nothing he could do anyway in their eyes. The only reason he knew his mother was alive was because he was speaking to her on the phone daily. But she was getting worse every day, and he could hear it in her voice. Even when she laughed and joked on the phone, he could tell. He knew the moment she would hang up the phone, she was going to be in tears and would grab her beads and began to pray. Once, she had caused him to lose a picture deal on one of his scripts. Nader was in a meeting with a production company in Beverly Hills; they were interested in one of his scripts. The deal was practically done. It was the last meeting to shake hands and work out the terms and leave it to the attorneys to draw up the contract. Everyone was happy and smiling. Then, he realized his mother had appeared in the corner of the office, right in front of his eyes, but sitting in her usual place in the living room in Tehran, on her colorful praying rug. She was looking up to God and praying. But this time was different, when her tears asked for help for others, for him. She prayed for forgiveness. In her frail hands, no prayer beads graced her fingers. One held a glass of water, the other a bunch of pills. He could see her hands shaking. Probably due to old age mixed with fear. He kept staring at the corner, where his mother was showing, and asked for a phone,

-Please, I need a phone; I must call my mother, she is killing herself, and I must stop her. Please, I need a phone right now!

All that time, he stared, watching her, while dead silence filled the room. All eyes in the room turned toward where Nader was staring, but no one saw anything. None of them knew about his ability to see things; most didn't. No one responded and stared blankly as if they were sure he was unbalanced. At the time cell phone was not popular, and only a few had one, and they were so big. So, he had to use the landline. He had to practically holler with all his might before someone presented him with a phone. He was still watching her in the corner. The phone rang and rang. Suddenly she shook and dropped all the pills. They scattered all over the floor as her image disappeared. She used to keep the phone by her bed so when he would call, she would not miss it. Then her voice echoed into the receiver, "Nader doobaareh that day" Nader, did you have a dream again? His mother was talking to him, now pretending she was laughing.

-Are you crazy? What are you doing? Do you want to go to Hell?

-I swear you are a messenger; I am sorry, I will ask God for forgiveness.

His brother-in-law, Dash Mahmod's voice is heard in the background, through the receiver, calling for Hajji Khanoom; it had happened that he arrived to visit her. He woke up and grabbed the phone from her. Nader told him what had just taken place and asked him to watch out for her. Nader hung up the phone and turned to see everyone was still staring at him like he was nuts, from another planet; of course, his conversation with his mother was in Farsi; therefore, he had no choice but to explain to them what had just happened. By seeing their reactions, he knew there would no longer be any deal. In fact, he had mentioned to his attorney before they went into the meeting that this deal was going to fall apart somehow. He turned to Nader as they walked out of the office empty-handed,

-Please stop having dreams, turn it off or something.

After they left that day, no one from the production company would accept their phone calls. He was an outcast from their elite little group; he had definitely lost the deal.

What his mother did caused Nader to begin to miss her terribly, and after the incident in the office, he knew he had to go and see her. He used to cry in private, sitting in silence, imagining her death with him so far away. If he went more than a week without talking to her, she would fall into a deep depression, and imprisonment or death could still be the outcomes of his return. He could return and cause her death by putting himself in danger, breaking her flood gate of stress, her body simply giving out, giving up. Or he could continue on with his days in America until the day she was gone for good. He began to communicate with everyone he knew to see if they could get some information in regards to the government blacklist at the airports in Iran. His thinking was if he could only get into the country for a few days and sees his mother, he could disappear and sneak out through the border. But he could not get any concrete answers if it would be safe for him to go back. His mother, brothers, and sisters were all worried about him returning since there were no concrete answers as to what would occur.

Within two days, he was seated calmly on a plane headed to Iran. He decided that prolonging and continuing the discussion about it with all could just set him up for failure. Word may get out that he was planning a return. It was better to do it quickly, hoping to surprise the government. He quietly informed some of his friends, who promised to step in and help if something were to happen. No one could guarantee him safe passage to his home. Such a funny thought, to not know if going home will be the end of you. He had informed his nephew and a few friends back home as well so they would expect him. The plane began its descent into the airport Nader had not seen in seventeen years. It looked smaller, of course. But the beauty of that which surrounded it was still the same. Still magical, still leaking out all the love and strength that defined the Persian Empire.

Persia. Then Iran. Conquered, rebuilt, conquered, rebuilt. What had been produced from such an intricate and commanding history still puzzled him. You could always get lost in Iran, the same way a person could become lost within the words of Rumi. It was in the air. And now, it was coming through the vents of Nader's airplane. Soon, he was in line at customs, waiting to pass through. He glanced around, worried to death of what might occur, but his face was straight, solid. The changes that had taken place in Iran since he had last been were huge. The individuals who were now running the customs office were even different. Now there were only bearded men wearing street clothing which was much different than the Shah's time. Before, they were clean-cut men wearing suits and ties, with beautiful ladies, and they all smiled, welcoming you back to your homeland. He could see the difference in feelings, in the energy. Before he reached the customs officer, he could see a sad look, the look of suspicion, the look that was questioning why you were coming back. It was the look that said without a single word, why are you back in this land? It is not your home anymore. Shortly he was speaking with a tall, lanky customs officer,

-Why doesn't your passport have a seal that you exited the country? Why haven't you returned for seventeen years? Why is there no information about you on our computer?

Questions were fired at him, left and right. But when the words there is no information about you in our computer pierced the skinny man's lips, Nader felt a weight lift off his shoulders. He could get out of this. He thought one of his friends must have erased all his info from the computer; there should be at least something. Thank god for his friends. He could now see a couple of his friends and two nephews through the glass window waiting for him. The customs officer guided him into an integration room and asked him to wait. Nader waited for over an hour. He became worried. What if they were contacting the Savana, that was practically the old Savak, just with a name change and more rootless, much more brutal now than before. He then noticed an older man that came and looked around, playing with his praying beads in his right palm. He stared at him, and for some reason, Nader approached him,

> -Hajji Agha, please, I cannot wait any longer. My mother is sick, she is dying, and I need to see her. If you guys do not have information on me on your computer, why should you be holding me here? Please, I have waited for seventeen years to see my mother, let me go see her, and I will come back tomorrow anywhere you wish, and if there is anything wrong you can have me tomorrow...

Nader knew he had gotten to him, especially when tears popped out of the corner of his eyes when he mentioned about his dying mother. His tears were real, and the man grabbed his passport and paperwork, looking it over. He began to search the computer as another officer entered the room. The old man turned to him,

> -Why are you holding the man if there is no information in the computer, and then he must be okay? Let the man go. His mother is sick.

His passport was sealed, and he walked out after two hours of waiting. The moment Nader stepped into the lobby, he was stormed by many of his relatives. They weren't supposed to know about his arrival. A multitude of hugs and kisses fluttered around; he could only hear names, people switching places, so many nieces and nephews who use to be children. He flashed his eyes quickly through the crowd; he was looking for Forogh. Through several bodies, her face appeared. Her round face was wet with tears. She looked so beautiful, so innocent. Nader felt the love for a daughter swelling out of his stomach. She did not want him to see her tears; they exchanged a hug and kiss as he took in the young lady before him; the children were all grown. His mother was not present. She was not aware of his visit yet, just in case something should go wrong upon arrival.

As he drove home through the streets of Tehran, through the new highway system, all the changes to the city had his eyes moving like fireflies. Their caravan of cars finally reached the houses. The cars turned into the private dead-end alley where the majority of relatives lived and stopped in front of his mother's house. The alley was packed with friends and relatives who were waiting for him or had just arrived from the airport. Older relatives who had not made it to the airport were waiting patiently at the house with the poise only elders possess. He slithered through the crowd of people throwing polite smiles in all directions. He wanted to see his mother and moved like an agile cat making his way inside the house. There she was, an old woman, barely able to stand upright. Leaning forward, tears in her eyes, words were stuck in her throat. She was attempting to push people out of the way with the spunk of a twenty-year-old as Nader kept looking for his mother. Nader noticed her, wondering who she was. It was his brother's voice who quietly reached and whispered into his ear,

-Nader, this is Hajji Khanoom, your mother.

Then, his eyes came back to her, she reached out, grabbing him. Sinking her small fingers into him. Her soft voice was barely uttering words,

Nader Jan. My Dear Nader, here you are.

He lost the strength in his knees and hit the ground. She was in his embrace, and he could feel her tears swapping her skin for his. Her hand ran through his hair and touched his face to be sure he was her son. He hated himself for having overlooked her. He would never forget that moment. He could not rise to go all the way inside. His brother and one of his nephews helped him up and into the house. He was mentally and emotionally numbed for more than a week. He did not leave the house for two weeks and just sat next to his mother. He watched her walk around the house, helped her cook, he ate, and talked with her about everything. Forogh was with them as well. His presence had brought peace between the two of them. They had set up a bed next to hers in the living room for Nader, and every night she would wake up three or four times and check him by touching his face to see if he was still there. But this particular visit with his mother and Forogh was the best, yet worst. They all relished in each other's presence, yet much had changed. Forogh was no longer a child. Arguing between her and Hajji Khanoom was constant. Forogh was a young woman in her twenties in med school living with a woman of the past, a very distant past. Her grandmother had no control over her emotions and was growing older and older, keeping the farm in her mind as if she set foot off it yesterday. She still believed she was the boss. Nader could see that Forogh loved her grandmother to the extremes. He could see Forogh, like millions of other young people who were little kids during the revolution, now grown, not obeying the Islamic rules and regulations set by the radical clergy. He could see that the younger generation of Iran was more aware, had much more understanding than the youth of his time. They were now aware that the rules and regulations set by the clergy were not acceptable for their own families. They knew the clergy was misusing their power for their own personal and financial gain. They were determined to challenge the clergy however they could. And Forogh was one of them. Nader felt pain for the youth who had to grow during the years after the revolution. They had truly suffered; they had missed out on so much. He sat watching Forogh and his mother argue, taking in the generational differences, wondering if they could ever sift through the grains to find common ground. They were both right in their logic, yet wrong at the same time. Families had been left tattered, scarred, aching because of the revolution.

*****

Chapter 31

After Spending So Many Years In Another Country; What Used To Be Normal Isn't...

Tears plastered faces, soft sighs were released. Hajji Khanoom and Forogh sat solemn. Nader was returning home, returning to the US. He knew he had to get Forogh out of Iran somehow. He also knew that if he did, his mother would die. She was her lifeline. Despite their constant arguing and differences, Forogh was the only company she had on a daily basis, the only joy, the only hope his mother had left to live on. If she were to lose Forogh, she would have no reason to live. He could see his self partly responsible for their situations and millions of others living the same kind of life. Nader was back in the States and could not do anything about it. He had given some thought to staying in Iran but realized there was no way that he could survive there. After spending so many years of his life in another country, you become used to a different kind of life and culture. What used to be normal isn't anymore? Perceptions change, and adapting is no longer needed; you become a part of the melting pot, especially since Iranian society was completely different than when he grew up. He could not go back. The economic hardships, hardcore Islamic law, finding any way you can to survive or feed your family; all of this had driven the people into insanity. For people like Nader, there was now a great struggle just to survive, to stay alive. No matter if you were in Iran or not. The only difference was in Iran, and you had to fight hard to stand for your beliefs and ideology. There was a new generation of people in Iran, and he did not know how to deal with them. Every moment their lives were filled with struggle and fear of being arrested or disappearing without a trace. To learn how to survive in these situations, you had to experience the hardships, and he was not there to experience the pain. He only knew that he was one of the millions of supporters who were responsible for enforcing the hardship upon innocent people, upon the new generations, like Forogh.

The consequence of witnessing what was happening in Iran had added more pain to his already broken spirit. He fell again into depression, sipped sadness on a daily basis. Hopelessness and loneliness prevented him from retaining a steady job. He began writing again, and by now, he had a couple of scripts already completed. Being from Iran, watching the news that was brought to the states made it unfeasible to break into Hollywood for him. Especially after the takeover of the American embassy. Every rejection made him stronger. A year after his visit to Iran, he realized his mother was losing her memory. He was still talking to her and Forogh every day. Then came another dream.

He was in his mother's living room in Tehran. Boloor, Forogh's mother, was cleaning the room. Nader noticed she was holding the Persian carpet up and splashing it with a water hose. He was surprised that she was using a water hose in the living room, so he went over to her and called out Zan Dadash, which means "his brother's wife," and he used to call her by that name,

-Zan dadash, what are you doing? You are ruining the rugs. Hajji Khanoom will be mad. What are you doing?

-I am cleaning Hajji Khanoom's house before she comes.

-But you are ruining the rugs.

Calmly Boloor pointed,

-This is not water. Look at it.

As she smiled, she held the carpet up higher for him to view as she was still was splashing the water through the water hose. He had reached and pushed his hand through the water and the colorful rug, but there wasn't anything there. His hand crossed through beautiful beams of light. Boloor was staring at him, smiling. And Nader woke up.

Again, he knew during the dream that he was dreaming, and he knew he was asleep in Los Angeles. But he was not aware Boloor was dead during the dream. But by having such a dream, he knew his mother was going to die. Boloor was preparing his mother's home after death. He did not know what to do. He immediately called his sister and brother, who assured him that she was doing well. He knew something was not right. At the time, he was engaged with a project that was supposed to be financed. He was finally preparing to do his first serious film in America, so leaving Los Angeles might mean completely jeopardizing the opportunity, and he really didn't want to lose the deal. Within a couple of weeks, he had a second dream; this time, it was about his brother Bijan.

Nader entered the narrow yet airy alley and was walking towards Hajji Khanoom's house, which was on the end to the right. He noticed his brother, Bijan, who was dead, pacing by the door, in front of their sister Parry's house, Parry, waiting. Puzzled, Nader went over to him,

-Bijan joon, what are you doing here? Why don't you go up?

He turns to Nader with a calm smile,

-I am waiting for Hajji Khanoom. I am taking her to her new house.

Nader didn't understand what he meant and asked him,

-Bijan Jan, what are you talking about? Are you going crazy? Everyone will be mad. They will not allow her to go with you.

Bijan smiles as he looks toward the dead end, where Hajji Khanoom's house was. Nader turned and noticed Hajji Khanoom sitting inside a beautiful carriage, made entirely of various flowers of all colors, moving toward them. But there were no horses to pull the carriage. She looked beautiful and healthy and young. Nader, frazzled as the confusion refused to dissipate, walked to her,

>-Hajji Khanoom? What are you doing? Everyone is going to raise hell? Where are you going? Are you going crazy? Let's go back up to the house.

She calmly reaches toward him,

>-Nader Joon, come hug me. I am going somewhere that you cannot come to see me anymore. Come give me one last hug.

Nader approached to stop her and take her back to the house, repeating she could not go; he would not allow it. But as they were about to touch each other, he woke up.

Nader sat up, his chest heaving softly; he reached for the phone and called his mother in Tehran. Forogh answered; she was crying; she had fought with her father and Uncle Kammal regarding her grandmother. She could not handle her grandmother's situation and wanted her to be in the hospital. But her doctor and others had come to the understanding that it was too late for her to heal.

Through Forogh's weeping, Nader could hardly understand her, but she managed to let out some comprehensible words; she is in a coma. He was told before she drifted to unconsciousness she had asked for him. Her wish was to see him one last time. Those were her last words. Nader knew he had to go back. He must be on the first flight back, hoping to get there before she was completely gone. The earliest day he could book a flight was on Monday afternoon. It was Friday night. He patiently waited to get to her. He prayed and prayed some more.

During this long year, Nader had worked hard and by now had his own house and a comfortable life. Money was not an issue anymore. He had talked to everyone on the phone back home before going to bed alone. He had a large, seven bedrooms home, which at the time was living all by himself. Just at the same time, a few of his friends Kenny and Kyle Saylor, were visiting him. This particular weekend their sister and a few of her friends had come to town for a visit. The house was full of guests, and Nader only wanted dead silence. He needed his privacy yet felt bad for them all. His mind was not thinking of being a good host. But he was. Around midnight Nader made his way to his room and fell on the bed. Then, the dream came again.

He was busy helping in the kitchen at his mother's house in Tehran. Suddenly he felt the sensation of burning and began to yell,

-I am getting hot. I am getting hot! Hot!...

As Nader continued to yell, a brownish steam sprung out through his entire body, flushing from his pores, just like grass from the ground. He noticed Boloor, very young and happy, who grabbed him by the hands, holding onto between her two hands on his both shoulders arm.

She calmly held him to calm him down,

-It will be okay, Zan Amoo. You are being freed.

Zan Amoo was a name she used to call his mother. She was holding on to him but calling his mother's name. Now his entire body was covered with brownish steam. He was still yelling, becoming hotter and hotter. He saw many creature-like people beginning to appear from the dark. They were approaching in a manner as if they wished to creep into his body. Boloor was concerned about the bodies, holding him tight and firmly as if to say you are not getting him. She kept repeating,

-Zan Amoo, it is okay you're finally being freed.

Nader noticed his other brother appear in the doorway, holding onto a wooden stick. He began to slam and jab at the creatures to get them away from getting into Nader's body. The brownish steam now filtered out of every inch, even the tips of his fingers and toes. As the steam became hotter, he was distracted by the fact that he was in California, asleep. And Boloor, she was dead. Suddenly he felt, his soul began to separate from his body, and he knew he had to wake himself up before it was too late. He hollered, telling his mind to push his body off the bed onto the floor. He finally heaved over, falling to the cold stone floor, eye wide open, disoriented.

He ran out of his bedroom, through the living room, and into his office. Kenny, his sister, and two other friends were in his office using the internet through a dial-up connection,

-Get off the internet. I need the phone. My mother is dead.

They looked at Nader strangely. Within few seconds, they all ran out of the office, and the phone was ringing in his mother's house. After the first ring, they all heard the phone. Then he heard Forogh's voice through the receiver, crying for her dead grandmother. It seemed as though Forogh had been sitting by the phone waiting for his call. After a bit of conversation, he walked back to his bedroom, not remembering the others in the house existed. He was in tears, yet no sound came from his throat. Somehow, he lay on his bed, closed his eyes, spaceless, lost in the time. A soft thud was heard at the door. Kenny wanted to know if he was okay. He simply answered, yes. And the next thing he knew, there was a soft thud heard at the door again and caused him to wake up, and it was Kenny again who wanted to know if he is okay. It was ten in the morning. Kenny joined him in, and Nader began apologizing for his abrupt behavior the night before. Nader inquired as to where everyone was. Kenny smiled and explained that after he had come out of his bedroom in his frenzy, everyone became scared and dispersed into different bedrooms. After Nader had gone to his bedroom, they all immediately left the house. Kenny was even scared. He saw Nader's entire hair sticking straight up in the air as if it was as dry and stiff as it could be. Even the hairs on his chest. And he continued to say, they all got scared and left the house last night. Now his mother was dead, something he practiced for many months to how to handle it. But would it work? He was confused and lost.

He was convinced by all his family not to travel back to Iran. He now wanted to be alone. He did not see many for a long while. He mourned his mother's death in silence. He cried, chanted, wrote poetry. He even tried to get in touch with her in a dream, to simply say goodbye. He could not handle her departure. It was not easy; he should have been by her side when she left him for good. A few weeks went by. He was on the phone for almost two to three hours a day talking to Forogh, who was also hit hard by her grandmother's death. He spoke to many, making sure all would go well and peacefully. It was the toughest time Nader ever had experienced. He had recently broken up with a woman who he really liked as well. He had spent a lot on his film projects, and every time something went wrong, it left him with financial distress. But he was not going to give up. Every time things were falling into place, when he needed support, something went wrong. That was just the way things were. And this time, it was his mother who came to him in a dream.

He was at their family's old home before the construction of their current one. He was missing his mother terribly. Hassan was sitting near him speaking with another friend, trying to pursued him to come and keep Nader company. Then the door opened softly. His mother appeared in the doorway. She looked healthy and young, her face dewy with the poised strength of someone who had seen something. She wore a white veil. Nader recognized it; it was her favorite through her late thirties. The white fabric was covered with various, simple and beautiful flowers. She looked as though she stepped out of a beautiful garden, which she was a part of. As she stepped in, he could see she was followed by several of his nieces and nephews. He began to cry, speaking as to why she left without saying goodbye. Her arms rose, taking him in a single embrace as they sat on each side of the single bed. Hajji Khanoom laid his head on her chest, just like she used to do when he was a little boy. Her hands began to pat him on the back as she was playing with his hair, just as she used to do when he was a little boy. He remembered this feeling as a child, a feeling of safety, of being grounded to the earth by a force so much stronger than yours. He imagined the arms of a mother must be like Gods. He was still crying, his tears being soaked up by her presence. She said nothing the entire time, not a word. When she had entered, Hassan became petrified and ran out of the room. Nader woke up from the dream.

Then, Nader called home. They told him several people were in the kitchen cooking dishes to take to her gravesite. Nader knew he had not been the same since his mother's death. When he felt her spirit leaving her body, his was doing the same. He knew that if he had not awakened himself, he would be gone as well. He began to feel as if their two souls were connected somehow. Maybe one soul in two separate bodies. People believed in soulmates, so why could two souls, those of a mother and a child, not be connected with a similar force? Forogh now plagued his mind. She was deep in depression as well. He knew no one back home really understood all that she was dealing with inside. To add to her own history of sadness was now her present circumstances. Life in Iran, life after the revolution, was a struggle for everyone. To add to the daily issues, you had to worry about the clergy. If someone did not like you and they knew a member of the clergy, they could talk to them and have you marked as being anti-Islamic, anti-revolution, or pro-America. And if you bore this invisible mark, you would be kicked out of school or perhaps jailed. Or you could simply disappear one day. It was all under the name of Islam, which sadly has nothing to do with Islam. There wasn't, and still isn't, anything stated in true Islamic ideology to support these actions. None of these rules and regulations set by the clergy had any real merit in the eyes of God. So much was manipulated, they would not hesitate to conveniently change the words around, make things flow their way. Something that was law yesterday could become a crime the next day. They created their own group of men called Hezbollah, and these were people who would come into the streets and strong-arm you. They would beat people up, destroy businesses, or whatever else seemed amusing. There were no laws to punish them. In fact, if you would retaliate, you would be the one jailed and punished. Defending your neighbor was a crime. Guilt weighed Nader down still. It would not release its solid grip from his body. He knew others, all over the world now, felt the same regret, remorse, and pained guilt as him. Love makes people do so many things, even blinds them down sunny paths that are hazy at the end. The deaths of his brother, mother, father, and Hussein would not let his spirit settle.

Nader was looking at the letter he had just received from Forogh. After reading it a few times, all he could do was cry. Learning about the life that she had to endure was even more painful than the suffering he saw on his mother's face at the hands of his father because he felt he was directly responsible for the pain and suffering that was inflicted on the Iranian people. What do you say when someone's twenty-two-year-old classmate and girlfriend was raped by the National Guard who was supposed to protect her? Then she was in jail for filing a complaint. What kind of response do you muster when a friend is sleeping with some old bearded fat man just to pay for her hungry little brother and sister to be able to continue school? Her friend had to drop out of college because she was spotted in a demonstration against Hezbollah. They were protesting because Hezbollah had entered into the university and beat up students,

-I wish you had watched the footage or photos of students being awakened and thrown out of windows from the second and third floors of the college dormitory at night by Hezbollah and the National Guard. Maybe you guys can ask your God to look out towards us because it seems God has forgotten us. I do not know how you all can live free of fear in your daily activities, can sleep without being worried about being kidnapped in your sleep? I hope you have read about young boys and girls that are being slashed to death just because they were in the same car. What kind of laws can take your dignity from you under the name of religion? If this is what they call Islam, then what was the Islam my grandmother was following all along? She was not this person, these people. I am wondering if my grandmothers were lying, or are they? I only know if this is what they call Islamic law, I am no longer interested in Islam. Nothing has let you and people like you off the hook for what you guys have done. You must be ashamed of yourself to be responsible for what is happening to the Iranian people. You must be ashamed of yourself....

By now, Nader's eyes ached as he read this letter from Forogh. If only she knew his whole life was not normal. He was not normal. His guilt filled every room he walked in. And what made it worse was that it was a helpless guilt. He had no way to help the Iranian people. He could not sleep; he was a prisoner of his own mind. He had everything a man could wish for, a large beautiful house, money, but he was losing every interest man could have, could not work, unable to concentrate, to focus. Perhaps, homelessness awaited him. He was a living dead soul with shadows all over his eyes, mind, and conscience. He watched the rest of his friends go on with their daily routine, making money, having parties, enjoying their card games, adding to their wealth, driving high model cars, gloating about their success to each other. Could he really blame these people for their in-action? Maybe they know they can't change things. Maybe they push it to the back of their minds and try to remain sane and enjoy life as the lucky ones. He was wondering if they were ignorant and selfish, only to think about their own happiness and comfort, or if perhaps he was wrong mining the god's business? Nader was up again late, almost every night, as usual. He moved from one area of the house to another. He was contemplating, deciding, then contemplating more. He came to the conclusion he had to go back. He had to fight in whatever way he could to make things right. Then, at midnight, there was a knock on the door. He opened it hazily, then stood stunned for a long moment, wondering if he could be dreaming,

-Can I come in?

He realized at least a whole minute had passed without him saying a word. At first, he was almost doubtful that it was Fariba standing in his doorway. She had aged so much within a short span of years, it had been about nine years since he had seen her last when she had left him while he was sleeping. He did look for her everywhere, but she had vanished as usual, and he could not find out anything about her. He knew wherever she was, she was happy because she had left her husband and was living alone, or at least this was the impression he had gotten. He wondered what had aged her so hard these past years as he beckoned for her to enter. Within seconds she threw her arms around him, holding him tightly as if she would lose him if she let go. It took him a good few minutes to kick the door shut with his foot, and he walked her to the living room.

 He helped her to sit on cushions by his desk as their embrace morphed into a different shape so they would not have to let go. But he didn't want to ask. Their entire lives, they had spoken with their silence, and they had not even exchanged twenty sentences between them in over thirty years. For some reason, they did not need the words. They just seemed to understand each other within. He had to break away to get her some juice, then instantly back by her, and she was in his embrace again. He was now feeling quite strange. He was very happy, but at the same time, he was worried. He was filled with a sad concern. But again, he could not open his mouth or think of any words to speak. Lovingly, she reached out and took his face into her hands, holding it and staring into his eyes for a few minutes,

 -I am sorry for your mother.

He was surprised that she was up-to-date about him every time she came back into his life. It seemed she had followed everywhere he was going or everything he was doing. That was the only conversation they had the entire night, but it was enough to get tears into his eyes, and there she was, wiping away and kissing him to give comfort. They did not move from the place they sat, and he only remembers moving to get a pillow and blanket for them, and that was after she had fallen asleep in his arms. She was sound asleep just like an angel, and he just watched her while past memories were played in his head. It was very early morning when he fell asleep.

 The telephone rang and awakened them. He could barely open his eyes. She was still holding onto him. Nader could see through the crack in the curtain that the sun had come up. Then, there was the sound of the answering machine playing and the voice of his friends complaining as to why he did not show up for their meeting. She rose her head up to let him know he could go. She did not need to speak this since he could understand from her eyes, but he did not want to leave. He placed his hand on her face and ran his fingers through her hair, placing her head once again on his chest for her to relax. Then, she reached out and began to play with his face, softly sliding her fingers through strands of hair, and soon her lips were touching his, and they felt each other's soul. It was not long before they were sensually human again, naked in each other's arms, feeling free as a human could feel, engaged in the holiest act in which a man and woman can participate in. There was never a feeling more beautiful than those moments.

*****

Chapter 32

I Miss My Son; I Want To See Him...

Traditional Iranian music with Rumi's lyrics being chanted echoed through the apartment. It was over a week now, and Fariba was still with him, but every time he closed his eyes, he wondered if he was going to see her again. There was something that seemed different this time. Maybe she was not going to run away. But he had many questions he wanted to have answers for. He wanted to know how this beautiful woman could have aged more than twenty years within just a few. Was any of it due to Abraham? What had happened to her happy spirit, which seemed to be threaded away? He did not want to question her directly, afraid she would be uncomfortable. He didn't want her to think he did not love her anymore or that he wanted her to leave. He made everything as comfortable as he could for her, and by now, he knew something was wrong. He had canceled everything he had to do. He forgot about work. No phone calls were returned, none were taken. He was only available to her and belonged to her for every hour, every minute. Days passed. He tried everything he could to create happy times for her. He played funny games, he sang for her, he danced and acted out foolish scenes for her. He cooked a variety of foods and created some of his own recipes for her. Whatever he could think of, he attempted. But none of it made a difference. She seemed to be losing more weight every day and was weaker. Her energy was non-existent, and now he was gravely concerned.

A couple of months had passed. She had remained with him. The night began with a light rainfall which became more intense as the night went on. She was uptight, almost afraid of the storm like a small girl. He watched her peer out the window, looking at the rain as if trying to make it stop with her mind. It was the first time he realized she was scared of rain, and if he had any power to stop it, he would have. She asked for the phone, and he brought it to her. He left her alone in the room and returned a few minutes later when he heard her hang up. He walked in to tears in her eyes. He sat by her, and she leaned over and laying her face in his hands and lap,

-I miss my son. I wanted to see him. He is flying in. He lives and goes to school in New York.

It was the first time he heard his son was living in New York, and now he is about twenty years old. He learned he was an artist who wrote and played music and sang. The rain continued to pour for the next few days, and every night he had her next to him. He was becoming exhausted; lack of sleep from worry was taking its toll. But the soft music was still alive and playimg through the house.

*****

The sun had just lit up when the bell of Nader's house rang and awaken him, he did not even know he had fallen asleep in a day time. Nader did not know if he should open the door or not, but as the doorbell rang again he opened it, his eyes left on a young man in his twenties standing in his doorway, looking at each other a bit to understand each other and concentrate the moments. It seemed Nader know that he must be Fariba's son, and as the young man's voice raised Nader had no more doubt who he was,

-Salam… I'm a Nader Fariba's son … when I received your letter and my mother, I flew immediately...

Nader looked at young Nader, Fariba's son, dumbfounded and did not speak or move. After hearing young Nader talking about receiving his and Fariba's letters, Nader recalled why Fariba's son was standing on his doorway. He remembered that in order to find Ibrahim or Fariba's son, he searched through Fariba's belonging she brought with her, to find the clue so he could reach them. There was not much to search through, Fariba had brought with her, just a bag and her purse. Going through her purse the first thing that caught his eyes was a sealed stamped envelope that Fariba had written and was going to mail it to his son, Nader, in New York. He immediately mailed the letter. Also, he attached a letter of his own to Fariba's letter, and now, less than a week after he mailed the letters, Fariba's son was standing in his doorway in front of him. But it was as if the presence of Fariba's son had caused a magical spell on Nader and taken control of his will and ability to move or talk, and had enchanted him. He could not breathe. With the presence and hearing Fariba's son. It was a sudden awakening into the past memories for Nader, he recalled his last days with Fariba and without knowing, he was lost into the passed thought and the memories as if he was no longer there… 'He remembered a knock on the door, awaken Nader from his deep sleep. He realized he had fallen into sleep late last night when he was holding to Fariba almost for the entire night watching and listening her breath, worried if she was oaky. But she was not in his hug any longer, he was alone, worried what had happened to her. Or is she left her again as she used to do? He stared at the door confused who could be and or if it was her, soon the door was open and she was standing there once again. She was the only soul that Nader was powerless when around. It seemed he had no control, as if her mere presence triggered a magical spell. She knew he was not happy about what had happened, and he needed to know why she left unexpected again. This time she did not wait for him to ask her to come in. She entered, sat at the kitchen table, and waited for him to sit across from her before beginning. He sat and listened to the words pour from her mouth. After a few minutes, he had heard all he needed to know. He knew it was painful for her to send it all into the air. He stood up and walked over to her putting his finger against her lips. Then, he kneeled down and hugged her waist, placing his head in her lap. Her hand immediately landed on his head, caressing it as if she was spreading love into his hair. He was crying inside, but he did not want her to know or have her see his tears. There was no way he would allow her to see his tears. She did not need to see that. She had more than enough to handle. Fariba had to settle things for her final days; she only had a few months to live. Liver cancer had spread and grown so rapidly was when she knew she had to find Nader, to spend the rest of her short remaining life with him. That is why she left to visited her doctor. She did not open up to him yet and now she was puring her pain out telling Nader why she was gone and then as she was playing with Nader's hair she whispered,

-What if I just claim you two as spiritual, as spirit...?

-We're, in fact, very spiritual. We believe it is all related, all so different yet exactly the same. We believe you can speak directly to the source, to God.

Nader's words made the priest's shoulders relax, a smile appeared on his face, and he continued with the ceremony. Finally, they were married. They kissed. It was a funny kiss, one that felt different than the rest. It felt as if they lost their freedom, were placed in prison, were victorious against their parents and tradition, and had a love that would not last more than months. It was funny how they both felt the same way, knowing they could not ask the priest for a divorce, they began to laugh.

On the way back home, as husband and wife, they continued to joke about it. She reached out, holding her hands high to catch the falling snowflakes, collected some, and began to eat them. There was snow on all the trees, on the roads; everywhere... the whole world was white. Soon they were back at his house. Then, awakened by the sound of a beautiful and familiar tone, something he had not heard for a long, long time. The sound paralyzed him as it took him back to his youth. It was the sound of her violin. He walked out to see her standing on the balcony under the snow that still was falling, just like a little child, like a rebellious young teenager, playing the song she always used to play when he would sit and watch her at his treehouse when they were too young and innocent. With the same violin she uses to play with when she was a young child and teenager, through the window for him, when she knew all along he was sitting on his treehouse watching and listening to her, it was a few days ago that Nader broke the news to her and showed her her first violin her mother gave it to him to keep her memory alive in his heart, she had kept and cherished it all along. And now, thirty-five years later, he was watching her fingers move across, gracefully and firmly controlling every sound. Neighbors opened their windows, and some even walked outside to hear the music more closely. He could not have been prouder a husband at that moment. She had captured not only his heart but all the neighbors' hearts as well. By now, many were out on their balconies, their backyard, behind their windows, watching the best concert of their life, and she did not even realize people were watching her. It was surprising to all. Few of the neighbors appeared on their porch, behind their window, and at their backyard, and they began playing their instrument to help her create a most beautiful concert, the moment of celebration to remember. One plays saxophone, one guitar, and another one also violin. It was a most beautiful celebration. Nader began to sing and dance, then she joined him dancing as she was still playing. She just played with all her heart, staring into his eyes. Their dance took them into the snow, but it did not bother them. Now few neighbors begin to dance at their porch or backyard as well, joining their celebrations. But just as they were living the most beautiful moment of their life, suddenly she lost her balance; it seemed she was so tired, he had to reach out and grab her so she would not fall. She whispered into his ear,

    -That was my wedding present to you.

Too bad he had not prepared a wedding present for her. Then she fell into his hug, the violin left her hand, landed into the snow and almost disappeared, the tone was dead, Nader did not know what was going on, he sat on the snow at the balcony holding on to his love,

-Fariba? Fariba...?

Now sadness replaced their celebration. He did not know what to think about this, having no idea if she would ever live long enough to enjoy the moments. He was furious with himself for not questioning her health, her life, or her sadness. He stayed in the snow for a while, holding on to her. They finally moved him inside.

Later he had made a bed right in the living room. She wanted to be able to watch the rain fall, she wanted to see the outdoors. She loved the ocean, the mountains, sitting in grassy fields, taking it all in. She had reminded him of the night they first made love on the cliff, with the rain was falling. She began to speak about it when she was lying in bed with him that same night. For some reason, she wanted him to know there was something special about that night and about that cliff, but he was not getting it, or she did not want him to get it. And why not? She spoke about that rainy night at the cliff, the night for the first time they made love. By remembering it, a smile would appear on her face. She said that night changed her life. Those moments together gave her new directions, a new meaning to her life. It was the beginning of thoughts of separation from Abraham. She even knew the date and the time. With every word, she was giving him a bit more understanding about the cliff and the effect it had on her life. She held him tightly,

-Nader? Do you think there is a God?

He thought about answering it for a while; in fact, he did not know what to answer. He already had experienced his doubts, but how could he tell her there was or wasn't. He always thought this was for each individual to come to their own understanding, but he knew she was waiting for his answer,

-We may only know after our death.

She continued,

-I am wondering if there is one, would God forgive them for what they had done to us? I want to forgive them.

-That gives you peace by forgiving them. You need to do that.

-Yes, I already did. But I know what I want done with my body after my death, and they must not have any say about that. You must be sure to honor my will.

-I will Azizam, I will, my dear, you are my wife, and I do have a say, just relax, you need rest.

She then wrapped her arms tightly around him again, positioning herself for sleep, for comfort. Her grip was tight, and she was creating so much heat Nader did not know what to do. He removed the covers a bit, thinking she may have a fever. Whatever it was, it was not normal, her heat intensified, and she held on tighter and tighter. He did not know what to do, but it was too much, his skin felt hot,

-Fariba... Fariba...

But there was no answer before he could make any move or think about what to do, her head fell onto his chest, and her hands were both lighter than a glass of water. He was startled and choking on air. He knew what had just happened but could not accept it. He knew she had left him, his tears running down his cheeks, he held for almost thirty minutes. He then laid his angel down, covered her as though she was going to catch a cold, and walked around her many times, stared at the snow, then back at her. He looked around the living room to see if he could feel her soul around. But it was just him and his angel, who now suddenly looked much smaller.

He softly walked into the bathroom and stared at himself in the rectangular mirror. As he turned the water on, tears filled the room. His deep crying echoed through the bathroom. He questioned if it all was real, why him, why again! He questioned God, unable to stop himself. The shock was setting in and wearing thin. He splashed freezing cold water against his face trying to pretend as if someone was slapping him back to reality. He had to call the hospital, and then he remembered first, he had to call her son. But he didn't have his number. He remembered the call she made to him from his phone. Stacks of unopened mail were lying on his desk, but he had no problem finding the phone bill. A few minutes later, he was holding the receiver, and it was ringing. A soft and calm voice of a young man spoke into his ear. It was her son. But suddenly Nader was speechless, he could not talk, he was trying to hold his tears, he was hearing her son's voice calling for his mother,

-Mom... mom... is that you? Are you okay?

Nader had to manage to get the words out. Telling him his mom was dead. He said he would be on the first plane to California. It took Nader a good two hours to get a hold of himself and call the hospital. It was later that the ambulance waited at the front of his house, just as everyone was beginning their daily routine. It was shocking to them to hear the dead person was the same beautiful violinist from the night before. He knew they all left for work with sadness in their hearts. Nader was left standing under the falling snow alone, watching the ambulance taking his heart away forever. The whole day was like a fog. Snow continued to fall. It just changed speeds and thickness. He did not know what to do with himself, he did not want to talk to anyone, he did not want to say a single word or see a single face. The phone was unplugged, and he stayed in his house, thinking and every once in a while, taking notes on his thoughts. He sat for hours thinking about his life, then hers. Then the life they never got to have.

A few hours into the night, he was awakened by a knock at the door. He did not even know he had fallen asleep. Nader did not know if he should open the door or not, but when he heard his voice, he knew he had to. There he was, Fariba's son standing in his doorway,

-Salam… Sorry to bother you but I had to… come to see you… I am Nader. Fariba's son…

A short while later, they both were drinking Persian tea, sitting by the window, staring at each other, mourning the death of the woman they both dearly loved. Then, he began talking,

> -I went to the hospital with my father to get my mother's situation handled, but we were not authorized. They say that her husband had to sign all the paperwork for what must be done with her body. My father replied he is her husband, but when they look at her driver's license, they said he is not, and then your name came up as her husband. By hearing your name my father and grandfather were so mad, but surprisedly my grandmother was smiling… but my father would not give in, and he was about to fight with them, then I stepped in, and I told them that my mother had left a will and we need to honor her wish… after I gave my mother's will to the hospital officials, things went south… he was so mad why I did not show him the will before? But I knew for sure if I revealed her will to them, it would be burned… so showing the will was not something that my father and my grandparents were waiting for… after reading the will, when they found out that my mother is married. Especially when they saw your name, which is her husband they almost died… they really want to kill me right that moment… but my grandmother was smiling, a happy smile that finally my mother took a stand for what she wished… to tell them no…

Young Nader waited for a second for Nader's response, but after there was no response, he turned toward Nader and continued,

> -I did not know my mother had gotten married. She did not tell me about it. In fact, this was the only secret she kept from me. They gave me your address. Maybe you could reveal to me what is going on, and I need to know...

Then, he handed him a letter. Nader looked at it, and it was from Fariba to him. After reading a few lines he realized, it was her will. Young Nader continued,

> -The will said that she wanted to be cremated and have her ashes sprayed over the cliff on a rainy day… but she did not say where the cliff is? Can I guess? Do you know what cliff she wanted her ashes to be through at the ocean?

Nader did not need to read or hear the rest of her will, he had a copy of it, and he knew which cliff she meant. He knew why that particular cliff was so important to her; Nader was broken away from his thoughts as Young Nader began to speak again,

> -My father Abraham, I do not know if you know him or not? He is furious. He doesn't want her body to be cremated. My grandfather and the whole family are outraged, but they could not do anything about it because you are the husband and her will gives you the power. It is your say.

Nader was debating what to say to Fariba's son. Should he open up and tell him what his father and grandfather had done to him, or should he let it go?

> -What about you? Nader quietly asked Fariba's son.

He had to ask the question and was delighted to hear his response,

> -I want to honor my mother's wishes; I have only my grandmother on my side…. And she wants to be present when we give her ashes to the ocean… For some reason, Nader reached out and hugged him. It was the most peaceful hug he ever could have had at that moment. It almost felt like he was hugging Fariba. Nadar asked.

-Who chose the name Nader for you?

-My mother, but my father wanted the name Abraham for me, so I go by Nader Abraham so both will be happy… but I prefer Nader.

It was then that Fariba's son was more curious about Nader and his mother,

-Do you want to tell me about you and my mother? I think I have the right to know.

This was the most difficult question to answer. How and where would he even start? Was bringing up the past such a good idea, especially if it stirred up hard feelings for this boy.

He decided to make it short,

-We were high school sweethearts. Then, she was sent away because I was Muslim and she was Jewish. But destiny finally brought us back together. There was a long silence, and the two men just looked on at one another, then at the blue-black sky,

-I hope they have learned not to make the same mistake. I hope we can all learn to understand one another as human beings, to not let beliefs separate the gift of love.

A few days later, the warmth of the fire burning her body was warming his face. Without any reservations and for no reason, Nader reached out and grabbed his hand to share the moment with Fariba's son, who was standing by his side. Then, his grandmother reached out and grabbed her grandson's other hand, keeping him safe as her daughter passed to the light. There were just three of them. The rest of the family did not want to be there. They stood until her entire body was cremated and the flame was dead. Her ashes sat waiting.

Chapter 33

To Claim What Once Belonged To Him ...

On a sad rainy day in spring, when the blooming flowers were glimmering in the beauty of nature's glow, a day when one's soul should be full of joy and happiness, away from an oceanfront cliff, Abraham stood away from view observing his son standing between Nader and Fariba's mother. If you could look into their thoughts, one could see the various memories scatter across their minds. Remembering Fariba in all her beauty. But everyone loved her differently; their pain was different, only the disappointment of losing her felt the same. Nader was unsure as to why Abraham was there. Maybe to claim the young man who was in deep reflection or claim what once belonged to him but was now gone. But they all knew that moment; her soul had belonged to nature. Her mother, standing tall, being one of the only ones who understood her all along. They stood in silence, waiting for the rain to subside. Nader firmly grasped the urn with her ashes. He looked at the ashes then peered up to the sky. Thinking, 'My God, is that all that is left of our body when we die?' Nader began to let the ashes go. They disappeared into the rain, mixing with water and traveling to a hundred different places from the top of that cliff. Suddenly the sound of her violin began echoing into his and everyone's ears and heart. It overtook his soul, and it was as if he was not even there. He traveled in the wind, becoming the sound of his violin girl, becoming her memory. He opened his eyes to see her son, playing one last song for her, and with her mother's first Violin having taken it from Nader's place. He wanted to say goodbye the right way. Young Nader closed his eyes and traveled with the tone and vibration of the violin. They manage for the song to play on for good long enough time to reach nature, the earth, the sky, her soul, and perhaps God. Then Fariba's mother reached over, grabbing the glass jar. She let the last ounce of ashes go to the wind, and she disappeared in the rain as if she was never even there. The sound of Violin was dead as her ashes were gone.

Finally, it was time to say goodbye. Her grandmother took her grandson's hand to walk him away. But young Nader stopped and turned around. They stood there for a long moment, and then he reached out to shake Nader's hand. Then they began to walk again, and as Young Nader began to make his way away from the edge, he stopped and turned again,

-Now I know why my mother chose this cliff… she said I was conceived here right underneath this cliff on a rainy day. That is why she wanted her ashes to be sprayed right here.

Nader was lost for a second in what he just heard. But he was broken away from his thoughts by Abraham.

-Son, we must go… we must let her have her peace after death.

It was Abraham who now was standing over the cliff, looking right at Nader; he was so broken apart Nader hardly could recognize him. He watched Fariba's son help his grandmother climb up the small hill, reach Abraham, who reached and grabbed Yong Nader's hand, claiming his son, and then they disappeared over the cliff. Now, standing alone, Nader was stuck, stuck in the realization that this cliff had an importance far beyond what he thought. To claim what once belonged to him but was now gone. A place where she would never be with any other man? A place she would never have come to with Abraham? Was she? Was Nader his son? Nader could not leave. He could not walk up the small slope to the top of the cliff. Sitting in the small cave underneath the cliff, he stared into the rain, thinking how fast time passes. It was almost as if time never really existed. As if there was no past or future, just passengers sliding by, struggling to be, then fading into the unknown. It still amazed him the impact struggles over religion had on all their lives. He doubted anyone even understood, after it all, that worship should be about peace, happiness. Respect and love. How could anyone claim to know what salvation is, how to truly get to heaven or God? Men who thought they knew destroyed so many lives, destroyed so many families. And they still do. Will God forgive those who blindly followed others? Will God forgive those who knowingly destroy others? I do not know. People can reach their own conclusions. But for Nader and Fariba, they knew something... they knew they were practicing love. They knew they were looking for peace, and that was all they wanted to know about being Jewish or Muslim. They were always human before they were Muslim or Jewish. An image of himself, with Fariba, and their son, crossed his mind. He imagined them together, happy, listening to the sounds from their instruments as they collided with the cool spring wind. For a moment, Nader could imagine a smile on Fariba's face. Now he was sitting alone, thinking about the past. A long, long history he had. The farm, Tehran, America. His friends and family, those that were alive, those that were dead. And his Violin Girl, his love... who now only existed in memories.

Standing alone, man is born innocent and will die innocent. He only learns to hate or love through his journey from birth to death, thinking about his son? Perhaps the truth should be revealed to him. How could he prove the truth? How could he know if young Nader is his son? Or have him as his son without tainting his heart with hate for others who love him? But he had no contact info to look him up. Now he has no choice but to wait; maybe one day, he shows up just like her mother did? Then, he heard the voice of a seagull crying, he turned to see a seagull, but this time only one, sad, crouched under the mockery right where they had seen two of them the first time he was there with Fariba. It seemed God had taken her partner as well, and she was crying in grief for her loss. Unbeknownst to Nader, his eyes traveled from the seagull into the air and the rain up toward

God. The rain caressed his face and perhaps washed away his grief to some extent, taking it to the sea and to his love; in his mind, he began talking to his God, "God is this what is left of us in the end ...? Nothing ...? Then there was a time of emptiness, time to begin thinking about the future if there really was such a thing as universal love or truth or peace. Now he had a new mission: In Search of Peace, In Search of Truth, In Search of Death, and In Search Of Love…

The End.

www.ingramcontent.com/pod-product-compliance
Lightning Source LLC
Chambersburg PA
CBHW070458120526
44590CB00013B/683